R⊕MANOVS

EUROPE'S MOST OBSESSIVE DYNASTY

'We have taught ourselves to ridicule all our past: we never acknowledge a good deed or a good intention in our history'
Alexander Solzhenitsyn, *The Gulag Archipelago*

'Unfortunate things often happen to Russian sovereigns'
The Emperor Paul's mother-in-law

THE ROMANOVS

EUROPE'S MOST OBSESSIVE DYNASTY

OLIVER THOMSON

TEMPUS

Cover images: St Basil's Cathdral courtesy of Neil Sutherland; Tsar Nicholas II, author's collection.

First published in the United Kingdom in 2007 by
Tempus Publishing, an imprint of NPI Media Group Limited
Cirencester Road · Chalford · Stroud · Gloucestershire · GL6 8PE

First published in the United States in 2007 by
The History Press, Charleston, SC 29403
www.historypress.net

British Library Cataloguing in Publication Data
A catalogue record for this book is available from the British Library.

Library of Congress CIP data applied for.

ISBN 978 0 7524 4421 5

Typesetting and origination by
NPI Media Group Limited.
Printed and bound in England.

CONTENTS

MAPS AND ILLUSTRATIONS

COLOUR ILLUSTRATIONS

Moscow
1 St Basil's Cathedral
2 Tsar Feodor's cannon
3 Trinity Tower
4 Annunciation Cathedral and Great Kremlin Palace
5 Bolshoe Theatre
6 Cathedral of Assumption and Palace of Facets
7 Bell Tower and Kremlin Wall

St Petersburg
8 The Bronze Horseman
9 Peter and Paul Fortress
10 Peterhof Cascade
11 The Winter Palace façade
12 The Winter Palace interior
13 Smolny Institute
14 Pavlovsk and statue of Tsar Paul
15 Spilt Blood Cathedral
16 The Cruiser *Aurora*

Of the black and white illustrations, 1 and 2 are reproduced by courtesy of the New York Public Library, 3–14 are from the author's private collection.

For the colour pictures I am indebted for 1 to my son-in-law Neil Sutherland and for the remainder to my old friend Lawrie Taylor.

For tolerance I am indebted to my long-suffering wife.

INTRODUCTION

The Romanovs were from the start in many ways a very dysfunctional family yet for several centuries they dominated what became the largest nation in Europe. Their incredible self-belief, their obsession with absolute control, their addiction to savage punishment, their self-indulgence and hedonism, their carelessness with human life and later their sheer incompetence caused enormous suffering. Their obstinacy cost millions of lives, particularly when they played a key role in starting the First World War, then wantonly exposed their massive but ill-prepared armies for slaughter. This book examines the extraordinary psychology of the leaders of this dynasty, their remarkable ability to survive major disasters, the strong and talented women they chose as wives and produced as daughters. They were not only an eccentric dynasty but their leading members were eccentric in remarkably different ways: from feeble, monk-like characters such as Tsar Mikhail to the workaholic giant Peter the Great or the hen-pecked mediocrity, Nicholas II.

The rewards for those members of the family who won the throne were enormous in terms of wealth and, if they had the character to wield it, almost unlimited power. Yet such was their sense of duty that they made great personal sacrifices for what they believed was right. The price of failure was also very high: for the men it often meant murder – six out of their eighteen crowned heads met violent ends – or imprisonment in remote fortresses for the rest of their lives; for the women it meant the dangers of frequent child-bearing, of compulsory incarceration in a nunnery or years of neglect as they had no choice but to tolerate the open adultery of their husbands.

Partly due to ill health and partly due to violence the average life-span of ruling Romanovs was not high: their average age at death was forty-four. Only two lived beyond the age of sixty, Catherine the Great (sixty-seven) and Alexander II (sixty-two) and none of them made it to seventy. The average length of reign was only seventeen years with Peter the Great having the longest – forty-three years – six others lasting five years or less.

Each chapter is a stand-alone mini-biography of each head of the family, so in terms of chronology there is some back-tracking, but that is because this book is more an analysis of character than a history of Russia. At the same time there is a thread running through all the lives, for each generation introduced variations on the theme of compulsive autocracy which cumulatively created an inheritance that made any softening dangerous, if not impossible, and led inevitably towards disaster.

The third main section of the book takes us on an armchair trip round the vast Russian empire which spread into areas which are now part of China and the United States as well as Poland, Finland, the Baltic States and a whole clutch of central Asian republics. Here we look at the extraordinary architectural legacy of a dynasty that did nothing by halves.

NOTE ON SPELLING

It is difficult to arrive at a style of spelling Russian names in our alphabet which is at once consistent, easily readable and true to the beauty of the Russian language. Some of the main characters in this book are so well known by their anglicised form of name like Peter or Nicholas that it seems pedantic to call them Pyotr or Nikolai, let alone Yekaterina for Catherine, whereas since the days of Gorbachev we have become used to Mikhail for Michael. Similarly we are well used to Tchaikovsky in concert programmes with a T and why change the final 'y' to a double 'i'? We are used to Moscow not Moskva, Crimea not Krim. Tartar is easier to say that Tatar. Odesa is more up to date than Odessa. Thus I have not been entirely consistent but have included a short glossary at the back of the book which lists those Russian words and names used with alternative spellings, especially those place names like St Petersburg that have been changed by different governments. I have also been slightly more pedantic in the gazeteer section so that people can find their way around.

NOTE ON CALENDAR

I have generally avoided complications due to the difference between the Julian and Gregorian calendars, though occasionally it does have some significance like the October/November revolution of 1917.

REFERENCES

Footnotes have not been included but wherever a source or writer is mentioned or quoted the details of the work referred to are included in the bibliography.

PART ONE

THE TSARS OF MUSCOVY

I

ANASTASIA ROMANOVNA
THE BEAUTY AND THE BEAST

'If they had not separated me from my little heiffer there would not have been so many victims'

Letter from Ivan IV to Prince Kurbsky

In February 1547 in the Cathedral of the Annunciation in the Kremlin, Moscow, the seventeen-year-old Ivan IV, the first ruler of Muscovy officially to be given the title Tsar, married his teenage bride Anastasia. Both his new title and his choice of bride were to be of great significance in the centuries that followed.

His new title Tsar, or Czar, was the russianised form of Caesar, first borrowed informally by his grandfather Ivan III after the fall of two great cities had presented him with a unique opportunity. The capture by the Turks of Constantinople, known as the Second Rome, meant that Moscow could put itself forward as 'the Third Rome' and one that would last for ever. The other city was Kiev which had been captured first by the Tartars, then the Poles, which meant that Moscow had a claim to be the capital of the Russian Orthodox Church. Put the two concepts together and the Grand Princes of Muscovy could justifiably call themselves Caesar. They could also start promoting Moscow as the new capital of the Christian world.

Even at the age of seventeen Ivan IV was ambitious and impatient, so that the concept of a jump in status from mere grand prince to Caesar appealed to him. As we shall see his career was in many ways to justify these pretensions although at considerable cost. He and his successors as tsars were to turn the small state of Muscovy into one of the most powerful and autocratic nations of the world.

Ivan's choice of a bride might not immediately have seemed so significant but was to have far-reaching and unexpected consequences, for the
girl's name was Anastasia Romanovna. Ivan, who had only just come of
age, had initially toyed with the idea of finding a foreign princess to be
the first tsaritsa, but there were none available that appealed. So he had
organised a short list of all the virgins of Muscovy who were of suitable
age and rank. Then he summoned the most likely 300 to Moscow for
medical tests, for personal inspection of their appearance and to check
on their table manners. He even sneaked into their quarters at night to
make sure they did not snore or sleep-walk. From this extraordinary
beauty parade, not the first to be held by a Muscovite ruler, many had
soon been eliminated and once Ivan spotted Anastasia he seems to have
plucked her like Cinderella from the crowd. It appears to have been a
genuine love match. He presented the handkerchief and ring that meant
she had won the contest.

Up to this point the Romanov family had been more minor gentry
than serious aristocracy. Anastasia's father Roman Zacharin, who had
died two years earlier, had provided the family with its new surname.
He was himself descended from an Andrei Kobyla who in around 1346
had migrated to Moscow from the area of the Baltic coast known to the
Russians as Prus (Prussia). That very year Estonia just to the north had
been sold by the Swedes to the Teutonic Knights of Germany who had
already overrun Lithuania from their crusading base at Marienburg. It
was in this atmosphere that the ancestors of the Romanovs, who were
almost certainly of Slavonic origin and the Orthodox faith, chose to
seek asylum in Moscow.

Andrei Kobyla was sufficiently respected for the Grand Prince
Simeon, ruler of Muscovy, to give him some ambassadorial duties to the
neighbouring principality of Tver which was not yet part of his growing
state. Andrei and his fifth son Feodor Koshka seem to have made money,
perhaps in the usual way in Moscow at that time by helping collect taxes
for the Tartar overlords, perhaps from trade, for having moved from Prus
they could not as yet be great landowners. They became influential but as
yet untitled members of the boyar class, the group of semi-independent
landowners who were entitled to advise the Grand Princes of Muscovy.
They could if they dared even seek the protection of alternative grand
princes in neighbouring states. One of Feodor Koshka's grandsons was
called Zachariah and from him were descended Roman Zacharin and

his daughter, the new tsaritsa, Anastasia Romanovna. Roman's brother Mikhail Zacharin (d. 1539) was a counsellor of Ivan III's and another uncle, Gregori, helped put Anastasia forward as a potential royal bride in 1547.

Nevertheless since Anastasia did not come from a top boyar family it was somewhat of a surprise when Ivan picked her from the final ten candidates and gave her the tokens which symbolised her triumph. Though their marriage was to last only thirteen years she was to make such a lasting impression that nearly half-a-century later it was to be her grand-nephew Mikhail who was elected the first tsar from the Romanov family and thus to alter the course of history.

It was Anastasia's pleasant personality that was the key to her success. An English visitor commented that she was 'wise and of such holiness, virtue and government that she was honored, loved and feared by all her subjects. He (Ivan IV) being young and riotous, she ruled him with admirable affability and wisdom.' Brought up quietly by her widowed mother she was not highly educated or sophisticated, but quietly pious, and in her own womanly way uniquely able to manage her unusual new husband. She behaved exactly as the textbook for Russian female behaviour, the *Domostroy*, said a woman should behave. Not that this entirely stilled the jealous tongues of the senior boyars.

We now turn to the teenager who had plucked Anastasia from obscurity. At this point Ivan IV was of course not yet known as Grozny (usually translated in English as Terrible though in Russian it means something more like Formidable which is not quite such a damning quality in a ruler). But already there were signs that his lonely childhood had left him psychologically scarred: he was rumoured to have dropped dogs from the battlements of the Kremlin. He was tall, but stooped and gawky with a hawkish face and close-set eyes.

Ivan had inherited the Grand Princedom of Muscovy at the age of three when his father Basil III (Vasili III ruled 1505-1533) died unexpectedly. Basil's first marriage had lasted twenty years but failed to produce an heir so he was already in late middle age when he put his wife aside and, to the horror of the Church, remarried. His new wife Helen was from Lithuania like the Romanovs and quickly bore him two sons, but as the bishops later chose to remind people, they had put the second marriage and its progeny under a curse which after Anastasia's death they were able to claim was fulfilled.

Meanwhile five years after Grand Prince Basil's death Helen, who had become regent for her son Ivan, was the victim of a palace coup. She was poisoned, her lover Prince Ivan Obolensky was stabbed to death and control of Moscow was seized by a faction of royal cousins and murderous boyars who were to create an oppressive atmosphere for the child tsar for the next few years.

Thus Ivan at the age of eight was made an orphan and until he came of age nine years later was left very much to his own devices. In particular as a bookish teenager he spent many hours sifting through the archives of the Kremlin and this gave him a unique awareness of the achievements of his father and grandfather in expanding the state of Muscovy. It was his grandfather Ivan III (1462-1505) who had captured Tver, subdued the princes of Yaroslavl, then conquered the city and mercantile republic of Novgorod 300 miles to the north-west. He had thus taken land-locked Muscovy to the Baltic Sea and right up to the White Sea where Ivan later founded the new sea-port at Arkhangelsk, albeit one that only functioned in the summer months.

Not only had Ivan III thus quadrupled the size of his princedom, but he had worked hard at its image as the focal point for the Slavonic nations. Rival Russian princes were gradually eliminated. The Great Bell of Novgorod was brought to Moscow and Ivan, instead of being the first amongst equals, began to emphasise his independence from boyar advice and his role as an autocrat (*samoderzhetz*) and sovereign (*gosudar*). Then Ivan also exploited the opportunity created by the fall of the two great cities which had previously been the centres of the Orthodox Church. Constantinople had been captured by the Turks in 1453 and Ivan in 1472 married Zoe, a princess from the old Byzantine dynasty, thus giving credence to the idea that Moscow would take over from Constantinople (the Second Rome) and become a Third Rome that would be everlasting. The other rival city which had previously been the centre for the Russian Orthodox Church was Kiev, but this had fallen to the Lithuanians and Poles who had turned it into a Catholic outpost directed against the heretic Orthodox. So the archbishops of Moscow could see their potential role as leaders of Orthodoxy and aped the elaborate ceremonials of the Byzantine Church. Princess Zoe was renamed Sofia (the Greek for wisdom) and Anastasia was christened in the same fashion for her name was the Greek for resurrection.

To sustain the new image of Moscow as a religious and ethnic capital Ivan III had imported Italian architects and masons to rebuild the city.

The vast triangular fortress of the Kremlin facing the Moscow River was given five huge square towers. With the tributary Neglinnaya on one other side and a wide moat on the third the Kremlin became an impregnable island. There were new dungeons and torture chambers including the Beklemishev Tower named after a boyar who had pushed his luck too far with Ivan III and been executed as an example to the rest. The main gateway to the Kremlin was the Saviour's Tower with its venerable icon and perpetually burning candles where all those who entered took off their hats in respect. In addition there was the new arsenal, not used just for the manufacture and storage of weapons, but also for a whole range of other crafts such as icon-making for the new cathedrals and jewellery for the royal family. Ivan also had three new cathedrals built. The largest was the Uspensky Sobor (Assumption) which contained the specially fabricated (but not genuine) throne of Vladimir Monomakh that was to be used for the coronation of all tsars. This magnificent white building with its huge four-arch façade had four onion-shaped domes surrounding a larger one in the centre. By the time of Napoleon the cathedral held 5½ tons of gold and silver for the French soldiers to steal.

The two other new cathedrals were the slightly Italianate Archangel Mikhail and the smaller but riotously domed Blagoveshchensky (Annunciation), the first for funerals and burials, the second for royal weddings for it was here that Ivan IV was to marry Anastasia. The three cathedrals bounded a square which also included a group of new bell towers, including the as yet half-built Ivan the Great Tower eventually 270 feet high and built to hold the monster Novgorod Bell, the symbol of Ivan III's greatest conquest. On special occasions this bell and three dozen smaller companions would ring out and receive a response from ten times that number of bells in the many other churches round Moscow.

For living quarters, Ivan III had built the Palace of Facets (it had diamond-shaped stones in its façade like its Florentine models) for state banquets and the display of dynastic wealth, while the new Terem Palace was for ordinary living and the royal females who were kept there in rigid seclusion. The two were partly connected by the Red Staircase.

As a long-term side-effect of Ivan's recruitment of Italian builders came the first introduction of spirit distillation, for the Italians brought that skill with them and the new beverage now produced for the first time in Russia was called little water or vodka.

The expansion of Muscovy continued under Ivan's father Basil III who conquered the states of Pskov and Ryazan and worked on the further embellishment of the Kremlin, but his death when his heir was only three years old created potential problems for the Rurik dynasty. However, after an uncomfortable period of regency young Ivan IV eventually asserted his adulthood in 1547 and donned the great crown of Vladimir Monomakh. He then very rapidly began to show that he had the character and ambition to make an effective tsar. After a brief honeymoon with Anastasia at the famous Troitse Monastery outside Moscow he settled down to work. Despite his subsequent reputation for cruelty and promiscuity his first marriage seems to have been a model of domestic normality. Though Anastasia kept herself mostly away from the public eye in the *Terem*, when she did appear she seems to have exuded an air of saintliness which was to boost the image of the Romanov family in years to come. In this she was helped by her brother Nikita Romanov or Romanovich Zacharin who became an influential courtier and friend to the tsar. Then in turn his brothers were also promoted, Daniel Romanovich becoming steward of the Grand Palace and his cousin Vasili Mikhailovich the steward of Tver, a move not too popular with rival boyars. There seems to have been a purge of the Glinsky clan, the relations of Ivan's mother, using as an excuse the accusation that their tricks had led to a fire that swept through the wooden houses of Moscow in 1547.

The first thirteen years of Ivan's rule which coincided with his marriage to Anastasia were successful in almost every way. He made a good choice of ministers who made intelligent reforms in the law and church. In his first major military campaign at the age of twenty-two Ivan accompanied by Nikita Romanov captured the important city of Kazan on the Volga some 500 miles east of Moscow from the Muslim Tartars. It was to celebrate this victory that he started work on another new cathedral outside the Kremlin in Red Square, the spectacularly domed Cathedral of the Intercession. It was later more usually called St Basil's after the wandering holy man Basil (Vasili Blazhennovy) who was befriended by Anastasia and was buried in a side chapel when he died in 1588. Thus by a strange coincidence both the first tsaritsa and the last were to be influenced by wandering holy men, in Alexandra's case Rasputin. Another church built for Anastasia was St Catherine the Martyr in the Fields and to emphasise her holiness she went on pilgrimages with Ivan to Rostov, Pereslavl and Yaroslavl.

Four years after the Kazan campaign Ivan also conquered Astrakhan which gave Muscovy its first outlet onto the Caspian Sea and meanwhile trade routes had been opened up to the rest of Europe from Arkhangelsk on the White Sea. Anastasia who so far had two daughters that had died in infancy at last produced the first of three sons, so the dynasty appeared to be secure. The only hint of difficulty was when Ivan himself was extremely ill in 1553 and tried to extract an oath of allegiance from the boyars for his infant son Dimitri. Anastasia and her brothers Nikita and Daniel were amongst the few who supported him and when he recovered there was the first hint of neurosis as Ivan realised how few of his boyars he could trust. Even then Daniel seems to have been dismissed briefly for a period soon afterwards. In a mood slightly suggestive of his later paranoia Ivan accused some of his less cooperative boyars of stirring up hatred of Anastasia by hinting that she was like evil princesses of the past. Implicated in this criticism of Anastasia were two key men in Ivan's entourage: Prince Andrei Kurbsky, for a long time Ivan's favourite general, but one who perhaps did not relish having to serve under Anastasia's brother, seems to have fallen out with her. Her other critic was the fire-eating Sylvester, the homophobic arch-priest of the Assumption Cathedral who ranted about the immoralities of court life, allegedly wrote the anti-feminist textbook the *Domostroy* and blamed Anastasia for her slow production of a male heir. Yet what exactly he had against her is not clear unless it was her patronage of the eccentric Saint Basil who like Rasputin nearly 400 years later was not part of the religious establishment.

The complexion of Ivan's reign started to change drastically when Anastasia fell ill herself. She went on a pilgrimage in the hope of recovery but died soon afterwards at the Kolomenskoe Palace outside Moscow, probably of natural causes, though there were the usual Kremlin suspicions of poison. Ivan blamed Sylvester and his allies for preventing her from going to other places of pilgrimage to aid her recovery, but at the time he was himself helping to put out another fire that was raging through Moscow. Yet since she had borne six children, four of whom died in infancy, it is hardly surprising in those days of minimal sanitation and uneven diet that she should succumb to illness.

Anastasia had been twenty-nine and Ivan still had twenty-four years of his reign ahead of him. Though little Dimitri had died as an infant there were still two sons: Ivan (1554-81) and Feodor (1557-98). But with his sister gone it was to be a major test for the key surviving male member of the Romanov family, Anastasia's brother Nikita.

It is hard to disentangle the image of a mad sadist from that of a ruthless Renaissance monarch, for Ivan IV was probably a bit of both. Certainly after Anastasia's death his personality seemed to undergo a drastic change. He began to attack his closest adherents, and when one of them, his ex-favourite Prince Andrei Kurbsky, went over to the enemy he exploited the situation to the full. He staged a mock abdication and refused to resume his reign until he had extracted more autocratic powers from the boyars. He then began to recruit an elite brotherhood of some 6,000 *oprichniks*, or enforcers, to purge those boyars who were holding back his plans to centralise the state. One of the prime movers of this new force seems to have been the Romanov cousin, Vasili Zakharin.

There followed a seven-year reign of terror during which the black-uniformed *oprichniki* tortured recalcitrant boyars until they confessed to disloyalty. It was during this period that Nikita Romanov who had himself been enlisted as an oprichnik, nevertheless enhanced the image of his family by restraining the sadism of his colleagues, so much so that a folk song about his adventures became one of the most popular of the decade. These acts of bravery in defiance of such a terrifying master were to stand the family in very good stead when the Muscovites were looking for a new tsar some fifty years later.

Meanwhile the *oprichniki*, like most private armies recruited to do dirty work, showed themselves to be cowardly and inept when threatened by real warriors from outside. In 1571 the Tartars attacked Moscow and the *oprichniki* failed totally to defend it. And since they had already done most of the purging that Ivan had wanted their days were numbered. Almost their final task had been to wipe out the population of Novgorod which had dared to rebel against Ivan's oppressive rule and objected to their business being snatched away by Ivan III's new port on the Baltic, Ivangorod. Now with the Tartar fiasco Ivan could abandon his protégées and allowed many of them to be massacred in Red Square. Operating from the Alexandrovo Sloboda Monastery they had encouraged Ivan's orgies as well as being the tools of his violence and had allegedly turned the building into a large brothel where the Tsar had, according to his critics, become a serial abuser of women. So when Ivan disbanded them there were plenty of enemies eager for revenge.

Five years later came perhaps the lowest point in Ivan the Terrible's career. For a man who had had six or seven wives and arranged for at least two of them to be murdered it was an odd act of prudery for him to protest about an immodest ante-natal garment being worn by his daughter-in-law, the pregnant wife of his eldest son the Tsarevich Ivan. According to the most credible account this was the cause of the quarrel which ended with the Tsar murdering his own heir in 1581. There may have been other reasons for there is some evidence that the Tsarevich had disapproved of the Novgorod massacres and been backed in this by the Romanov clan. One of Anastasia's nephews, Protasi Zacharin, was executed in 1575 whilst both Vasili Zacharin's daughter and grandson were also executed so there may have been a connection, perhaps the beginnings of a plot to replace Ivan with his half-Romanov elder son.

The murdered Tsarevich Ivan, a Romanov on his mother's side, was sometimes portrayed as violent and promiscuous like his father but he had at least been healthy and of enough intelligence to be a competent tsar. The same could not be said of the new Tsarevich Feodor, Anastasia's youngest son. He was small for his age, suffered from dropsy, had weak legs, probably had severe learning difficulties and was apparently only interested in bell ringing. Moreover he had spent his youth with no mother to guide him in the brothel-cum-police headquarters, the notorious Alexandrovo Monastery.

Meanwhile Ivan IV, apparently full of regret that he had killed his son, still had another three years to reign. Like Henry VIII of England (who died the year Ivan married Anastasia) he was a serial collector of queens. Nikita Romanov who had married an Evdokhia Yaroslavovna was still in sufficiently good odour to be sent to negotiate with the ambassador of Queen Elizabeth for the hand of Mary Hastings, a relation of the Tudors. The English conditions were too demanding however and Nikita was dismissed from his position in 1582, the negotiations coming to nothing. Ivan was by this time fifty-three and showing signs of decrepitude. He died in 1584, a character blackened by many subsequent chroniclers though his achievements were considerable if not necessarily beneficial and his behaviour was probably only marginally worse than many other rulers, including Romanovs, who were later described as great.

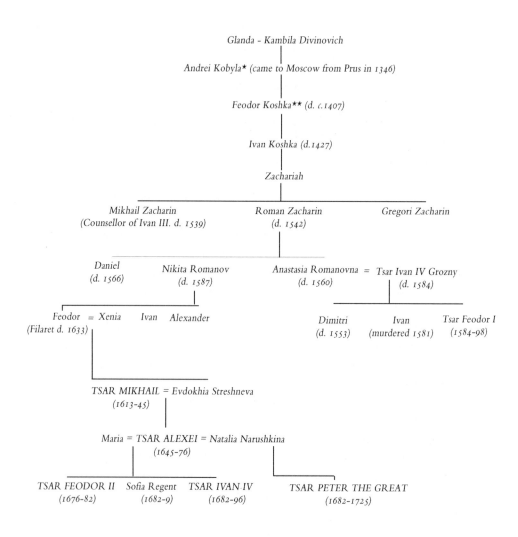

Glanda - Kambila Divinovich
|
Andrei Kobyla★ (came to Moscow from Prus in 1346)
|
Feodor Koshka★★ (d. c.1407)
|
Ivan Koshka (d.1427)
|
Zachariah
|

| Mikhail Zacharin | Roman Zacharin | Gregori Zacharin |
| (Counsellor of Ivan III. d. 1539) | (d. 1542) | |

Daniel   Nikita Romanov   Anastasia Romanovna = Tsar Ivan IV Grozny
(d. 1566)   (d. 1587)   (d. 1560)   (d. 1584)

Feodor = Xenia   Ivan   Alexander   Dimitri   Ivan   Tsar Feodor I
(Filaret d. 1633)   (d. 1553)   (murdered 1581)   (1584-98)

TSAR MIKHAIL = Evdokhia Streshneva
(1613-45)

Maria = TSAR ALEXEI = Natalia Narushkina
(1645-76)

TSAR FEODOR II   Sofia Regent   TSAR IVAN IV   TSAR PETER THE GREAT
(1676-82)   (1682-9)   (1682-96)   (1682-1725)

★Kobyla = mare
★★Koshka = cat

II

FEODOR
THE HALF-ROMANOV TSAR

'Without the tsar the land is a widow, without the tsar the people are an orphan'

Old Muscovite Proverb

When Ivan IV died in 1584 he left his much increased state of Muscovy to a virtual invalid of about twenty-seven. Significantly Feodor (ruled 1584-98) was of course half a Romanov for his mother had been Anastasia. One thing in his favour was that Russians had a certain affection for saintly idiots like the holy beggars who tramped the country roads round Moscow, and the new Tsar Feodor I (his name meant Gift of God in Greek, the language of the Church) fitted this category though he was to live on until he was over forty. Perhaps he was not as stupid as people chose to suggest for he could speak Polish as well as Russian and was an avid reader of the latest Polish romances.

All might still not have been lost for the old dynasty of Rurik for initially Feodor had an able and popular regent, his uncle Nikita Romanov, but sadly within two years Nikita died and Muscovy was heading for chaos.

The new head of the Romanov family, Nikita's son, shared Christian names with his first cousin the Tsar Feodor, but sadly he was a mere teenager and in the hurly burly of Kremlin politics he stood no chance of replacing his father as Regent for the sickly tsar. Certainly he was intelligent, well educated and perhaps even more able than his father the popular Nikita. He commissioned the first Russian-Latin dictionary to help his study of the ancients but this was of little value in the current crisis. Thus he was packed off to the Lithuanian front to gain some military experience, leaving Moscow to the mercies of a succession of ruthlessly ambitious boyars.

Instead of any member of the Romanov family the new star of Muscovite politics was a former aide and chess-playing companion of Ivan the Terrible's, Boris Godunov. He had contrived to get his sister Irene married to the new tsar and had himself earlier gained favour by marrying the daughter of the chief *oprichnik*. Though of Tartar descent and not a ranking boyar he was in his early-thirties both able and decisive, so he quickly established himself as the new regent.

The next twelve years saw the gradual decline of the ailing and almost imbecilic tsar. Since he had no surviving children, and there were no other acknowledged legitimate male heirs, it spelled the end of a dynasty that had ruled Muscovy since its migration there in 1263. The only other surviving son of Ivan the Terrible had been Dimitri, the product of his seventh and ecclesiastically challenged marriage, and he had died in mysterious circumstances at Uglich in 1591 aged nine. It is quite clear therefore that the ambitious Boris Godunov had used his period as regent to prepare himself to take over and found a new dynasty. He had his own man Iov appointed as Patriarch of the Russian Orthodox Church. He allowed the Muscovite peasants to become the virtual property or serfs of local landowners, whom he exempted from tax to help create his own power base.

By 1597, the year before Tsar Feodor's death it was clear that Boris had only one serious rival as a potential replacement tsar, Feodor Romanov. Feodor had excelled in the army and now in his early-thirties, a decade younger than Boris, he was a popular figure. But as yet he lacked the networking skills of his rival who one way or another had most of the senior boyars in his pocket, the civil service and the Church well under his thumb. Boris also had the supreme advantage of having the Tsar's widow as his sister and had no intention of losing his advantages.

III

FEODOR ROMANOV
THE RELUCTANT MONK

'He is irritable, mistrustful and so overbearing that the tsar himself is afraid of him'

Comment on Feodor Romanov by Archbishop Pakhomi of Astrakhan

Feodor Romanov and his allies made one last effort to stop the election of Boris Godunov as tsar. He was apparently involved in a scuffle where it was said he tried to stab Boris. The Romanovs also encouraged a smear campaign which implicated Boris in the strange death of Dimitri, the son of Ivan the Terrible's final marriage which had never been fully accepted by the Church. The boy Dimitri was epileptic and according to one official version had accidentally slit his own throat during a fit at Uglich, but naturally there were rumours of murder. The odd circumstances of his death meant that in future years it was easy enough to suggest that the whole thing was fiction and look-alikes were found so that Dimitri could be brought back to life to the discomfort of future tsars. So from suggestions that his death had been a murder organised by Boris Godunov it was a natural step to make the additional, though even less likely accusation, that Boris had poisoned Tsar Feodor as well.

In the meantime however Boris was successful. He was crowned Tsar in September 1598 with the full approval of the *Zemski Sobor*, the assembly of notables. Initially he was not vindictive to his former rivals such as Feodor Romanov and Alexander Romanov was actually promoted to boyar rank. But within two years Boris had failed to deliver on many of his promises to his supporters and there were rumours of unrest to which it is probable that the Romanov family contributed. In October

1600 Feodor's brother Alexander Nikitich Romanov was accused by one of his own servants of practicing witchcraft against the Tsar and poisoned herbs were conveniently discovered in his store house. It was a standard ploy encouraged by Boris in his campaigns against restive boyars and one regularly used by him when he had been an *oprichnik* officer for Ivan the Terrible. The accusations of witchcraft were mere cover for the real crime of the Romanovs which had been to create a private army made up mainly of their personal slaves and to begin to concentrate it round Moscow.

Feodor, Alexander and two other Romanov brothers were arrested and charged with plotting to kill the Tsar. One of the main Romanov houses in Moscow was burned down. All four brothers were sentenced to exile – Ivan to Pelym in Siberia – and two of them died mysteriously in the process. All their lands were seized and redistributed amongst boyars who favoured Boris. Their private armies were disbanded and their adherents similarly punished in a major purge. Then most calamitously of all for the family its senior member Feodor was forced to become a monk, an especial disaster for him, because in the eyes of the Russian Church such a step was irreversible and it meant that all Feodor's hopes of a royal career were permanently dashed. In addition his wife Xenia was forced to become a nun and after four infant deaths in the family they had only one sickly son left alive, so it looked as if the Romanovs as a potential royal dynasty were no longer a possibility.

Thus the new monk, renamed Filaret (lover of virtue in Greek) and the new nun renamed Marfa had to go their separate ways, Filaret initially to the Antoniev Sissky Monastery and Marfa to faraway Onega. It was to be one of the remarkable feats of history that this family whose star had been so drastically eclipsed should eventually triumph thirteen years later.

This is not the place to discuss in detail the tribulations of Tsar Boris as he struggled to retain control till his death five years later. He was far from being an ineffective ruler for he continued Muscovy's expansion southwards and kept good control of finances despite the expense of trying to subdue the Cossacks. But he struggled always with the fact that he was a newcomer and fairly or unfairly was tainted by the slanderous accusations about the death of the Tsarevitch Dimitri. Our concern is more with the extraordinary guile shown by the monk Filaret as he fought to regain the political initiative despite his huge disadvantage. In this he was aided by two factors. One was the increasingly unpopular rule of Boris himself, which became reminiscent of the bad days of Ivan the Terrible as he felt it necessary to use torture to gain confessions and encourage false accusations by slaves and servants against their masters. The other was the mischievous assistance of one-time rival and now close ally, the unscrupulous ex-oprichnik Bogdan Belsky. He and other Romanov allies exploited the growing unpopularity of Boris when Muscovy was hit by a disastrous famine which wiped out nearly one-third of the population. Ordinary Russians were reduced to eating hay, roots, dogs and cats. Belsky and Filaret revived the irritating rumour that the Tsarevitch Dimitri had not died at Uglich but was a living legitimate tsar who should be called back to replace the usurper Boris. This was the theme of Mussorgsky's much later opera *Boris Godunov* based on a play by Pushkin.

Then unexpectedly Tsar Boris died in 1605 and was replaced at once by his sickly son the sixteen-year-old Feodor II Borisovich who handed out 70,000 roubles to the populace in a vain effort to enhance his popularity. Bogdan Belsky, the Golitsyns and other allies of the Romanovs produced the replacement (or just possibly genuine) Tsarevitch Dimitri and proclaimed him the legitimate only son of Ivan IV. A mutiny in the Tsar's army at Kromy and a popular uprising in Moscow led to an almost bloodless takeover by the supporters of this first look-alike Dimitri. Tsar Fedor II and his mother the widow Godunov were strangled on the orders of Golitsyn and 'Dimitri' was crowned Tsar.

As his reward for help in this coup the humble monk Filaret Romanov was instantly promoted to Metropolitan of Rostov. The other Romanovs recovered their estates and Ivan Romanov the senior lay member of the family was promoted back to the rank of boyar.

The success of this first 'Tsar Dimitri' did not last long however. There were perhaps well-founded rumours that he was a Pole and therefore a Catholic, possibly even an ex-monk. Another version was that he was Otrepev, a monk and a former servant of the Romanovs who had specially groomed him for the job. In 1606 he was assassinated.

The Romanovs were not ready for this new vacancy on the throne. Filaret as a monk could not be a candidate; his son Mikhail at the age of nine was too young; while the only other senior male Romanov, Ivan, had made himself too unpopular and was ill anyway. So Vasili Shuisky leader of the boyar coup which had ousted 'Dimitri' came forward as the champion of Russian Orthodoxy against the Poles.

The wily Filaret was not to be outdone. He quickly organised a new look-alike Dimitri. Despite the objections of Tsar Vasili he managed to have himself made Patriarch of Moscow and when he was sacked by the Tsar simply took the job back for himself with the help of his tame new alternative tsar, the second 'Dimitri' based at Tushino to which Filaret had been brought as a prisoner in 1608. This time it was Tsar Vasili's turn to be forcibly shorn in Red Square and condemned to life as a monk.

Despite the fall of Tsar Vasili, there was little gain for Filaret Romanov. He was sent to the Polish capital of Krakow to negotiate the peaceful appointment of a Polish candidate, Ladislaus, as the new tsar, an offer that was to be conditional on the Pole converting to Russian Orthodoxy. Most Muscovites thought this a desperate measure and the Poles probably had no intention of letting their man abandon Catholicism. In this messy situation Filaret was arrested in Krakow and was to spend the next eight years as a prisoner in Wawel Castle. The fate of the ex-tsar Vasili, now monk Varlan, was even worse for he was murdered in Poland.

With four tsars in three years, the onset of another famine, a spreading plague and an invasion by the Poles which threatened Moscow itself, Muscovy appeared in 1611 to be in terminal decline. The Swedes captured Novgorod. The so-called Time of Troubles had reached its deepest trough. However Moscow was saved by a gallant contingent under Prince Dimitri Pozharski who was given financial support by a demagogic butcher named Kuzma Minin from Nizhny Novgorod. They drove the Poles out of Moscow.

The next year a third look-alike Dimitri was in prospect and the Cossacks were involved. They were the amorphous body made up mainly of ex-serfs, casual workers and wandering hunter-gatherers who had turned themselves into a part-time militia and had helped colonise the dangerous steppe country previously controlled by the Tartars. They also probably included many of the ex-slave soldiers previously part of the Romanov family's private army. They could in times of unrest wield considerable influence and supported the latest false look-alike Dimitri, the third to make his appearance since the days of Boris Godunov. There was also another part-time militia, the *Streltsi* or marksmen, founded by Ivan the Terrible in 1550 as a group of 3,000 specialists trained to use the *arquebus* – guns so heavy that that they had to be fired from a stand. Mostly they were city tradesmen who were given a basic wage and tax privileges in return for military service, but when there was a power vacuum as at this period they could use their bargaining power, just like the Cossacks. By this time there were around 7,000 of them in Moscow alone as well as at least the same scattered through other Russian cities. So now they also ranged themselves alongside the new Dimitri who made his base at Pskov. Despite this a counter-coup soon afterwards resulted in the capture of the third Dimitri in 1612 and he was put on display in a cage for some time before being hanged.

By this point the state of affairs was so chaotic that the need for a genuine, legitimated tsar became desperate. The *Zemsky Sobor* was summoned, backed by the threatening presence in Moscow of belligerent Cossacks, frustrated *Streltsi* and large numbers of the more prosperous peasants. A three-day fast was ordered to clear the heads of participants. There were as usual plenty of boyar candidates for the tsardom, but none that had any special claim or outstanding ability. The Patriarch Filaret Romanov was not on the list partly because of his tonsure and partly because he was still a prisoner in Poland. His brother Ivan Romanov was not popular as he was blamed even more than Filaret for trying to sell out to the Poles. But with the residual image of the Romanovs' connections to the old dynasty, particularly the memory of Anastasia and Nikita, and more recently some of the more popular ploys of Filaret, there was a swing of mood towards the Romanovs. The Cossacks in particular dominated the meeting of the *Zemsky Sobor* and were desperate for the installation of a proper tsar and the restoration of normal life.

Their only candidate was Filaret's son Mikhail Romanov, aged sixteen, but no one even knew his whereabouts. Many of the boyars had been alarmed by the extravagant support given to all three of the false Dimitris and dreaded the concept of a populist tsar. They thought that Mikhail would be another puppet submitting himself to their whims, so they seem mostly to have supported the new candidate. All that remained was to find him.

How and when Filaret in his distant Krakow prison heard the news that his son was to be the first Romanov tsar we do not know. But it must have been with mixed feelings, for the lifespan of recent tsars, even capable ones, had been extremely short, and Mikhail was young, inexperienced, untrained and physically weak.

IV

MIKHAIL FEODOROVICH ROMANOV
THE ELECTED TSAR

'Let us have Misha Romanov for he is young and not yet wise; he will suit
our purposes'
> Alleged remark made by one of the boyars at the assembly of 1613

The boy chosen without his knowledge to be the new tsar was at the
time living 200 miles from Moscow in the remote Ipatiev Monastery
at Kostrome, the latest place of exile for the reluctant nun, his mother
Xenia or Marfa. Here he had spent much of his childhood and naturally his education had veered towards the ecclesiastical rather than the
military or political. The fact that he had been a sickly child with no
prospects but a monastic career had made this seem eminently sensible.

When the boy Misha and his mother were told about his selection as
Tsar by the Zemsky Sobor it is hardly surprising that at first they both
rejected the idea. It was not just the usual act of playing hard to get
which had been used by both Ivan IV and Boris Godunov. They were
both aware of the high death rate amongst recent tsars and Misha had
been exposed to some of the violence when he was briefly resident in
the Kremlin during the Polish occupation. But despite initially shedding
tears at his fate Misha was eventually persuaded that it was his divine
duty to accept the title of Tsar Mikhail.

To add romance to the story of his election there was the somewhat
embroidered tale of how he had been saved from a group of murderous
Polish soldiers by a local peasant, Ivan Susanin, who had at the cost of his
own life lured the Poles off the track into the deepest and coldest part of
the forest. This incident provided the new dynasty with its first martyr

and centuries later gave the composer Glinka the ideal theme for his patriotic opera *A Life for the Tsar*.

Meanwhile the emphasis was not on Mikhail being the first of a new dynasty, but much more about his continuity with the old one. Six months after his selection by the Zemsky Sobor he was crowned in the Cathedral of the Assumption or Uspensky Sobor in Moscow and the elaborate sacraments were all tuned to emphasise his relationship as cousin of Feodor, the last legitimate tsar of the dynasty of Rurik and as the proper upholder of the Russian Orthodox Church. In this context it was appropriate that his father was an imprisoned patriarch and he had himself been largely educated in the Ipatiev Monastery. Significantly as he and his mother had made their first stately progress to Moscow they had passed through Yaroslavl, then Rostov his father's first Episcopal see and finally the famous fortified Troitse Monastery. At each stopping point they had ostentatiously received oaths of allegiance from the surviving inhabitants, for vast numbers had been killed or died of starvation and lay unburied by the roadsides. Many farms and villages had been burned by passing Polish platoons or rebel Cossacks.

Several major problems confronted the new tsar and his boyar advisers. The first was the virtual bankruptcy of Muscovy due to the depredations of the Poles and the extravagance of successive short-term tsars. As a temporary expedient Mikhail borrowed a considerable sum from the Stroganov family who had made their fortune in the Siberian fur trade and metal foundries in the Urals. This source was soon put on a more formal footing by imposing a levy of 10 per cent on all fur traders. It brought in 45,000 roubles a year and even that doubled by the end of the reign, as the trade thrived with exports of ermine, sable, otter, lynx and marten to the west. The only problem was that the animals were hunted out of existence and the trappers had to move ever deeper into Siberia to make a living.

The second problem was the fragile credibility of the new tsar, accentuated by the fact that the Russians had listened to so many lies from the three false Dimitris and other claimants to the throne that it was hard to distinguish fact from fiction. Moreover the Romanovs were still somewhat tainted by their recent support of a Polish candidate to the throne, particularly the double dealings of Ivan Romanov and to a lesser extent the dubious mission of Filaret to Krakow. It had only been redeemed when he was arrested by the Poles and could now be portrayed as victim rather than perpetrator of treason. So a major propaganda campaign was orchestrated to emphasise the credentials of Mikhail as an oblique descendant of the old Rurik dynasty and as a supporter of Russian Orthodoxy against the encroachments of the hated Catholic Poles. At the same time there was a network of informers set up to search for any new Dimitris who might try to make an appearance. Torture, beatings and executions were used to intimidate anyone who might question the Romanov tsardom.

The third major problem was that so much Muscovite territory was in the hands of foreigners or rebels. Of the rebels the most immediate threat was from the Cossack leader Ivan Zarutsky who had been plundering the southern frontier with some 2,000 men and was championing Ivan – the posthumously born son of the second look-alike Dimitri – as the new child tsar, helped by Tsaritsa Marina, the look-alike Dimitri's widow. Even before Mikhail's coronation one of his armies had headed south to Voronezh and defeated Zarutsky in a closely contended battle. Many of his Cossacks at once changed sides, and Mikhail's advisers, who had a healthy fear of them made sure that they were quickly re-employed on Muscovy's dangerous western front or kept happy with ample supplies of vodka and gunpowder. Zarutsky himself survived for a while in Astrakhan before he was eventually captured. The child would-be tsar Ivan was hanged outside the gates of Moscow, Zarutsky was impaled and the self-styled Tsaritsa Marina was locked up to die in a Kolomna tower, showing that for all his alleged saintliness Mikhail had a streak of ruthlessness. As usual there were stories that little Ivan had survived and would make a come-back, but effectively this was the end of false tsars for the immediate future and for most onlookers marked the end of the Time of Troubles.

With Zarutsky out of the way Mikhail and his boyar advisers embarked on a purge of the remaining troublesome Cossacks, this despite the fact that the Tsar owed them his throne and Moscow owed them its release from Polish captivity. It was the usual system of bribed informers to root out troublemakers. There was also a drive to seize back all identifiable runaway serfs who had joined the Cossacks. Then Cossack units were broken up by luring their leaders to Moscow for negotiations only to execute them without trial. Others were accused of brigandage, some of them but by no means all fairly, and were similarly executed. The remainder wherever possible were sent off to fight the Poles and Swedes, even though the southern frontier was now so weak that the Tartar slave raiders were carting off such a large number of Russians into slavery that the price of them on the Istanbul market in 1642 fell by 70 per cent.

So far as foreign invaders were concerned the Swedes, under their able king Gustavus Adolphus were the most serious threat but were the most likely to negotiate, for Gustavus was more interested in conquering parts of Germany than the frozen north-east and was also seriously short of money. Gustavus had also failed to capture the city of Pskov despite hugely outnumbering the garrison and was getting weary of trying to subdue the area, especially since its Russian inhabitants had all vanished, leaving behind nothing but burned fields and empty granaries. Thus by a treaty signed in 1617 Muscovy recovered, for cash, the important city of Novgorod, Ladoga and Starie Rusa but not the coastal territories on the Gulf of Finland including the important harbour of Ivangorod, which had been lost in 1583.

The other major threat was from Poland. Prince Ladislaus, son of King Sigismund of Poland-Lithuania, had long been a candidate to be Tsar and now made one final attempt at invasion to achieve his ambition. Many Cossacks deserted to him in the wake of the boyars' efforts to turn them back into serfs and also because of their extreme tardiness in paying wages. As the remaining Cossacks refused to fight for any Russian commander except the trusted Prince Pozharsky, Mikhail was forced to acknowledge him as commander-in-chief and to make more effort to placate the Cossacks. As a result Ladislaus was beaten back. Like Gustavus the would-be tsar Ladislaus was running out of money so he agreed to negotiate and won a surprisingly good treaty from the Muscovites. Mikhail even surrendered several Russian towns which were still holding out against the Polish army. Altogether some thirty towns were transferred to Poland-Lithuania, including the areas round Smolensk and Chernigov. The only explanation for the supine behaviour of the Muscovite negotiators is that Mikhail was petrified of yet another look-alike tsar, Ivan Dimitrivich, who was being groomed by the Poles and he was also desperate for the release of his father Filaret from Polish custody. In the long run the return of Filaret was more important for the future of the Romanov dynasty than the loss of thirty towns.

A third major area of foreign incursion was in the south where the Crimean Tartars still ran a major slave-trafficking operation which snatched thousands of Russians from the steppes and shipped them down to Istanbul for a substantial profit. Not for nothing was the word slave derived from the ethnic term Slav. For the time being Mikhail could do little about this problem and the defence in the south was left to the irregular Cossacks.

The fourth major problem besetting Mikhail was that Moscow, including the Kremlin, had been badly damaged during the Polish siege and subsequent fires. Many of the palaces had lost their roofs, the wooden housing had been destroyed and there was need for a considerable amount of reconstruction and expense. In addition he needed to build a number of new fortresses to guard the redrawn frontiers of Muscovy.

Miraculously Tsar Mikhail had now survived six years on the throne, a tribute perhaps more to the revulsion felt by most Russians for the chaos of the Time of Troubles than for any skill on the part of the young tsar. He had surrendered substantial areas of territory to the Swedes and the Poles, but Muscovy was once more at peace. Above all he was now able to welcome home his father Filaret who was to provide the new dynasty with a backbone for the rest of his life. At this point the Tsar was still a weak-kneed twenty-two while his father, now restored as Patriarch, was a robust, energetic sixty-six. After their long separation they greeted each other apparently with tears of joy on the outskirts of Moscow.

Up to this time Tsar Mikhail had been heavily dependent on the council or *Duma* of boyars which had urged him to be ruthlessly suppressive. He had still been summoning the *Zemsky Sobor*, the body which had first elected him, on an annual basis. But with his father at his side he could begin to get rid of both bodies. The boyars had a reputation for corruption and many of Mikhail's advisers had been, as Isaac Massa described them in 1614, 'young and ignorant men' anxious to line their pockets after the long years of turbulence. His officials were 'ravening wolves who pluck and pillage the common people most of all.'

Bribery was standard. With his urgent need to reduce his military dependence on the Cossacks the Tsar had been obliged to continue the policy of giving out land to service barons who were empowered to prevent any escapes by their serfs in return for helping his military campaigns. Since the time of Boris Godunov serfdom had become more rigidly enforced to ensure a tax-paying basis for the economy with a superstructure of landowners obliged to do military service. Initially there was a spate of serf escapes to Siberia and the Ukraine which slowed down the recovery of agriculture but gradually this haemorrhaging of peasant tax-payers was stemmed.

Filaret now had himself officially consecrated by the Patriarch of Jerusalem and installed himself near his son in the Krutiskoe Podvor, the traditional residence of the patriarch and had the additional title of *Veliky Gosudar*, Great Ruler, the same as his son, so that he became joint-Tsar in all but name. He also built up a large staff and a substantial portfolio of property, making himself a very rich man. His wife the nun Marfa came back to the Kremlin but was now regarded as slow-witted and taking her religion too seriously, so she was kept out of state affairs. As always Filaret was still image-conscious and had his hair and beard trimmed every other month for twenty-four kopecks by a monk from the Chudov Monastery. His strategy was to eliminate altogether the *Zemsky Sobor* which had come into existence in the Time of Troubles, and to reduce very considerably the size of the *Duma*. It was shrunk to the *Blizhny Soviet*, a privy council of four or five boyar advisers.

The other prong to Filaret's strategy was to make use of the Russian Orthodox Church of which he was the Head as the backbone of the new autocracy. Both his and his wife's relatively new profession as well as the religious predilections and non-aggressive temperament of his son made it relatively easy. The Tsar liked to pray and attended church services two or three times every day. Even his visits to his wife and children in the *Terem* were dictated by the church agenda. He smothered his frail body in vast ceremonial garments so that it took two boyars to help hold him up. Most of the time he hid himself away in the Kremlin to cultivate his godlike status, only appearing on special occasions like the December Festival of the Patriarch and the Epiphany blessing of the waters. This meant that the populace only saw him in the dim distance and could revere him as someone beyond normal life. The number of prostrations required of those seeking an audience just added to the image of remoteness. By the same token Filaret as head of the Church was punctilious in insisting on triple-immersion baptism and other features that made it distinctive, making sure that any Protestant mercenaries in the army were kept well out of the way and persecuting any religious deviants.

Despite his general austerity Mikhail did allow himself a few frivolous indulgences. He was fond of folk song and enjoyed listening to the new organ he had brought in from the West, the first in Russia, to the horror of conservative priests. Like many of his successors he liked at times to be entertained by jesters, dwarfs and people like negroes from exotic lands. He also had a passion for jewellery and encouraged skilled goldsmiths to settle in the Kremlin. Though neither a great eater nor drinker himself he did like to organise elaborate feasts for his guests. The general standards of Russian court life at this time as observed by Westerners like Olearius were heavy drinking, minimal hygiene, constant swearing and although the women were kept in almost oriental seclusion there were other forms of sexual indulgence that horrified the foreigners.

Meanwhile the aging but still energetic Filaret attended to the detail of government. Taxation was reformed and trade encouraged by tax exemptions for foreign merchants trading in the summer through Arkhangelsk. Alcohol production was nationalised and became a huge revenue-earner for the state. Freeborn tax-payers were prevented from turning themselves into Church serfs in order to evade taxes and Filaret organised a major census of serfs so that escaping could be reduced. As a result the Tsar was able to spend money on the further beautification of Moscow with a fine new palace in the Kremlin as well as an extension of the *Terem*, additions to the massive Saviour's Gate and the installation of the great Kremlin chiming clock which became a focal point for the city. There was also money to spend on a new stone bridge over the Moskva River based on a Swedish design. On a more utilitarian front construction projects included a chain of fortresses and twenty-nine garrison towns from Belgorod and Voronezh to the Vorskla River on the western frontier. At the same time heavy expenditure on armaments stimulated the growth of large new metal works at Tomsk, foundries, rope-works and ammunition factories. Moscow itself had a new cannon factory powered by water in 1632.

If the populace saw little of the Tsar they saw even less of the Tsaritsa who spent most of her life in the Terem and if she emerged at all only did so in a windowless carriage as decreed by the *Domestroy* of the archpriest Sylvester. Despite his lack of fitness and his apparent lack of interest in women Mikhail certainly did his duty in the production of heirs. His first wife Maria Dolgoruka whom he married in 1624 died in childbirth and with his second wife acquired two years later, Evdokhia Streshneva, he had ten children of whom sadly six died in childhood.

The improvement in the economy and the gradual replacement of the boyars by an officer class of newer landowners with strict obligations meant that Muscovy could re-arm. Professional officers from the rest of Europe were attracted by good salaries and prospects to help enhance the skill levels of the Russians. The *Streltsi* or marksmen were expanded to around 20,000. The uneasy truce with the Poles was due to end and there were still problems with the Crimean Tartars. In 1637 there was a rebellion of Cossacks in Polish territory who objected to religious persecution by their Polish catholic masters so they moved nearer to Moscow or went to help the Don Cossacks in their wars against the Tartars.

Significantly peace had ended in 1632 when Filaret at last died aged seventy-nine having undoubtedly contributed very substantially to the establishment of the Romanovs as a viable dynasty. After major initial successes under General Shein the Russians suffered a humiliating defeat by the Poles at Smolensk. The entire Russian force surrendered and Shein was beheaded by the Tsar for incompetence. Equally ineffectual was Mikhail's record in the south. There an army of 4,000 Cossacks had used their own initiative in 1637 to mount a daring attack on Azov, the main Tartar fortress guarding the approach to the Black Sea. They captured it, massacred the Muslim defenders and freed the Christian slaves. Then they twice offered it to Mikhail but each time he hesitated to accept. Much though he hated the Muslim Turks he had no great love for the independent-minded Cossacks and after passing the buck of decision-making to his council he finally refused the valuable but perhaps dangerous prize.

Mikhail's final years were therefore spent without any dramatic successes. Even his efforts to marry his daughter to a foreign royal came to nothing because the chosen bridegroom, Prince Waldemar of Denmark refused to give up his Lutheran faith and the Russian churchmen went back on their promise not to force him to do so. Then in 1645 came further disaster when both Mikhail's two eldest sons died in quick succession. He was reported to have cried himself to death within a couple of months. He was forty-eight, had always supposedly been of weak constitution and below average ability, could barely walk due to an early riding accident and yet had ruled Muscovy with unexpected competence and firmness for thirty-two years. He had also managed to name his surviving son Alexei as his official successor.

V

ALEXEI
THE QUIETEST TSAR

'So vile are my deeds I am not fit to be a dog let alone a tsar'
Tsar Alexei in letter to Patriarch

By coincidence Alexei Mikhailovich Romanov (Alexis) succeeded to
the throne of Muscovy at exactly the same age as his father had done;
sixteen. By coincidence also he ruled for the same number of years and
died at the same age – forty-eight. In many other respects however
they were very different. Alexei was much healthier and probably more
intelligent. At adulthood he reached a height of about six feet and was
inclined to be overweight. As a child he wore toy armour and played at
soldiers, later he loved hunting, falcons and gardening. Yet as we shall see
he was a very complex character and there were marked changes in his
attitudes as the years went by.

At least in his piety he was similar to his father for from the age of six
his education in the Kremlin was supervised by his grandfather, Filaret
the Patriarch, so that he became a fanatical observer of every detail of
orthodox ritual. To achieve this he normally rose at 4 a.m. for prayer, then
attended matins with his wife and another two-hour service later in the
day at vespers. He often conducted business with his boyar advisers during intervals in the middle of services. If any priest made even the most
minor slip in conducting worship he would become apoplectic with
rage, screaming at the culprit or even using physical violence, though
when he calmed down afterwards he would sometimes apologise. In
the same way he was obsessive about court protocol, never appearing
unless he was wearing full state garments of the most elaborate kind,

sable with silver and precious stones, never listening to a petition unless the person made the requisite thirty obeisances before him. His throne was seven steps above the floor to emphasise the massive difference in status between himself and even the most senior of his subjects. Yet he led from the front and was known to make as many as 1,000 obeisances himself during major church celebrations and could stand for five hours or more listening to the sacraments. He was abstemious in both food and drink even at normal times, but during Lent even more so, taking only three modest meals a week. He was also an avid reader of theological texts including the Bible, now just recently translated into Slavonic from the Greek for the first time. So he was, from a religious point of view, perfectly prepared to take on the job of a priest-king and divinely ordained autocrat. The first step towards making other people believe it was for him to believe it himself.

His mother Evdokhia died in 1645 very soon after his father, Tsar Mikhail, so young Alexei took over the throne of Muscovy with no parental support. He did have one surviving royal uncle the popular Nikita Romanov but he was kept at a distance. So as a teenager he quite naturally turned to his tutor Boris Morozov who became the effective head of government for the first three years of his reign. While Morozov shared Alexei's religious conservatism he was far from being an incorruptible politician, for he seized the opportunity to make himself the richest man in Moscow. He bought himself one of only three English-made carriages in the whole of Russia. Two of his pet officials, Pleshcheev and Trakhaniotov were put in charge of key departments with a brief to increase taxes by whatever means, as the costs of the army continued to rise. Since more than half of all Russians were exempt from most taxes, the remainder found any increase very oppressive. A new salt tax that quadrupled the price of salt was particularly unpopular and so much food was allowed to rot that there was a severe shortage. There were signs that sooner or later dissatisfaction would bring the tax-payers to boiling point.

Meanwhile in early 1648 Alexei had decided to marry and there was the usual beauty contest of several hundred suitable virgins. This was narrowed down to a shortlist of six from whom after close inspection Alexei, now nineteen, selected a girl called Feodosia. Sadly she fainted on the spot and was suspected of epilepsy but perhaps her drink had been spiked by the family of her closest rival. Thus Alexei took his

second choice, Maria Miloslavskaya and his chief minister the rapacious
Morozov craftily married her sister a week later.

Then, while the tsar and his new tsaritsa were away on their honeymoon at the Troitse Monastery, the populace erupted. Alexei was
waylaid by rioters on his way back from Troitse. A massive fire broke
out in Moscow and Morozov was blamed for starting it. The revolution
spread to Pskov and Novgorod. The Cossacks on the Ukrainian border
joined in and just as in the Time of Troubles the rebels found themselves
an alternative would-be tsar, the supposed son of Vasili III. The *Streltsi*
refused to fire on the rioters. Nor was Alexei cheered up by the news
from Britain that their King Charles I had just been decapitated by order
of Parliament.

In this crisis the Tsar sought the help of his uncle Nikita Romanov
who was famed as a good landlord and was more popular with the
crowds. He succeeded in deflecting the anger of the people away from
the Tsar towards Morozov who was banished to a monastery in the arctic.
His fancy carriage was destroyed, his house set on fire and his wife, the
Tsar's sister-in-law ejected naked into the streets. Both Pleshcheev and
Trakhaniotov were surrendered to the anger of the mob in Red Square
and met grizzly ends in the *Lobnoe Mesto* – execution place.

The crisis deepened as the violent mobs took control of all Muscovy's
major cities and murdered the offending tax collectors. Tsar Alexei was in
no position to retaliate. At this juncture he received sensible advice from
Nikon, the Metropolitan of Novgorod who was to feature prominently
in the next stage of the Tsar's reign. His advice was to turn the other
cheek and grant amnesties to the thousands of rioters who had committed atrocities. By this time they had had their fill of revenge and were
now ready to settle back to normality. The *Streltsi* were given extra pay
to make sure they would back the establishment. The *Zemsky Sobor* was
once more relegated to the background and the Boyar *Duma* reduced to
a minor talking shop.

Once order had been restored Alexei and his new advisers set about
drawing up a new law code designed to prevent such disorder ever
breaking out again. Severe punishments were ordered for all future
acts of treason and any disobedience by serfs was to be met with the
knout whip or death. The urban classes were even more restricted in
their movements to prevent tax evasion. In addition, since the Church
asserted that the people had resorted to riots because of their addiction

to 'the games of the devil' Alexei introduced a whole series of puritanical laws designed to ban almost everything which might overexcite the ordinary citizens: tobacco, card-playing, music other than the chanting of psalms, performing animals, jugglers, jesters and all other entertainers, as well as many other apparently trivial pastimes. Alcohol consumption however brought in so much money to the exchequer that it was not curtailed, despite the fact that alcoholism was a serious problem throughout Russia.

A possible solution to the dangers of an unruly populace led by ill-educated boyars was offered by one of Alexei's new advisers, Feodor Rtishchev. This remarkable man built a new monastic school outside Moscow and attracted as its staff some thirty Kievan monks who brought with them from the old religious capital of Russia a much higher standard of scholarship than had been available in Moscow. They were encouraged for the first time to translate foreign texts into Russian and at the same time teach Latin, Greek and other languages as well as a broad curriculum of general knowledge. Not only did Rtishchev thus substantially improve education but he set a fine example by freeing his own serfs, giving shelter to alcoholics and others destitute on the streets of Moscow, and encouraging the building of almshouses to care for the disabled. Perhaps he was too radical and too ahead of his time to have vast influence but he did at least have some.

The other major influence on Alexei was the Croat priest Iuri Krizhavich who argued that Russia was such a large and complex country that no system of government could work there except total autocracy. Not surprisingly the Romanovs chose to accept this theory and amplified it over the next two centuries. Meanwhile one of Alexei's initiatives was to force all the foreigners in Moscow to live in one special area, a kind of ghetto known as the *Nemetskaya Sloboda* later much beloved by his son Peter. Yet most of the city remained a stinking fire-hazard, with piles of garbage and excrement.

Another by-product of the troubles was the elevation of Nikon to be Patriarch of Moscow. He had made a good impression on the Tsar for it was his sage advice which had enabled him to damp down the fires of rebellion. In 1653 he was brought down from Novgorod where he had been Metropolitan and set about a substantial reform of the Russian Church. His motivation as Patriarch was that if he could bring the Russian version of orthodoxy into line with the churches in Jerusalem and Istanbul then it would be realistic for Moscow to become the senior patriarchate, fulfilling the idea of the Third Rome predicted in the previous century and with great appeal to the ambitions of Tsar Alexei.

Many of the changes Nikon introduced now seem extremely trivial, like the number of fingers a person used to cross himself or specific words and spellings used in the sacraments. They were mainly just minor variations on the Greek model which had crept into Russian practice over preceding centuries. Yet as so often in religious practice the reaction of Church members to even the most minor changes can be explosive. The idea of going back to Greek forms of ritual seemed almost as horrific as the idea of conforming to Rome and the hated Catholics. Despite the fact that the gospels and service manuals had only recently been translated from Greek to Russian, the average Muscovite thought the Greek versions were the novelty and the Russian based on age-old tradition. So opponents of Nikon's reforms identified themselves in large numbers as the Old Believers and were willing to die rather than accept the changes advocated by Nikon. One cynical boyar even taught his pet dog to do the Nikon blessing and in this kind of atmosphere Nikon became not only obsessive but paranoid. In 1666 he was forced to resign but the discipline of his reforms was maintained.

The most virulent opponent of the new reforms was a charismatic Moscow preacher named Avvakum, a man whose reputation for putting his hand over a live flame to help him suppress sexual desire had spread widely and who also disapproved of beer, tobacco, art and the Greek fashion of worship. He was punished with prison, exile and nearly with mutilation but was to survive to become a martyr, burned at the stake, in the next reign. Many of his followers were martyred much sooner, including numerous congregations who barricaded themselves in their wooden churches and allowed themselves to be burned to death rather than surrender. A sister-in-law of the Tsaritsa, Theodosia Morozova, a widow who owned around 8,000 serfs, suffered torture for cursing the Tsar and supporting the Old Believers or *Raskolniki* (Sectarians). She and her sister were eventually starved to death in prison. The monks of the massive Solovetsky Monastery on the White Sea refused to accept the changes and were besieged by the royal army for eight years before being forced to surrender.

Apart from these largely unnecessary troubles created by religious reform there were plenty of other problems to bedevil the reign of Alexei. 1653 was a year of plague and famine and in the financial crisis

Alexei introduced highly unpopular copper coins to debase the coinage, partly because he was once more planning a war against Poland. In addition his Romanov cousins and his wife's numerous relations saw in the debasement a further opportunity to line their own pockets.

Alexei was encouraged to contemplate a war with Poland because the previously neutral Zaporozhian Cossacks based at Pereyslav had in 1648 fallen out with their Polish Catholic overlords in the western Ukraine and successfully rebelled under Bogdan Kmelnitsky. They defeated several Polish armies, ransacked Kiev and incidentally massacred around 200,000 Jews in one of the world's first great acts of genocide. However the energy of the Cossacks ran out in 1654 and the Poles made a come-back. In this situation the Cossacks turned to their old enemy Muscovy for protection, thus effectively handing over Ukraine to the Romanovs on the under-standing that they would enjoy local self-government and their traditional freedoms. It was a form of delusion that the Romanovs were to exploit regularly over the next three centuries. For Alexei it was an opportunity to wage a crusade to protect the Zaporozhian Cossacks from both the Catholicism of Poland and the Mohammedanism of the Turks and Tartars. The war that followed was, however, extremely brutal and largely ineffec-tive. By far the largest number of casualties was caused by plague which swept Russia in the wake of war causing losses of up to 30 per cent of the population particularly, but not exclusively, men. Alexei himself fought at the front on several occasions but did not distinguish himself as a general. In 1659 the Zaporozhian Cossacks reverted to the Polish side and destroyed a large Russian army at Konotop in north-eastern Ukraine.

The succession of military failures and the consequential plagues which cost around 700,000 lives must surely have challenged even Tsar Alexei's obscurantist conviction in his own divine mission. In one battle his general lost all the sacred icons taken to inspire the troops and then surrendered with some 20,000 men. The Tsar's urgent pleas to his offic-ers to lead pure lives so that God would help them had all been in vain. His own plying of the ordinary soldiers with sacred mead, his tearful blessings and prayers had made no difference. Yet though the Russian armies had been so badly beaten they had perhaps contributed to the exhaustion of their enemies and certainly to their financial problems. The plague was so virulent in this situation that few who caught it sur-vived: for example in the Vozneshenski Convent ninety nuns died and only thirty-eight survived.

That is why when Alexei's able negotiator Athanasy Ordyn Nashchokin was sent to sue for peace he was not nearly so severely treated as he expected. By the treaty of 1667 Muscovy regained Smolensk and won control of Kiev, the other great holy city of Russia plus most of the Ukraine with the Zaporozhian Cossacks once more welcomed into the fold. Instead of being weakened by his huge losses of men and the deaths of so many from the plague Alexei was more powerful than ever. He soon forgot his promise to preserve the freedoms of the Cossacks and steadily moved Muscovite governors (*voevodi*) and garrisons southwards into Cossack territory, doling out land and spreading serfdom in the process. Yet this failed to have much impact on the continuing spate of Tartar slave raids which in 1666 had seen 100,000 Ukrainians kidnapped into slavery.

Unlike the crisis eighteen years earlier when he had had to bow to the pressure of the mob, this time when there were riots in Moscow caused by the debased copper coinage he simply had 7,000 of the rioters executed.

Significantly the reward of Ordyn Nashchokin, a man of humble origins who had given excellent service, first in repressing the rioters of Pskov back in 1649, then as a general against Poland, and finally as envoy to Poland, was to be sacked and sent as a monk to Kiev. So far as Alexei was concerned he had outlived his usefulness, and had been more interested in trying to win back some Baltic coastline than the cathedrals of Kiev, a policy which did not appeal to the saintly Alexei's sense of priorities.

More to Alexei's taste, this same year of 1667 was the new trade relationship built up when the first big caravan was sent to China. This was the first occasion when tea was introduced to Russia and subsequently became the country's other great national drink.

No sooner was one crisis over than another developed. This time it was the Don Cossacks further to the east. Their remarkable leader Stenka Razin was quite indiscriminate about which side to fight, as he slaughtered large numbers of both Russians and Poles before turning his attention to Persia from where he returned with huge booty. Though he was later the hero of folk-song and legend, a symbol of resistance to the Romanov autocrats, in reality Stenka Razin was a sadistic murderer, at times a drunkard and he famously cast his Persian wife into the Volga when he had had enough of her. Meanwhile he had captured both Tsaritsyn (later Stalingrad) and

Astrakhan on the Volga, carving out a new Cossack republic in defiance of the Tsar. It was to be some years before he was eventually captured and executed in Moscow after excruciating torture.

In 1669 when Alexei was forty there came a turning point in the life of the Tsar – the death of his wife Maria Miloslavskaya who had borne him a dozen children in the course of their marriage. The most promising of their sons, Tsarevich Alexei, a teenager with many signs of ability, had died tragically in 1667 and the two surviving sons Feodor and Ivan were neither of them very fit, the first physically subnormal, the second mentally, whereas ironically the five surviving daughters seemed perfectly robust. They and the boys were tutored by the progressive Kievan scholar Simeon Polotsky who denounced the low educational standards of the Moscow clergy.

It was to be nearly two years before Alexei started looking for a replacement tsaritsa but his choice was to have an extraordinary effect on his character and was to have momentous consequences for Muscovy.

As usual the search appeared to begin with a beauty parade of available virgins, but not such a big one as usual, because the Tsar had already made up his mind and the parade was just for the sake of protocol. The lady he had already chosen was Natalia Naryshkina who was the ward of his new chief minister Artamon Matveev at whose house he had met her and been instantly attracted. The crucial difference between Natalia and the previous tsaritsa was that she had been educated in, for Muscovy, a very liberal atmosphere, largely because Matveev was an ardent Westerniser and had himself married the daughter of a Scottish mercenary officer called Hamilton. Thus Natalia, herself the orphan of a minor Tartar land-owning family, had been brought up in a way totally different from the style of the Terem and the strictures of the *Domostroy*. It was Alexei's infatuation with this girl that led to an extraordinary turnaround in his attitudes and it was this Westernising background that later formed the character of the couple's baby son who was thirty years later to drag Muscovy reluctantly towards Europe.

The new marriage was of course most unwelcome to the Miloslavsky clan which had thrived financially on its relationship with Alexei's first wife. They deeply resented their dismissal from the court and were to cause trouble in subsequent years. Also deeply resentful was the cleverest and most strong-willed of the Tsar's daughters, Sofia, who was much the same age as her new step-mother and hated the idea of kissing her hand.

To make matters worse Sofia had shared the education of her brothers to quite an unusual extent for a Muscovite woman and dreaded the fate normally reserved for tsarevnas: not to be allowed to marry but instead to be confined to the *Terem* and eventually transferred to a nunnery. It was an illogical habit of the tsars that while they usually picked wives from the wider semi-aristocratic community, they would not allow their daughters to find husbands of a similar type. Only foreign royalty was good enough and at this point in Russia's history no foreign princes saw any advantage in marrying into such a distant and backward dynasty. This too meant that there was trouble in store.

Meanwhile Alexei enjoyed a whole new lease of life. The list of pleasures that had been banned twenty years earlier was drastically reduced. Music and song were allowed once more as were performing dogs and dancing bears, football, fencing, games and jesters. Even paintings other than icons began to make their appearance. It was for a while no longer a criminal offence to shave or wear Western-style clothes. Wine and fine banquets were enjoyed. Within a year of his marriage Alexei allowed the construction of a theatre at his Preobrazhenskoe Palace outside Moscow and soon afterwards another one in the Kremlin itself. Like his minister Matveev the Tsar became fascinated with all the novelties brought to Moscow by immigrant craftsmen and artists. Due to general anti-Western prejudice amongst the Moscow populace and its church leaders all the immigrants had been moved into a specific suburb to the south of the city known as the *Nemetskaya Sloboda*, sometimes translated as German District though Nemetskaya originally meant just dumb (i.e. unable to speak Russian). Here Alexei found enjoyment in fancy German toys for his children, new gadgets, mirrors previously regarded as a temptation to sin, brass band instruments and fancy carriages like Matveev's. Instead of the traditional stylized icons, painters were encouraged for the first time to produce realistic portraits and Bible scenes.

Alexei also became an obsessive builder and his passion for hunting meant that he loved country houses. He had already started on the new Kolomenskoe Palace outside the city, a huge wooden structure that recycled all the traditional onion shaped towers, overlapping roofs and fancy arches of the Russian church. Unlike traditional Russian palaces which were dark this one had thousands of mica windows, the walls were decorated with murals, paintings and mirrors. The rooms were comfortably furnished along Western lines. The palace was surrounded by ornamental pleasure gardens and its gate was guarded by two copper lions that roared and rolled their eyes when a servant operated the bellows. The poet Polotsky called it the eighth wonder of the world.

Similarly at his new Izmailovo summer palace Alexei ordered a small zoo of unusual animals and a special garden to grow exotic fruit and vegetables as well as other potentially useful imported plants such as cotton, pepper and mulberry. He had experimental windmills, a glassworks and ingenious heating devices to keep his banana and pineapple trees from dying in the winter.

Thus the last five years of Alexei's reign saw a radical change of outlook and prepared Muscovy a little for the even more drastic changes which were later to be introduced by Peter, the son born some fifteen months after his second marriage. As the little boy was soon obviously much more able and healthy than either of the two surviving sons from his first marriage, this gave Alexei a lot of hope. But sadly less than four years later he caught a chill in the Moscow winter of 1675-6 and died soon afterwards, still only in his late forties, leaving Peter too young to take over.

Alexei's career had shown many inconsistencies: a passion for the traditional Russian liturgy yet encouragement of the reformers to clean it up despite the objections of his people; the cultivation of a saintly image yet savage repression when it suited him; huge expenditure on rearmament but incompetence in war; a willingness to make promises like his offer of protection for the Zaporozhian Cossacks yet no intention of keeping them; extravagant Puritanism during the first part of his reign and sheer extravagance towards its end; an oscillating love-hate relationship with the clever foreigners confined to ghettoes on the outskirts of his capital; and the ability to turn disaster into victory and victory into disaster.

VI

FEODOR III
THE UNDERESTIMATED TSAR

'No one expected him to live'
Contemporary account

The remarkable, if short, reign of Tsar Feodor III (1674-82) has sadly been greatly overshadowed by that of his bullying, extrovert half-brother Peter. For a person with such dreadful disadvantages Feodor's achievements were very considerable and had he been just slightly fitter the later history of Russia might have been very different and much misery might have been avoided.

Feodor was fourteen when he succeeded to the throne, having been declared as the successor by Alexei just before his unexpectedly early death. He suffered constantly from swollen legs which meant it was often impossible for him to stand, he had scurvy and his face was badly disfigured. Yet he had an excellent mind and was the best-educated tsar who had to date ruled Muscovy. He could speak both Latin and Polish and like his dead brother Alexei, he had studied Aristotle under their tutor Polotsky together with affairs both of Church and State. It could be argued that the reforms introduced during his reign were the work of his ministers, but it was he who appointed the ministers and he who backed them, and the reforms bear the stamp of his enlightened attitude, certainly not that of the crowd of squabbling relations who tried to manipulate him.

At this point Russia's population was approximately 15 million but spread over a vast area stretching a thousand miles from north to south and already double that from west to east. Moscow had 100,000 people and 1,500 churches.

Naturally in the aftermath of the old tsar's death there had been a bitter confrontation between the Miloslavsky clan, the family of Feodor's mother, Maria, who had been ousted from court five years earlier and their replacement the Naryshkin hangers-on of Alexei's second wife Natalia. Matveev, who was still chief minister at the time of the tsar's death, naturally supported his protégée Natalia and it would have suited him for her son, four-year-old Peter, to become Tsar. It could be argued that both Feodor as physically unfit and the other brother Ivan, a brain-damaged epileptic, should be left out of the succession. But the boyars would not let Matveev overrule the dying command of Alexei, so it was the Miloslavskys' turn to make a come-back, led by the tsar's extremely capable sister Sofia who had always hated Natalia and had no reason to love little Peter.

Thus Feodor's accession went ahead even though he could not stand for the official rituals. Matveev was dismissed by Feodor and sent as governor to the very distant Verkhoture region near the Arctic Circle across the Urals. He was blamed for failing to taste Alexei's medicine before his death and thus letting him run the risk of being poisoned if not deliberately poisoning him. Natalia, her Naryshkin relations, her little son Peter and her two baby daughters were thrust into the background in the Preobrazhenskoe hunting lodge on the Yauza River outside Moscow.

Though often bed-ridden, young Tsar Feodor soon appointed his own group of advisers: Ivan Yazykov, Alexei Likhachev and Prince Vasili Golitsyn. The latter was a rich, high-ranking and charismatic Westerniser very much in the mould of Matveev, the chief minister who had just been sacked. Like Feodor himself he was highly educated, multilingual and well aware of Western culture. Together with the young tsar he set about a programme for modernising and liberalising the state of Muscovy. The slavish style of multiple obeisances to the tsar was abolished. Shaving and the wearing of Western dress which Alexei had allowed in his brief flurry of liberalism were once more acceptable. There was a move to end the use of mutilation like the chopping off of hands as punishment for relatively minor offences and replace it with exile to Siberia as a more humane alternative. The maltreatment of women by their husbands, the widespread habit of wife-beating and other forms of abuse were tackled, though it would take a much longer time to eradicate them. There were even plans to reverse the drift of the Russian peasantry into serfdom and make a fairer system of taxation but that would have aroused massive opposition from the land-owning class.

The reform of the Russian Church also continued with special emphasis on weeding-out the heavy drinkers from the clergy and tightening up discipline. The rebel priest Avvakum who had dared to pronounce that Tsar Alexei would be in hell because of his reforms was burned at the stake.

Most radical of all was the major attack on the privileges of the boyars, who up to this time had always been able to claim instantly the same rank in the army or government as any of their ancestors, resulting in the appointment of young, incompetent generals and officials. This system of *mestnichestvo* was abolished and in this reform at least we know the young Tsar played a key role for he is recorded as having made a highly effective speech to the council of boyars in 1682 shortly before his own death. Backed by the patriarch he threatened the boyars with both civil punishment and excommunication if they rejected the new system and he won his case. There was a ceremonial burning of the old rank books outside the palace and at least one step had been taken towards reducing the inefficiency of the Muscovite army.

The need for competence in the army had been demonstrated in the war started by the Turks and Tartars in the second year of Feodor's reign, 1676. The Turks with an army of over 100,000 had invaded the Ukraine with a view to capturing Chigirin and the heartland of the steppes. The Russian army facing them was half the size but Feodor summoned the Don Cossacks and sent further reinforcements, so that for the first time the Russians with the help of superior artillery defeated the Turks. For once the Poles had been asked to help the Muscovites against the infidel, but had demanded that Kiev be returned to them and that was too high a price for Feodor, even for what he regarded as a crusade against the infidel. A second Turkish attack with an even bigger army the next year did succeed in capturing Chigirin, but by this time it was in ruins and the Turks had endured massive casualties. Both sides now wanted peace and the terms were favourable for Muscovy as the Turks now recognised its claim to western Ukraine, the left bank of the river Dnieper, and those parts of the eastern Ukraine controlled by the Don Cossacks.

At least in theory the Russians now applied themselves to the better development of artillery though perhaps they tried too hard, for their new forty-ton cannon, the largest in the world and known as the Tsar Pushka, was too heavy to move and never left the Kremlin.

Meanwhile in 1680, aged eighteen, Feodor had chosen his own wife Agafa Grushevska, the daughter of a minor court official of Polish origin from Smolensk. She shared the liberal attitudes of her husband and set the tone at court by encouraging hair-cutting, shaving and the wearing of Western-style clothes. Within two years she produced a son Ilya, but sadly both she and the baby died a week later. Encouraged by his family, particularly his sister Sofia, Feodor quickly found a replacement tsaritsa, Marfa Apraksina, but this time it was his own health that gave way. He died at the age of twenty-one having done much more than anyone could have expected.

VII

TSAREVNA SOFIA AND TSAR IVAN V

'And there triumphed then the great contentment of the nation'
Lopukhin

So long as Feodor was alive his sister Sofia and the members of their mother's family, the Miloslavsky, were happy enough. Their father's hated second wife Natalia and her precocious son Peter could be kept out of the way. But when Feodor died without having named his successor an assembly hastily convened by the Patriarch ruled out his mentally retarded brother Ivan as his successor and voted for the ten-year-old half-brother Peter. This meant that Natalia would be Regent; Matveev would be back as Chief Minister, while the Miloslavskys and Sofia would be in the wilderness.

At this juncture Sofia began to implement an astonishing *coup d'etat*. She was twenty-five, unmarried and extremely intelligent, a big woman, and probably, though accounts vary and no portraits survive, not particularly attractive but certainly confident and articulate. The unkind gossip about varicose veins and facial hair probably came later. Like her two elder brothers Alexei and Feodor she had received a very thorough and liberal education and realised that unless she now took some action her fate would be perpetual boredom either in the *Terem* or a nunnery, for she was too close to the throne to be allowed to marry. Her step-mother Natalia on the other hand was perhaps a little complacent, underestimated the guile of Sofia and was too slow in grasping the opportunity that the Patriarch's decision had offered her. Her designated chief minister Matveev made things worse by his slow return journey from his place of exile.

Matters came to a head at Feodor's funeral procession to the Arkhangelsk Cathedral, which would normally have been an all-male affair, but where the two rival ladies tried to upstage each other. First Natalia made a discreet but unscheduled entrance with her young son, the new Tsar Peter aged ten. Provoked by this, Sofia made an equally unscheduled but much less discreet entrance and stole the show, Natalia and her son beating a hasty retreat. Sofia followed this up with an impromptu speech about the plot against her family including the alleged poisoning of Feodor and appealed for help. Meanwhile her Miloslavsky uncles were briefed to start doling out bribes to Moscow's home guard, the part-time musketeers, the *Streltsi* of whom there were now around 20,000. At the same time Natalia's relations, the rapacious Naryshkini, were showing undue impatience to seize the perks of office and Sofia started a rumour that they had murdered her unfortunate brother Ivan. Matveev had by this time arrived in Moscow and produced Ivan to prove that he had not been murdered. Natalia in a panic allowed the *Streltsi* to knout their colonels but they were still not content. They refused to accept orders from their pro-Natalia commander Prince Michael Dolgoruky, especially when he threatened them with the knout, so they tossed him over the palace walls onto the pikes below. Soon afterwards Matveev himself was also murdered by them in the Granovitaya Palace (Facet) and they began to knout their other officers in Red Square. Natalia and her son Peter sought safety in the Terem Palace, but not before Peter had witnessed the beginnings of a massacre of his mother's close relations and supporters by the *Streltsi* which in the end lasted three days. To stop the slaughter Natalia was forced to ask her surviving brother Ivan to surrender himself for an excruciating death.

The triumphant Sofia rewarded the *Streltsi* with an amnesty, increased pay and a monument to their bravery. She then had herself declared Regent for the two joint-tsars, her brother Ivan V aged sixteen who suffered from what are now called learning difficulties or perhaps Down's Syndrome and her half-brother Peter aged ten who was fit but too young to understand what was happening.

Sofia had won at least temporary power but her position could not be secure so long as it depended on the unpredictable *Streltsi* who were now almost totally out of control. Their new commander Prince Ivan Khovansky thought that his next move was to marry Sofia and make himself Tsar, but though Sofia had undoubtedly exploited his feelings and ambition, she had no intention of losing power to any man. Her other problem was that the *Streltsi* had aligned themselves with the Old Believers and now believed they could do anything they wanted. When they entered the Kremlin to deliver a turgid list of demands for Church conservatism, she turned the tables with another brilliant speech, saying that such demands meant that both she, her father Tsar Alexei and her brother Tsar Feodor were heretics, in which case she would abandon Moscow to its fate. This persuaded the fickle *Streltsi* to murder their ecclesiastical spokesman. Soon afterwards Sofia started rumours of yet another murder plot against the boy tsars and used this to arrange the fall of the new commander of the *Streltsi*, her ally Prince Ivan Khovanski who had pushed her gratitude too far when he dared to suggest he might marry her. She organised his murder and the mutinous behaviour of the now leaderless *Streltsi* began to lose momentum, the streets became quiet again and she was able, after a brief sojourn outside the city, to return to the Kremlin in total control of Muscovy. It was one of the most remarkable political feats achieved by any woman in world history, but particularly in Russia where women had never been expected to take part in public life.

Sofia then resumed the modernising, Westernising work done by both her father in his later years and her brother Feodor. Prince Vasili Golitsyn became effectively her chief minister just as he had been Feodor's, but to balance him she had Feodor Shaklovity as new commander of the *Streltsi* and thus essentially her enforcer at home. Both were probably at some point her lovers, but while Golitsyn was married and might otherwise have been of sufficient rank to be her husband, Shaklovity was a bachelor but of too low a rank. So whatever her inclinations it was too politically dangerous for her to marry anyone. It was however absolutely essential for her masterplan that her unfortunate brother Ivan V should marry and try to produce an heir who could be given preference to her hated half-brother young Tsar Peter. So Praskovia Saltykova was procured as a bride and whatever his other alleged deficiencies the wretched Tsar Ivan V did manage to procreate two daughters: Catherine (d. 1728) and Anna (d. 1740) who were later to be significant in the survival of the Romanov dynasty.

Only on very rare ceremonial occasions did Sofia allow the junior of the two joint-Tsars, Peter, to appear in public with Ivan and she provided twin thrones with a hole behind their heads so that instructions could be whispered to the two of them about what answer to make to envoys or appellants. In the case of Ivan this was the only way to get him to say anything at all; in the case of Peter it was to make sure he said nothing inappropriate. For most of the next seven years he was kept out of the way at the Preobrazhenskoe hunting lodge on the outskirts of Moscow where his mother Natalia and those few of her near relations who had survived the *Streltsi* massacre had sought shelter. Peter, who up to the age of ten had received a typical tsarist education, was left very much to his own devices and spent much of his time with other young teenagers amongst the busy streets of the foreign quarter of Moscow, the Nemetskaya Sloboda which was perhaps more useful to him than any formal training as later became evident.

The modernisation programme which Sofia and Golitsyn continued to implement included some modest improvements in the taxation system, an attack on drunkenness, an attempt to improve the rights of women in which Sofia's own example was a key factor and an effort to tackle the sewage problems of Moscow. She also continued the suppression of the Old Believers but despite apparently good intentions did little to halt the steady spread of serfdom.

Thus Sofia consolidated her position as virtual tsar and in 1687 actually took the title Gosudaraya or sovereign and was planning a coronation. Her one problem was the existence of joint-tsar Peter and the fact that in 1689 he would come of age. Ivan had already done so but was completely dominated by her and had two daughters whom she could potentially also use as puppets. Her hope lay in the fact that Peter was behaving as a hooligan teenager with uncouth manners and a penchant for heavy drinking and seemed to have no particular interest in the duties of a tsar.

In the end Sofia's fall resulted not from any domestic problem but from her conduct of war. Poland had been under attack from the Turks and wanted Muscovy as an ally. Sofia agreed to support the Poles and won as her reward the agreement of the Poles that Kiev and its surrounding territory be permanently ceded to Muscovy. This success was however not matched by Golitsyn in the field, for he was perhaps a better diplomat than a general. Besides, Muscovy had yet really to master the logistics of taking an army 700 miles away to fight the Crimean Khan. The motivation was to stop the Tartar raids which still took place in that area to serve the slave markets of Istanbul. But in his first campaign

Golitsyn set off with an army of 100,000 only to lose nearly half of them before he reached the battle area. He failed to capture Perekop, blamed the Cossacks for mysterious fires on the steppes and at the same time greatly exaggerated his so-called victory when he returned to Moscow.

Golitsyn's second campaign two years later was slightly more success-ful but he still lost some 20,000 men and was forced to retreat due to lack of supplies. By this time rumours about his false claims of military prowess were circulating in Moscow, no doubt aided by the Naryshkin family. The fact that Golitsyn had ceded some territory to the Chinese this same year did not help. So it was in this atmosphere that young Peter, doubtless briefed by this mother's relatives, took the risky step of refusing to endorse Golitsyn's triumph when he returned for the second time from the Crimea. This act of defiance against his half-sister Sofia triggered the confrontation which brought about her downfall. For the first time, now that Peter was at seventeen officially an adult, Sofia's con-stitutional position was seriously vulnerable.

As ever in her moments of crisis Sofia called on the *Streltsi*, but they were now much less of a cohesive force and some of them, particularly those based round the foreign quarter where young Peter was a familiar figure, were more inclined to his side than hers. This time it was Natalia's turn to spread rumours of a murder plot against Peter and herself and perhaps with reason, for Shaklovity certainly wanted them out of the way. Shaklovity responded by suggesting there was a plot by the Naryshkini to murder Ivan V. Peter and his mother escaped from the Kolomenskoe Palace and hastened to the safety of the Troitse Monastery which was built like a fortress. Sofia gathered some 700 *Streltsi* in the Kremlin and Lubyanka but Peter could call on nearly as many. He also won over some key officers such as the Scots-born Patrick Gordon, adding to them a group of loyal and now highly trained soldiers from the regiments which he had been building up for several years at Preobrazhenskoe. Two vital allies of Sofia deserted her in her time of need; the Patriarch and Vasili Golitsyn. Her *Streltsi* were disorganised and poorly trained to cope with a crisis. Shaklovity proved a poor leader and the end for Sofia was as rapid as her rise. The ultimate desertion was that of her weak-minded brother who under Naryshkin pressure agreed to her arrest. Her regency was over.

Strangely this coup which removed Sofia from power does not seem particularly to have been inspired by Peter or to have inspired him with political ambition, for after it as we shall see he continued much as he had before. But for Sofia who was still in her early-thirties it meant internment for life in the Novodevichy Convent. She made one attempt at a come-back in 1698 but it was easily crushed. As punishment she was forced to become a nun and the bodies of her followers were left hanging outside her cell window. Shaklovity and others of her supporters had already been executed in 1689 while Golitsyn won a reprieve but was sent into permanent exile. Sofia died in her cell in 1704 at the age of forty-seven, just over the average age of death for Romanov rulers, but having set a remarkable precedent for women to assume supreme power in Russia.

VIII

TSAR PETRUSHKA OR BOMBARDIER PETER ALEXEVICH

'He is a ruler both very good and very evil at the same time'
Electress Sophia Charlotte of Brandenburg

Peter the Great was probably the most unusual hereditary monarch in the whole of human history. In many ways he behaved very much more like a self-made despot such as Napoleon or Hitler. In his early life he seemed to reject almost every aspect of his inheritance and in his later career he did his best to change it out of all recognition. Much of this may be attributed to the extraordinary events of his childhood.

His first three years while his father Tsar Alexei was still alive followed the usual Muscovite pattern of life in the *Terem*. At the age of three he was given a golden miniature coach pulled by five dwarfs and was unaware of the fact that he had almost been chosen as the new tsar. Then during the seven-year reign of his half-brother Feodor II he was not perceived as posing any kind of threat and was given as his tutor Nikita Zotov who later became a stalwart drinking companion. It was when he was ten that his life underwent a traumatic change. During the coup by which his half-sister Sofia became Regent he was present for the three days of mayhem when the *Streltsi* massacred many of his closest relations as well as their own commander and his father's former Chief Minister. Though he was appointed junior co-tsar with his retarded half-brother Ivan, the new regent Sofia had every intention that he should be kept well in the background and ideally should never become an adult tsar. Thus his formal education was brought to an end and, except for very rare formal visits to the Kremlin to sit like a puppet on the specially built twin throne with Ivan, he was kept for his own safety in the more remote Preobrazhenskoe hunting lodge on the river Yauza. This he shared with his mother Natalia, his sisters and the surviving Naryshkin hangers-on who were for the time being deprived of the perks of power.

Never has any potential monarch made better use of self-education. There were three strands to this. The first was the freedom that he enjoyed to wander round the streets of the nearby Nemetskaya Sloboda (foreign or literally dumb quarter, later used mainly for Germans) where he acquired a lasting fascination and considerable skill in all forms of craftsmanship from carpentry and masonry to printing, blacksmithing and even dentistry. His curiosity was boundless. The second hobby developed from his toy army and metamorphosed from the drilling of boys into fully-fledged mock battles with significant numbers of his boyhood friends to train as members of real regiments, sometimes incurring real casualties. This introduced Peter not just to infantry techniques but also to fortification and artillery as he gradually acquired more serious equipment from the unsuspecting or compliant keepers of the Kremlin arsenal. It also introduced Peter to a number of boyhood friends like Alexei Menshikov, according to gossip the son of a meat pie salesman but in reality of a minor civil servant, who were to grow in stature alongside him and become talented lifelong supporters of his regime. By the time he was twelve he had a life-size fortress to besiege and by seventeen 600 properly paid and highly trained guardsmen in the Preobrazhensky Regiment to which he shortly added the Semenovsky Regiment named after another nearby village. And though not interested in schoolwork for its own sake he did ask to learn some geometry when he managed to procure an astrolabe from the West and found that it would help calculate the ranges for his artillery.

The third hobby was sailing. This began with a model of his father's warship the *Orel* which had been sunk by Stenka Razin on the Volga. Then he came across an old sailing dinghy, probably made in England and sent as a gift to the tsar in Tudor times. Some versions of the story have him find the boat in an attic belonging to Nikita Romanov, others rotting by the lake at Ismailovo Palace.

Either way that was where he first sailed it and realised that because unlike any Russian boat it had a retractable keel it could sail against the wind. This was to have a profound influence and together with his fascination for the foreign craftsmen was to create his life-long yearning to come closer to Western Europe and win proper access for Muscovy to the sea. Meanwhile he rapidly graduated to sailing in a bigger boat at Pereslavl on Lake Pleshcheevo.

Three significant bi-products of Peter's freedom from discipline were an early introduction both to alcohol and sex plus a total disdain for even the most basic Muscovite manners. He ate with his fingers, belched, broke wind and was utterly careless with other people's prized possessions. From his early teenage years be became a prodigious drinker though he rarely let it impair his judgement or reduce his energy for the following day. A commanding figure at six foot seven he had huge strength and vast reserves of energy. He also acquired his first mistress, Anna Mons, the libidinous daughter of a vintner in the German quarter. Soon afterwards he allowed his mother to choose him a bride, the relatively colourless Evdokhia Saltykova, but within a few months he had returned to the more adventurous Anna Mons. Evdokhia did bear him two sons, one of whom died almost immediately and the other Alexei (b. 1690) was to be the subject of much controversy twenty years later.

As we have seen, apart from refusing to endorse the undeserved military honours bestowed on Golitsyn in 1689, Peter was not much more than a passive observer during the manoeuvrings which led to the downfall of Sofia. His own installation as an adult tsar alongside his half-brother Ivan ,who had never demonstrated any interest in the position except for the ceremonial, did not seem to cause much change in his habits. He returned as if nothing had happened to his exercises with the Probrazhensky, his carousing with Anna Mons, Menshikov and his other favourites – the Genevan-born mercenary Francois Lefort and the Scots soldier Patrick Gordon, members of his Universal Drinking and Joking Society. He spent the next four years in a succession of orgies and bizarre pranks interrupted only by his continued pursuit of technical knowledge. Often his banquets showed signs of the sadistic streak in his character as he forced guests to imbibe near fatal doses of spiked beverages or overcome nausea at the sight of vermin or filth deliberately included in their meals. Sometimes to add to his voyeuristic pleasure he disguised himself as one of his own servants and invited all kinds of dwarfs and other unfortunates to add a freakish frisson to the occasions. Mock weddings between unsuitable couples and obscene versions of religious ceremonies were normal fare. Later in Holland he was to make a man bite a corpse. And given the affectionate Russian style of their correspondence some alleged there was a homosexual element to Peter's friendship with Menshikov. Yet despite late nights and heavy drinking his manic energy was undiminished and he would be up early next morning to pursue some new obsession.

Meanwhile the government was left to his mother Natalia and her corrupt relations while Ivan happily continued with the ceremonials. In 1692 having spent some time working as Master Shipwright Peter Alexeevich he helped launch a frigate at Pereyaslav south of Kiev. Then in the summer of 1693 Peter undertook his first trip to the sea where he developed his sailing skills off Arkhangelsk in the White Sea. So inspired was he that he ordered a fourty-four-gun frigate from Holland and supervised the construction of his own first salt-water warship.

Even the death in 1694 of Natalia, of whom he was genuinely very fond, seems only to have caused a brief break in his routine and was followed by his biggest ever military exercise with his two palace regiments, so realistic that some forty men were killed. Soon afterwards came his first two genuine campaigns which were aimed at the great Turkish fortress of Azov near the mouth of the Don, sacked by the Cossacks sixty years earlier and turned down by his grandfather. The first led by General Lefort with Peter acting as mere Bombardier, was a failure. The second, before which Peter personally laboured in the shipyards at Voronezh to accelerate the launching of two frigates and twenty-three galleys, was much more successful. This time Peter gave himself the rank of captain and took charge of eight of his galleys. Azov was captured to great acclaim, but in the triumphal procession afterwards Peter walked in the uniform of an ordinary mercenary pikeman.

The death of his half-brother Ivan V who, despite his infirmities, had lasted to the age of thirty and produced four daughters, did perhaps draw Peter's attention to the duties of tsardom, for Ivan had at least attended to much of the ceremonial. But at the age of twenty-five Peter was still not ready to settle down. He was obsessed with finding out more about ship construction and other European technologies and used the excuse of looking for alliances against the Turks to propose an elaborate tour round the courts of the West. He also started despatching craftsmen to the West with instructions to improve their skills and each come back with a Western recruit in their own trade.

Meanwhile he inaugurated a crash programme of naval ship building to protect Azov and the new harbour he was having built at nearby

Taganrog using the forced labour of 20,000 Ukrainian serfs. To guard it he sent down 3,000 *Streltsi*, much to their disgust, since normally they regarded themselves as only part-time soldiers. To pay for the ships there was a new tax on landowners, including the patriarchs, bishops and heads of monasteries. While his hold on Azov remained quite weak it did suffice to reduce for a while the ability of the Tartars to make slave raids into Russian territory.

Once this work was in hand, however unpopular in many quarters, he was ready to set off for the West. Thus an embassy of over 200 delegates headed off early in 1697 under the nominal command of Lefort with Peter listed as an ordinary seaman, though this did not prevent him from reverting to royal status whenever he fancied. Their route took them via Novgorod into Swedish Livonia where Peter was offended when the governor refused to let him inspect the fortifications of Riga. Then it was south to Libau and by ship to Konigsberg and a gunnery lesson in the arsenal of the Elector of Brandenburg. Next came Berlin and Celle where he was entertained by Sophia the half-Scottish Electress of Hanover and mother of the future George I of Great Britain. Peter now took a smaller party down the Rhine to Holland where he resumed his apprenticeship as a shipwright at Zaandam under the name of Peter Michailov. During several months in Amsterdam he oversaw the finishing touches to the frigate which he had earlier ordered for his navy and went out on exercise with a Dutch East India Company warship. It also made him realise the potential of Russia as an exporter of naval stores like tar, pitch and hemp to the other nations of Europe.

In Utrecht Peter met William of Orange who invited him to England and in Leiden he spent time in anatomy classes, an engraver's workshop and a nearby paper mill. In London he became an avid admirer of Christopher Wren's rebuilding work, studied watch repairing and coffin making before another session of ship building at Deptford and a visit to Woolwich Arsenal. Not a moment was wasted unless on a casual affair with an actress called Miss Cross or the usual carousing which left considerable damage in the mansion which had been loaned to him by the diarist John Evelyn. It was in London that he was given the idea of a monopoly of tobacco imports to Russia as a means of raising revenue.

By the time Peter was nearing the end of his mission he had recruited around 700 experts in different fields to take back to Moscow with him, particularly mathematicians and experts on navigation or artillery to help establish his proposed new colleges. He had also bought numerous examples of the latest European technology from blocks and tackles for rigging to flintlock hand-guns, cannons, anatomical instruments and dentistry tools, so that he had to charter several ships to send his purchases back home. Then he headed off by land to Vienna where he met Emperor Leopold but failed to persuade him to back the anti-Turkish alliance. Here in mid-July he heard about a major mutiny by the *Streltsi* in Moscow and Azov where they objected to new orders drafting them to Lithuania. The *Streltsi* of Toropetz, west of Tver, joined in and were soon close to Moscow. When he heard news that Sofia was perhaps involved in a new plot spreading rumours that he was dead Peter hastened towards Krakow. He learned en route that his old friend General Gordon had defeated four regiments of *Streltsi* at Voskresenskoe Monastery sixty miles from Moscow and executed the ring-leaders. Peter was angry because he had wanted them tortured first.

At Rawa he stopped off to meet the newly elected king of Poland, Augustus II who was slightly keener to join in an alliance, but against Sweden rather than Turkey. So fortified by this interesting prospect, towards the end of August 1698 Peter at last returned to Moscow after an absence totalling fifteen months, a long time for any ruler to be away. Significantly it was not the Kremlin where he spent his first few days but Preobrazhenskoe and later the German Quarter, home of his old mistress Anna Mons.

With his usual obsessive energy Peter at once set about moulding Muscovy to the standards he had found in Western Europe. Immediately he started cutting off beards and made the wearing of a beard a criminal offence for all but priests and peasants until he found it was more profitable just to tax it. Next he ordered the banning of traditional Muscovite robes which were too cumbersome for doing the skilled tasks which he now wanted the population to undertake. For reasons of taste and because she symbolised the old order he finally managed to get rid of his tsaritsa Evdokhia whom he forced to become a nun, at the same time denying her access to their surviving son, Tsarevich Alexei.

Next he unleashed his fury on the *Streltsi* whom he had always hated since their massacre of his relations in 1682. He had provoked them in turn by failing to pay their wages, sending many for service far from home in Azov and generally preferring his own professional regiments. This time he set up torture chambers and furnaces at Preobrazhenskoe so that he could inflict every conceivable form of pain to elicit confessions of guilt, particularly to try to implicate his half-sister Sofia, whom like his wife he had compelled to take the veil. Burning, the knout, the wheel and flaying were followed in due course by execution of nearly a thousand *Streltsi* with Peter and his friend Menshikov themselves acting as axe men on several occasions – Menshikov personally executed twenty. Nor was there any question of hiding the corpses, quite the opposite, they were hung as prominently as possible to ensure mass intimidation as Peter made his people and particularly Sofia outside whose cell he strung several of the bodies, realise that the entire population had to submit to his ambition to westernise Muscovy and create a totalitarian modern state with access to ice-free harbours. Those of the *Streltsi* who survived were dismissed and exiled to distant parts of the country to prevent them causing further trouble.

With the effective elimination of the *Streltsi* Peter now had to replace them in his army with a new volunteer force of full-time professionals. He could not afford to start his war against Sweden until he had made peace with Turkey and this took over a year, though not long enough to reach more than half his target of 64,000 fully trained men. He also no longer had the help of his trusted old officers Patrick Gordon and François Lefort, as both had died, probably exhausted by the demands of Peter's own carousals. However he was under some pressure to act against Sweden before his allies, the Danes, Poles and Saxons lost patience and what is more he naively expected the new teenage king of Sweden, Charles XII, to be a mediocre opponent. In this he was to be proved very wrong.

Thus Peter began his attack on the Swedes in 1700 with a siege of their fortress town of Narva on the Gulf of Finland just within what is now the Estonian border. It was already October, too late to start a campaign and as it turned out Charles XII had in the meantime just defeated both the Danes and Saxons, thus taking out two of Peter's main allies. Narva turned into a serious disaster for under cover of a snow storm Charles suddenly appeared with 8,000 men and the Russian army with three times that number of troops but much less experienced, panicked and was defeated with huge losses. Peter, who was not present at the battle, lost all the valuable artillery which had been used for the siege.

At this point Charles XII could have marched on Moscow as soon as the weather improved and Peter would have been unable to stop him.

This might well have meant the end of Peter, perhaps even of the Romanovs, but Charles was short of funds for such an exercise and instead spent the next few years conquering the Poles and Saxons. Peter thus had the opportunity to regroup and over the next two years managed to inflict minor defeats on two Swedish armies which had been left behind by Charles in Livonia. At least it proved that Russian troops could stand up to the Swedes. By October 1702 he felt confident enough to send Marshall Sheremetiev to attack the Swedish island fortress of Noteborg on Lake Ladoga. It was captured, renamed Schlusselburg and became the base for Russian conquest of Ingria, the area round the eastern Gulf of Finland. Then another Swedish fort at Nienschantz at the mouth of the Okhta was taken, plus two Swedish warships that were based there on the Neva.

Peter started building a small fleet on Lake Ladoga and in 1703 at last ordered work to begin on a major new city set among the nineteen islands of the marshy mouth of the Neva. Hare Island or Zayachy Ostrov, was chosen for the new Peter and Paul Fortress. Peter sailed a boat among the islands himself sounding the depth of the water with a lead to help plan the city layout like a new Venice. He had his own small first house which still survives just to the east of the fortress yet within a year he had started work on his Summer Palace on the other side of the Neva using the Italian architect Domenico Trezzini who had helped dig similar waterlogged foundations in Copenhagen and had been doing that too in St Petersburg since 1704. The Kronverk fortifications, the Smolny Dvor and Admiralty soon followed. In 1707 Peter gave his lieutenant Menshikov the whole of Vasilyevsky Island with its arrow-like spit, the Strelka, and Menshikov as governor of the city soon built the first of its great palaces for himself. The city got its first stone church in 1710 with Trezzini's magnificent Peter and Paul church begun in 1714. By 1715 Peter was lining up the Nevsky Prospect as the main boulevard for the new city and a year later the Alexander Nevsky Monastery to commemorate a much earlier victory over the Swedes on this site. Then the first Winter Palace was started. The pattern was set that all houses had to be made of brick or stone, they would have steeply pitched roofs as in Holland and a colour-wash, usually Peter's favourite rich yellow with detail picked out in white which still contributes to the city's spectacular beauty. The Twelve Colleges were finished by 1718 as offices for Peter's twelve new government departments, again designed by the hard-pressed Trezzini. This would fulfil Peter's great dream of providing Muscovy with an access to the Western seas that was ice-free for at least most of the year. He named it after his patron saint, Peter.

The cost of building St Petersburg both in monetary terms and in human lives was enormous. Vast numbers of slave labourers housed in primitive encampments worked till they died in conditions which varied from extreme cold and wolf-ridden in the winter to stagnant, muggy and disease-ridden in the summer. There were great technical difficulties laying the foundations of large stone buildings in the middle of a muddy estuary which was prone to flooding. Eight miles out into the Gulf of Finland Peter built the fort of Kronstadt on Kotlin Island to guard the entrance to his new port. Such was Peter's drive and ruthlessness that within ten years the new city was to be more or less ready to replace Moscow as capital of his empire. It is estimated to have cost around 200,000 lives and the sufferings endured were later brilliantly captured in Pushkin's epic poem *The Bronze Horseman.*

Meanwhile there had been developments in Peter's private life. Amongst the prisoners of war picked up at Marienburg (now Aluksne in Latvia) was the locally born wife of a Swedish soldier, Martha Skavronska. Aged perhaps in her late teens, an orphan of peasant stock but well trained in domestic duties she attracted the attention first of the local Russian commander Field Marshal Sheremetiev, then of Peter's close friend Menshikov, and finally of the Tsar himself. Thus she became successively the mistress of the three most important men in Muscovy, each one pulling rank on his predecessor. This remarkable woman, with the homely skills of an illiterate Lithuanian peasant was not only in due course to become Tsaritsa, but also later a sovereign in her own right and with Peter, ancestress of all the Romanov rulers from 1741 onwards. By becoming his 'little mother – matushka' she perhaps also contracted venereal disease which may have been the reason why eight out of her ten children did not live beyond childhood and why she herself died at a relatively young age. For the time being her great capacity was to sooth the manic moods of the Tsar, to curb some of his extravagances, to create a more populist image for the Romanovs particularly amongst the troops and provide a comfortable home life which probably prolonged his otherwise hyperactive and self-destructive existence.

While all this was happening Peter's situation was still far from secure. The main Swedish army was still undefeated and it was just a matter of time before Charles XII turned on Muscovy. At the same time there was severe unrest in the south to which peasants had been absconding in large numbers, driven to rebellion by Peter's heavy taxation, annoyed by his flagrant disrespect for the old religion and the threat of forced labour in his new forts and shipyards, plus the fact that a large number of peasants since 1705 had been conscripted into the army. Search parties sent to the south to round up escapees were met with strong resistance. The nomadic Bashkir tribes and the Volga Cossacks round Astrakhan were suppressed with great brutality but the conflict escalated as the Don Cossacks and the Zaporozhian Cossacks joined forces in a widespread rebellion in 1707 which it took a considerable effort to suppress.

It was in the following year, 1708, that Peter began his disastrous quarrel with Tsarevich Alexei, the son of his abbreviated marriage to Evdokhia. The boy was now eighteen and had already for four years been serving as a private in the army though his character was rather more academic than soldierly, a tendency that was perhaps accentuated by Peter's overbearing impatience and evident lack of affection. The first crisis came when Alexei, without Peter's permission, visited his mother in her nunnery. Peter was apoplectic with rage, perhaps the more so for Charles XII had at long last fulfilled his threat to invade central Muscovy. Charles had by this time the reputation of an invincible general and he expected to conquer Russia with ease. Even Peter must have been anxious and the fact that he had an unpredictable heir just added to his stress.

Initially the Swedes were successful and beat the Russians at Golovchina but Peter organised a guerilla response and a scorched earth retreat which slowed down the Swedish advance. Charles XII headed south to try to join up with the Cossacks under their leader Prince Ivan Mazeppa who had been promoted by Peter but then come to resent his erosion of Cossack freedoms. Peter himself managed to defeat Swedish reinforcements heavily at Lesnaya and the Cossack response to Charles was weak, especially after Menshikov had been sent south to discourage any treachery by a timely massacre at Baturin. Even in the south the Swedes suffered a harsh winter and by spring 1709 when they besieged Poltava some 400 miles south of Moscow in the Ukraine their army was less than half its original strength of around 50,000 men and some were suffering from frostbite. Peter arrived with an army twice as large but hesitated to attack until the Swedes made the first move. The Russian infantry had been drilled not to retreat and Peter's artillery did considerable damage until the remaining 14,000 Swedes were forced to surrender. Charles escaped but was never again a threat, while Peter who had been in the thick of the fighting was for the first time now genuinely the master of a much expanded Muscovy which could henceforth be described as Russia. Poltava was also a crippling defeat for Mazeppa who despite his subsequent treatment as a hero-figure also made his escape with Charles and died soon afterwards leaving the Ukrainian Cossacks in much less of a position to assert independence.

Peter now felt sufficiently pleased with his progress as a soldier to promote himself to Lieutenant General. He followed up in 1710 with further victories at Vyborg the fortress which protected Finland, Cape Hanko where the Russian navy had its first success and Riga, meanwhile sending his heir Tsarevich Alexei to Dresden to learn more about mathematics and the technology of war.

The fact that Peter now controlled the Gulf of Finland enabled him to start work on the exotic new series of palaces west of St Petersburg at what was later called Peterhof. The coastal site looking across to Kronstadt was landscaped in the Versailles style with exotic water features and Peter himself helped in the building of his favourite new palace the Montplaisir. Later he added the Marly Palace and the Hermitage as guest accommodation while Menshikov, not to be outdone, built his Oranienbaum.

Now it was Peter's turn to be overconfident in his military abilities. Partly because he still wanted to eliminate Charles XII he embarked in 1711 on an attack of Turkey, a crusade blessed in the Uspensky Cathedral. His own health was suspect as at this time he had the first of a series of alarming fits. Nevertheless lured on by the expectation that the Christians in the Ottoman Empire would rise to support his invasion he headed south with too small an army and inadequate supplies. It was an absurd risk and he paid for it when his army of 38,000 was surrounded by a Turkish force five times its size on the Pruth River near the Moldovan border. Peter faced the loss of all his previous gains and was saved only by the corruptibility of the opposing vizier and the calming effect of his mistress Martha who was on campaign with him and added her jewels to the cash which bought his escape from certain annihilation. Apart from that all it cost him was the surrender of Azov back to the Turks and a promise to marry Martha as soon as they got back to Moscow. They already had two daughters who would thus be legitimised.

Meanwhile Peter had taken advantage of his new international credibility to arrange prestigious foreign matches for his son Alexei with Charlotte of Wolfenbuttel, his niece Anna with the Duke of Courland, and his niece Catherine with the Duke of Mecklenburg. It was to be a fashion for mixing Germanic blue blood with the Romanovs' that was to persist for two centuries.

Thus in 1712 Russia in theory at least acquired a new capital – the still unfinished St Petersburg – and a new tsaritsa, Martha now renamed Catherine. Peter proceeded to conquer more of Finland and sent the reluctant tsarevitch up there to supervise ship-building on Lake Ladoga. So frightened of failure was young Alexei that he shot himself in the hand as an excuse in case his marine drawings were sub-standard. The wretched boy had only another miserable four years left to live as his relationship with his father drifted into terror on one side and contempt on the other. Peter might at long last be a successful conqueror and was building a huge new city from scratch but he was still the same hard-drinking bully and obsessive who could not adjust his behaviour to cope with the most basic of relationships, that of father to son. That failure was in the end to undo many of his other achievements.

Up to this point Peter's career was such that it has evoked great praise from historians brought up to admire rulers who increased the size of their country and who modernised, since size and progress have so often been regarded as criteria for greatness. Yet there was a basic anomaly in Peter's actions: he was certainly increasing the size of Russia and in some respects justifiably for he was taking it back to frontiers that had existed in the past and many of the new inhabitants of his empire were ethnically Russian or at least Slavonic. But even in this sphere he tried to play God by transplanting Germans to the Black Sea, settling Swedish prisoners on the Don and encouraging Serbs from within the Turkish Empire to move to the Ukraine.

At the same time as increasing Russia he was demonstrating his intense dislike of most things Russian: he preferred other languages, other cultures and other customs. It was the persistence of this anomaly under his successors that was to provide the Russian empire with its greatest flaw: the larger it grew the more it seemed to be ashamed of its own core. What is more the huge sacrifice that was being made to enable the Romanov dynasty to become ever more powerful was self-perpetuating. It depended on serfs, conscription, stultification and intimidation. Most of the people it conquered were offered little better while those that asked for protection were cheated into subservience. It could command fear but not loyalty. Even the Church was taken over as an instrument of suppression made mysterious and remote by retaining the old Slavonic language. Any form of education that allowed rational thought was out of the question. For the time being the state of Muscovy was destined to rise to further levels of sadistic magnificence. There was no turning back.

PART TWO

THE EMPERORS OF RUSSIA

'We have come out of the darkness into the light'
Peter the Great
St Petersburg

I

PETER THE GREAT
FATHER OF THE FATHERLAND

'The Russians as fashioned by Peter were rotten before they were ripe'
Diderot

With his wars all but over Peter had much more time during the last dozen years of his reign to focus on domestic matters. By the taxing of clothes, the creation of state monopolies and other measures he had more than doubled his revenues to 8 million roubles per annum and he increased this by introducing a poll tax in 1719. This helped pay for a standing army of around 200,000, five times what it had been under his predecessors. He was also building up his navy to two dozen frigates and a large galley fleet with 16,000 men to crew them. There was administrative reform as the bureaucracy reluctantly relocated to St Petersburg. Russia was divided into eight provinces and from 1721 there were to be nine colleges or boards responsible for different aspects of government. The cumbersome Cyrillic alphabet was tidied up and Arabic numerals introduced so that Russians could more easily multiply and divide. Similarly the calendar was modernised. There were the first newspapers in Russian, printing and publishing made rapid strides. Women were no longer restricted to the *Terem* and there was a renewal of Church reform.

At the same time there was continued encouragement for Russian industry as iron mining and foundries expanded rapidly, textile, china and glass manufacture developed and foreign trade quadrupled. Peter's Scottish engineer Farquharson built a new road from Moscow to St Petersburg. The next task would be education.

All this success did not seem to moderate the manic impatience and intolerance which were at once Peter's greatest strength and his greatest weakness. The year 1718 saw both his supreme triumph and his worst demonstration of inhumanity.

On the one hand with the death of Charles XII he was at last able to start negotiating a proper settlement with the Swedes which confirmed all his gains except Finland, so that he controlled all the Baltic States. It was this treaty which led his senators in 1722 to beg him to assume the title of Peter the Great, Emperor of All Russia, Father of the Fatherland. In the meantime he had in 1719 annexed Kamchatka and Titus Bering's expedition had reached the Pacific coast, though it did not report back his discoveries till after Peter's death. Another force in 1722-3 had made gains from Persia round the Caspian. So he should have been content with his expansion achieved in the west, south and east.

Yet 1718 had also despite his huge successes been the year when Peter vindictively and with great sadism killed his own eldest son, Alexei. Ivan the Terrible had murdered his son 250 years earlier, but he did so in the heat of rage and regretted it afterwards: Peter on the other hand did it over a period of several days during which he had plenty of time to change his mind. The trouble had always been that Peter expected his heir to be a multi-talented workaholic like himself, so he had treated him as he did himself. Overwhelmed by these expectations and unable to cope with the huge physical and intellectual demands made on him Alexei though by no means stupid shrank into himself. The more his father berated him, the more he became terrified and evasive. In this frame of mind he began drinking heavily and took out his feelings on Charlotte of Wolfenbuttel, the German wife whom Peter had made him marry. Charlotte produced two children for him but he callously ignored her, just as his father had done his first wife, and just like him took a peasant mistress, Efrosinia.

Yet far from endearing him to his father this behaviour by the Tsarevich made things worse and the death of Charlotte in 1715 brought their quarrel to a head. Peter wrote to Alexei threatening to disinherit him 'Better a worthy stranger than an unworthy son.' Alexei wrote back renouncing his claim to the succession which infuriated Peter further, as that had not really been his intention. Alexei went further and asked to become a monk, but was so terrified of being killed that he absconded with his mistress Efrosinia and sought asylum in Vienna.

Peter's spies eventually found the young couple in a Tyrolean hide-away. Peter, who was at this time strutting around Versailles with the French king, was busy noting down ideas which he could take back to St Petersburg. As a man used to the total obedience of millions he found it deeply humiliating that he should be publicly defied by his own son. He threatened war with Austria unless Alexei was handed over. Eventually under a variety of personal threats Alexei, who had by this time moved to Naples was persuaded that he had to return to the Kremlin where he renounced his claim to the succession in favour of his three-year-old son Peter.

It looked perhaps as if the crisis was over but not for a man as paranoid as Peter. Just as he had obsessively persecuted Sofia and the *Streltsi* back in 1698, desperately looking for evidence of even more plots than were obvious, so now he did the same with Alexei and his friends. Efrosinia had been allowed back to live with Alexei in St Petersburg, but Peter had her brought first to the Peter and Paul fortress then to Peterhof for inter-rogation. Here, for whatever reason, she poured forth every grievance which Alexei had ever muttered to friends about his father and every confidential letter that she had either seen or with the help of Peter's interrogators invented. One damning snippet was that Alexei had said that when he became Tsar he would shift the capital back to Moscow, the sort of accusation, however unreliable, that would send Peter apo-plectic. In June 1718 he ordered Alexei's arrest and imprisonment in the Peter and Paul Fortress, making a token effort to distance himself from the trial that followed, yet there is no doubt that he was responsible for the interrogation by torture to which his son was subjected: twenty-five flesh-cutting strokes of the knout, another fifteen strokes five days later so that his back was raw, then further torture two days after that with his father probably present – all this despite the fact that by this time he had already been sentenced to death. The sentence was hardly necessary for by this time he was close to death. He died seven days after the inter-rogations first began. A state funeral and burial in the Cathedral of Saints Peter and Paul hardly made up for what he had undergone.

Peter simply went back to work pursuing his endless stream of reforms. A series of new academies were founded for specialist subjects like navi-gation, engineering, artillery and the sciences. Attendance at one or other of them was made compulsory for all the service aristocracy. Reform of the Church continued. Then in 1722 there came the new Table of Ranks so that there were now fourteen grades established for both military and civil service appointments. By this time the number of heads of land-owning families had risen from 20,000 to 200,000 partly due to Peter's military promotions and partly due to the lack of a primogeniture system that led to the splitting of estates between all sons. At the same time there was still a standing army of 130,000 with 100,000 Cossacks also on call. Peter's tame bishop Prokopovich was preaching the new creed, what Lincoln calls 'the concept of universal sacrifice' – the sole purpose of existence was to serve the emperor. For the landowners that meant not just learning to be efficient soldiers or naval officers but also how to sail a dinghy, dance the minuet, build an appropriate town house in St Petersburg or play whist.

That same year Peter was down in Astrakhan increasing the pressure on Persia that ultimately led to the cession of Baku on the Caspian to Russia. It was on this campaign that he first showed signs of the acute prostate problem that was to bedevil his last few years. Yet he was still putting in a fourteen-hour day either chasing up his new shipyards, harrying the senate, acting as clerk of works in the huge building site of St Petersburg, constantly taking notes, and checking that his underlings followed up any failures that he had noticed.

Meanwhile as his health faltered he became more aware of a succession problem which was largely his own fault. His own baby son Peter had died in 1719 and his grandson Peter was still only seven. In 1722 he had an *ukaz* passed which decreed that he could choose his own successor and two years later he had his wife Catherine crowned as Empress in the Uspensky Cathedral. She was rewarded with huge quantities of valuable gems. Even she however disappointed him, as did his best friend Menshikov and his old friends the family of his former mistress Anna Mons, for all of them were involved in a corruption scandal that made a total mockery of his lifelong efforts to eliminate bribery from the government. A shortage of able but honest officials was always one of his problems. Peter had hanged his own governor of Siberia for a similar offence. Catherine was half-forgiven though the decapitated head of one of the Mons brothers was installed in her bedroom in case she thought of straying again, but Menshikov remained out of favour and the lesser members of the scam such as the Mons family all suffered the knout or execution.

Peter's strangury problem, perhaps exacerbated by an earlier vene-real infection, did not go away. He underwent bladder surgery with no anaesthetic, yet soon afterwards headed off to inspect his new Olonetsky ironworks in Karelia and work on the new Ladoga-Volga Canal. After being personally involved in the rescue of a boat full of soldiers near Lakha on the Gulf of Finland, despite a soaking in near freezing conditions he carried on with another factory visit. By January 1725 he was delirious and confined to his bed in the Winter Palace, St Petersburg where Catherine nursed him till the end. His daughter Anna, who had just become engaged to the Duke of Holstein, was summoned to take down his final wishes but by the time she arrived he was delirious with pain. He died on 8 February 1725 aged fifty-three.

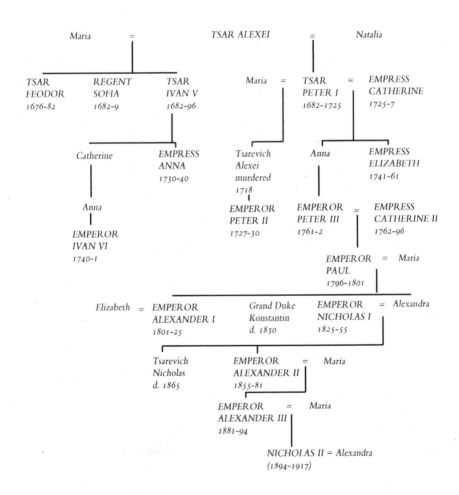

II

THE EMPRESS CATHERINE I
A LITHUANIAN PEASANT GIRL

'She had much mother wit and simplicity'
Robert Graham, *Peter the Great*

Strictly speaking the next two years (1725-7) represented a hiatus in the
reign of the Romanov dynasty for Catherine, previously known as Marfa
Skavronska, was the orphan child of Lithuanian peasants with no trace
of either Russian or Romanov blood in her veins. Yet the pliable senate, massaged by Menshikov, her one-time lover, and other old allies of
Peter, decided that it was Peter's will that she should succeed him rather
than any of the available genuine Romanovs. If they needed any further
persuasion this was provided by the sight of the two famous regiments
founded by Peter, the Preobrazhensky and the Semenovsky drawn up at
the ready outside the senate house, apparently on the orders of Catherine
herself. Just as Sofia had made use of the *Streltsi* back in 1682, Catherine
now did exactly the same with the two regiments founded by her late
husband. And the instability created by having two easily bribed regiments so close to the capital was to result in a prolonged weak period
in the Romanov dynasty's tenure of power. One mistake that no new
dynast for the next few decades could make was to neglect the wage
payments of the Prebrazhensky.

There is no doubt that Catherine wanted power and also dreaded the
consequences of not getting it: death or incarceration in a nunnery. The
humdrum work of government she was more than happy to leave to
Menshikov who now became the virtual ruler of Russia. Having first
come to Peter's notice as a sergeant in the Preobrazhensky and as a keen

drinking companion, Alexashka as he was known, had then shared the early hardships of ship building and campaigning, ultimately becoming an extremely successful field commander in the Northern War, meanwhile surrendering his mistress, the future Tsaritsa Catherine to his master. As a result of his loyalty and success he had become the richest man in Russia but still wanted more and now used this new opportunity to add to his huge wealth.

The other potential, but for the time being rejected candidates for tsardom remained lurking in the background. They included the Tsar's young grandson Peter now aged ten, as well as his and Catherine's two surviving daughters: the tsarevnas Anna aged eighteen and Elizabeth sixteen, both of whom though technically illegitimate were obviously capable and Romanovs. There was also the amiable Tsarevna Natalia, the daughter of Peter by his first wife Evdokhia who at sixty was still nursing her wrath in the Schlusselburg prison. There were also three other tsarevnas, the daughters of Peter's half-brother the mentally feeble Ivan V: Catherine the Duchess of Mecklenburg, Anna the widowed Duchess of Courland and the youngest, the sickly spinster Praskovia named after her mother.

While Menshikov and his elderly ally Tolstoy ruled Russia Catherine who was still not yet forty devoted herself to drinking and to two replacement lovers, Peter Sapieha and Reinhold Lowenwolde. At the same time she made herself slightly independent of Menshikov and his aging cronies by establishing a privy council of seven. She also imported many of her old Lithuanian relatives to the court and loved to treat them to banquets until the early hours of the morning, a habit which did nothing to improve her health. She enjoyed the country estate at Tsarskoe Selo, originally an island farm 20 miles south of St Petersburg first acquired by Menshikov in 1707, then passed to Peter who gave it to Catherine before their marriage. The costs of maintaining the royal palaces rose to over 6 million roubles, many times what it had been under Peter and as a result savings had to be made on some other projects like the Ladoga Canal. The tax burdens on the peasants were bringing them close to boiling point so Menshikov sensibly suggested the cancelling of arrears to avoid a rebellion.

In foreign affairs during Catherine's reign there were only two minor crises and each was related to one of the two Annas. The first was when the English tried to curb the ambitions of Holstein where Catherine's elder daughter Anna was the duchess, but Russia made the English back down and anyway, this Anna was to die soon afterwards in Kiel. The other Anna, widowed Duchess of Courland and daughter of Ivan V, was involved in a scheme to marry a German adventurer and Menshikov was sent with an army to chase him away, thus at least leaving this Anna as a potential long-term candidate for supreme power in Russia.

As Catherine's health declined rapidly there was another succession crisis. After a hefty bribe from the Austrians, Menshikov persuaded Catherine in her dying moments that the crown should go to Peter's grandson instead of her daughter Elizabeth who had been the favoured candidate of both of them and of Menshikov's colleague Tolstoy. Menshikov's main objective was of course that he himself should remain the power behind the throne. Catherine died at the end of May 1727, just over two years after her husband. It had been an extraordinary career for a Lithuanian peasant girl. She died without implementing a decree which she had published to expel all the Jews from Russia and the Ukraine.

III

EMPEROR PETER II
THE TSAR WHO NEVER GREW UP

'I will see whether you or I am emperor'
Peter II aged twelve to Menshikov

The succession of Peter the Great's grandson Peter II in 1727 at the age of eleven was not due to any legal precedence over other candidates, particularly his more popular aunt Elizabeth, but purely to the machinations of Menshikov. He was so desperate to remain in power that he ditched his principles, changed from the modernising wing of the political spectrum to the conservative and abandoned his old colleagues like Tolstoy. He backed little Peter to save his own skin and gain the bribe promised him by the Austrians, a seat in the electoral council of the Holy Roman Empire. To make things easier he was one of the few people in Russia who could quickly lay hands on enough cash to ensure the loyalty of the Preobrazhensky Guard.

Menshikov's machinations continued and in the end his efforts to control the Tsar were so oppressive as to make the boy react the wrong way. The first mistake was to send away the Tsar's aunt Anna, the Duchess of Holstein who was packed off to Kiel with her husband where she shortly produced a son, another Peter, and another grandson therefore of Peter the Great. Sadly she caught a chill at the firework display to celebrate the birth and died. As Peter II had lost both his mother the German princess Charlotte, and his father the wretched Tsarevitch Alexei, at a very young age, his aunts Anna and Elizabeth were his closest relatives apart from his sister Natalia, so the loss of Anna was another blow.

The second mistake Menshikov made was to push his own daughter rather over-aggressively as a potential bride for Peter who was too young to be interested but now getting old enough to resent manipulation. These two grudges against Menshikov added to a third, encouraged by court gossip which reminded Peter that Menshikov had played a part in the brutal torture and death of his father the Tsarevitch Alexei. From these beginnings as the Tsar approached his teens he developed an intense dislike of Menshikov and everything that he and his grandfather Peter the Great had stood for, particularly the new capital city and the navy. In all this he came under the influence of the charismatic Ivan Dolgoruky who became his favourite hunting companion.

Matters came to a head when Peter was still only twelve. He publicly snubbed Menshikov who responded with a huge party at his country chateau the Oranienbaum to try to bring the boy round. It failed to do so. Then Peter who at this young age was already drinking snubbed Menshikov again at Elizabeth's eighteenth birthday party at Peterhof. Egged on by Dolgoruky and his other would-be minders at the St Petersburg Summer Palace Peter boldly ordered Menshikov's arrest. The privy council was summoned, and it condemned Menshikov to exile in Berezovo beyond the Urals where he died a year later.

Peter and his new advisers now swung the conservative policy into action, moving the government back to Moscow from St Petersburg, which because of his father's terrible death there had painful memories for him. The fleet was neglected, the troop levies were cancelled and the interrogation chambers of the Preobrazhensky closed down.

In Moscow Peter lived in Lefort's old palace and the Dolgorukys aimed to keep him happy by indulging his favourite pastime, hunting, one of the reasons he preferred Moscow to St Petersburg which was short of good game. They provided him with 600 dogs to make it more exciting and obscene numbers of animals were slaughtered. They tried to persuade his flirtatious aunt Elizabeth to marry him despite the fact that she was seven years his senior, but perhaps wisely she refused. Then, just as Menshikov had tried to build himself into the dynasty by marriage, so now the Dolgoruky clan provided a fiancée of their own for the thirteen year-old Tsar. But all was in vain as the boy's health deteriorated. They even tried the last minute ruse of inserting the fiancée in the dying Tsar's bed for a last minute effort to beget an heir. It cannot even be said that he therefore died happy for he had contracted smallpox. He was still only fifteen. In defiance of his grandfather's new tradition he was buried in the Kremlin instead of St Petersburg.

IV

THE EMPRESS ANNA
THE HUNTRESS

'There are few murkier pages in Russian history and the murkiest blot was Anna herself'

Vasili Klyuchevsky, *The Course of Russian History*

Nobody was more surprised than Anna, the widowed Duchess of Courland to be invited back to Moscow in 1730 to become ruler of Russia (1730-40). She had lived in Mitau (now Jelgava in Latvia) the capital of the Germanic Duchy of Courland for twenty years, most of it in near abject poverty, for her husband had died on the way back from their alcohol-fuelled honeymoon. Not only was she taken aback by the summons but she had been so remote from Russian affairs for so long that she accepted as gospel the implication that the terms of the offer had been agreed by some sort of national assembly, not just a very small privy council of aristocrats. In fact it was all just part of a plot by Dolgoruky and a few friends to hold on to power for themselves.

Anna, the daughter of the mentally inadequate Tsar Ivan V and his wife Praskovia was by this time thirty-seven. Married at the age of seventeen to the Duke of Courland she had become an almost instant widow and since then despite many requests for much needed cash had been deprived of any subsidies by her Russian relations who at the same time prevented her from marrying again. They feared that a new Duke of Courland might be a nuisance and the most likely candidate, a German prince, had been chased away on Menshikov's orders in 1726. This did not however stop her taking lovers of whom the best known were Peter Bestuzhev, the Russian ambassador and then a local riding master Ernst

Johan Buhren who followed her to Russia and changed his name to Biren. She also allegedly had a passionate friendship if not a lesbian affair with a Mademoiselle Oginska.

As might be expected of a widowed duchess in her late thirties who had been stranded in a rather dull provincial town for two decades, she had put on weight. Since she was anyway of well above average height for those days she returned to Moscow as an imposing if no longer quite so attractive physical presence and this was accentuated by the fact that her years in virtual exile had left her very bitter, humourless and not given to smiling.

Anna was however far from unintelligent and it did not take long for her to realise that the Dolgoruky set had tricked her into signing a document which they had no real authority to impose. The eight conditions or *Punkti* for her gaining the throne had included quite sensible ones such as that without the council's consent she should not go to war or make peace, raise new taxes, marry or choose a successor. If this had meant the consent of an elected parliament this would have given Russia a useful constitution but in fact it just meant the consent of a very small, self-perpetuating clique mainly made up of Dolgorukys and led by Prince Dimitri Golitsyn.

So Anna rapidly worked out that the main body of the senate had no greater affection for an oligarchy of eight aristocrats than they had for despotism by one autocrat. What is more, the Dolgoruky-Golitsyn faction was sufficiently unpopular for her to flout their terms with impunity and tear up the *Punkti*. So this significant attack on Romanov absolutism came to nothing with probably disastrous long-term consequences for Russia. She set about disbanding the privy council and encouraging instead the Senate and a cabinet of ministers led by the German Andrew Osterman while most senior positions in the civil service and army also went to Germans. She even founded a new regiment the Ismailovsky, manned mainly by Courlanders or Germans and commanded by Count Lowenwolde to offset the previous influence of the Preobrazhensky. Thus did she begin to take her revenge on the Dolgorukys and Golitsyns.

Once the coronation in Moscow was over Anna moved the seat of government back to St Petersburg where she settled in the Winter Palace to which she began to make substantial expensive additions.

Having been deprived of what she regarded as fun for so long Anna now proceeded to enjoy herself. Her style of living was ostentatious and

opulent with little regard for cost. Her ex-lover Biren the riding instruc-
tor was promoted to the post of High Chamberlain, given vast estates,
palaces both in Russia and Mitau and a huge new riding school to practice his craft. Not only was he made a Russian count but also Duke of
Courland, the title once held by her dead husband many years before.
None of this however gave him any deep sense of security so he used
some of his new wealth to set up a private police force which he used to
extract confessions from those old Russian aristocrats whom he perhaps
rightly regarded as his enemies. Many of them were never seen again.
This just added to the unpopularity of the German clique.

Meanwhile the peasants were also disappearing in large numbers, for it
was estimated that in fifteen years as many as half a million decamped to
Siberia or the Ukraine to escape from the heavy taxation imposed by the
Romanovs. Anna was extravagant in her building projects, encouraged
by the great fire in St Petersburg which destroyed many wooden buildings in 1737 so that many were replaced with stone or brick. She also had
the two new palaces in Mitau built by Rastrelli for Biren and herself. As
well as her huge extension of the Winter Palace in St Petersburg she also
built a new opera house.

Anna's favourite pastime like her predecessor's was hunting so she now
had the opportunity to shoot as many birds and animals as she pleased,
often from the windows of one of her palaces. She also enjoyed gossip, card games, banquets, fêtes, fireworks and dances. She added hugely
not just to her own expenditure but to that of the rest of her courtiers
by insisting on expensive new imported drinks like Champagne and
Burgundy, ostentatious new clothes which could only be worn once
before they were thrown away, and exotic new furniture made from
tropical hardwoods instead of the traditional Russian oak. Her own
golden and jewel-encrusted commode was just the most risible example
of uncontrolled extravagance which rapidly depleted her own treasury
and led to an embarrassing balance of payments deficit. Biren's proposals
for harsh extra levies from already hard-pressed tax payers simply made
the regime even less popular.

Yet in Anna's expensive festivities she still gave vent to the bitterness which had clouded her early life. Like her half-uncle Peter the
Great she took pleasure in the discomfiture of hired dwarfs or other
unfortunates and later in the ritual humiliation of those courtiers to
whom she had taken a dislike. One such ploy was to make elderly

aristocrats sit on eggs and cluck like a hen. Chief amongst her victims was Prince Mikhail Golitsyn whose Catholic conversion had annoyed her and whom she forced to marry an allegedly repulsive Kalmuck Tartar and spend the wedding night with her naked in an ice house.

If she disliked Catholics she also, like Catherine I, disapproved of Jews, many of whom had been brought within Russia after the acquisition of the Ukraine in 1667. A number of them were burned for witchcraft or heresy during her reign.

Surprisingly, despite her devotion to pleasure, her regime achieved some modest successes abroad. Her armies reached the Rhine to help intimidate the French in 1735 though that was of no great benefit to Russia. A force under her German general Marshall Munnich scored a victory against the Turks in the Crimea which resulted in the Azov area once more becoming part of Russia. But as on previous occasions the financial cost of funding a war so far away had been huge and the campaign had cost 100,000 Russian lives. After this Munnich was transferred to oversee the completion of the Ladoga canal.

Anna was overweight and suffered from kidney stones yet as her health began to fail her main concern was the survival of Biren with whom she still seems to have been besotted, despite the fact that he had taken a wife. In her final moments she warned him that his plans could be dangerous but she still agreed to nominate his choice as successor. This was the baby Ivan recently born to her niece Anna of Brunswick. The alternative, her cousin Elizabeth of whose looks and personality she had long been jealous was rejected in favour of a baby whose blood was three-quarters German.

Anna was still only forty-seven when she died.

V

IVAN VI
THE PRISONER OF SCHLUSSELBURG

'The palmiest of days for the favourite, the intiguer, the lover, the instigator
of plots … '

Kochan

Many previous tsars had been incapable figureheads and led miserable
lives, but through no fault of his own Ivan VI (1740-41) was to endure a
worse fate than most if not all of them. He became Tsar in October 1740
as a helpless infant with the grasping, arrogant Biren as his regent, a man
with no other qualifications for the post than an expertise in riding and
the favouritism of his late mistress.

Of baby Ivan's four grandparents only one was Russian and a Romanov,
Catherine of Mecklenburg, the sister of Empress Anna. The other three
were German and given the existing unpopularity of the three senior
German officials, Biren himself, Ostermann and Munnich, not to mention the numerous other Germans scattered through the army and civil
service, this did not bode well for him. In fact the three main Germans
had no trust or liking for each other and were soon to fall out.

Meanwhile Biren continued to antagonise nearly everybody but
his worst mistake was to try to dispense with the Preobrazhensky and
Semenovsky Guards. He tried to break them up by sending detachments
to different parts of the country and they appealed to Munnich to intervene. He did so and within three weeks of becoming Regent, Biren had
been arrested at night in the Summer Palace and was lucky to have his
life sentence commuted to a stay in the Schlusselburg prison fortress and
then a penniless exile in Siberia.

The new regent was the Tsar's mother Anna Leopoldovna of Brunswick – Wolfenbuttel who had very little interest in the task, not even to help her little son survive. She oscillated between an allegedly gay relationship with a German lady-in-waiting, Julie Mengden, and a torrid extramarital affair with a Saxon called Lynar. In this chaotic situation the remaining two Germans fought for power and Ostermann won at the expense of Munnich. Once in sole control along with the compliant and totally uninterested Anna of Brunswick Ostermann found that he was facing new intrigues led by the French and Swedish envoys who were plotting for Elizabeth, the surviving daughter of Peter the Great, to take over. She was not particularly interested but Ostermann overreacted by summoning her for a meeting with the regent and arresting her go-between, the physician Armand Lestocq. Elizabeth who had previously been nervous about joining any coup aimed at placing her on the throne now realised that there was a stark choice: either run the risk of supporting a coup or face being shut in a nunnery for the rest of her life.

The Preobrazhensky, already unsettled by the threats of Biren, were more than ready to back her, because like her mother Empress Catherine she was popular with the army, a pleasant, sociable girl who had often been willing to act as godmother for the soldiers' children. Late at night on 24 November 1741 she travelled by sledge with a small group of friends to the barracks. The men responded eagerly to her presence and within hours were heading for the Winter Palace where still under cover of night they arrested the Regent Anna, her cuckolded husband, the infant Tsar and the two unpopular ministers Ostermann and Munnich. Anna of Brunswick and her wretched husband were exiled to Kholmogory near the White Sea.

Their unlucky son who had been Tsar for thirteen months and was still not two years old was locked up in the island dungeon of Schlusselburg for the next eighteen years and never saw his parents again. He was not even allowed a cell-mate, was kept short of food, badly clothed and humiliated by his warders as he grew up with only the vaguest idea of what had happened to him. When Emperor Peter III visited him in 1762 he found him a gibbering wreck. The misery of his solitary confinement only came to an end because the guards had orders to kill him at the first hint of an attempted rescue. Whether there really was an attempt or whether it was just finally considered better to have him out of the way he was quietly murdered in July 1764.

VI

THE EMPRESS ELIZABETH
THE PLEASURE LOVER

'She always had one foot in the air'
R.N. Bain, *The Pupils of Peter the Great*

When she came to the throne Elizabeth was thirty-two and still one of the great beauties of the Russian court. With blue eyes, light brown hair, good dancing legs and a fine figure, her two priorities in life were physical pleasure and devotion to the Orthodox Church. Affairs of state were very much further down the list as was any form of study, for she blamed the early death of her sister Anna, Duchess of Holstein-Gottorp, on too much reading of Latin poetry. Nevertheless despite very little education apart from religion she did manage to pick up three foreign languages, German, Italian and French, which she made use of when she came to power.

She had been born at the Kolomenskoe Palace outside Moscow in 1709 just after her father Peter the Great's famous victory at Poltava. He and her mother, the former Lithuanian peasant girl Martha/Catherine, had not yet married by this time and even when they did so three years later there were question marks, for he had never actually divorced his first wife Evdokhia who was then still alive in her nunnery.

Certainly a nunnery was always the last place where Elizabeth would have wanted to spend her life and indeed fear of such a fate had been the main motivation behind her at last supporting the coup which brought her to the throne. She had already been passed over three times in previous succession crises: in 1727 for her half-nephew Peter II, in 1730 for her cousin Anna, and in 1740 for her other cousin the infant Ivan VI –

the other Anna's son. She had also missed out on two potential husbands: the big prize Louis XV where it was reckoned that she came a creditable second in the list of eighteen candidates and a German princeling who tragically for both of them died just as their engagement was to be announced. Since she was too important to marry any normal Russian aristocrat, and anyway few of them seem to have appealed to her, she had to content herself with lovers. The first was a sergeant in the Semenovsky who on Anna's orders had his tongue removed and was sent to Siberia when the affair was discovered. Her second choice was equally unorthodox, Alexis Razumovsky a humble Cossack musician from near Kiev who became a singer in Empress Anna's court chapel. This affair was to last the rest of her life. It is probable that once Empress she contracted a secret marriage with him and they may even have had children, though apparently none survived to adulthood except the mysterious Avgusta Tarakanova who was smuggled abroad and then kept in solitary confinement in the Ivanovsky Convent outside Moscow till her death in 1810.

Meanwhile the fifteen years between her father's death in 1725 when Elizabeth was sixteen and her accession in 1740 were all spent in reasonable comfort. During the reign of her young nephew Peter II she became his close companion even when the court was moved back to Moscow from St Petersburg. Her greatest passion remained dancing, particularly minuets and quadrilles, at which she had excelled since she was eleven or twelve. But she was also extremely fond of the outdoor life: riding, sailing, the wolf hunts around Kurgan, the gardens at Izmailovskoe, sledging and dancing in the local peasant festivities. In due course she also fell in love with the country estate outside St Petersburg left to her by her mother, Tsarskoe Selo.

During the reign of her cousin Anna, she was under a slight cloud for it suited the Dolgorukys to portray her as only a bastard daughter of Peter the Great. Anna was jealous of her youth and good looks, disapproved of her flirtations and her addiction to dancing. So her twenties were in some respects her least happy decade. Even in this period however she won the regard of the guards regiments for with no real ulterior motive she had natural warmth like her mother and was often ready to act as godmother for a soldier's baby or exchange a friendly word.

This was to stand her in very good stead when at thirty-two she was at last faced with the dilemma of risking a dangerous coup or spending the rest of her life in lonely, probably celibate, obscurity.

When the moment finally came for her to oust Ivan VI and his mother there was one other driving force which was to colour the whole of her reign. Ivan VI had been three-quarters-German, his mother half-German and since the reign of Anna, who had spent half her life in Germanic Courland, there had been a steady increase in the number of top positions in Russia held by Germans. Thus Elizabeth and many of the displaced Russians felt a real sense of grievance. If there were two strands to the policies of Elizabeth as Empress other than simply continuing to have a good time, they were to purge the Russian government and army of Germans, a move that was greeted with wild celebrations, and to stop Prussia from becoming a dominant power in Europe. There was a general feeling, which she shared, that the emotional and generous if sometimes inefficient nature of the Russians was preferable to the cool and disciplined ways of the Germans.

One group she did specially make sure were rewarded for their help in her coup, the Preobrazhensky Guards, were well paid for their efforts. For the rest of her reign she never neglected to pay their wages and thus had little to worry about when there were plots to restore Ivan VI as in 1742-3.

Despite her desire to purge Germans from senior positions in Russia there was one instance of the reverse. Almost as soon as she was in power she sent to Kiel for her orphaned nephew Peter, the now thirteen-year-old son of her dead sister Anna and her husband Charles Duke of Holstein Gottorp. At least he was half-Russian, a grandson of Peter the Great and high enough up also in the Swedish royal family to be a candidate for that throne as well as one of Russia. But he had been born and brought up in Kiel where since the loss of his parents he had been bullied by obsessive and abusive German tutors, so he had been brain-washed into adulation of all things German, or more specifically Prussian. This passion which it proved too late for his Russian tutors to reverse was years later to have considerable consequences both for Russia and for his own life. But for the meantime it was clear that unless Elizabeth married officially and had a legitimate child, Peter was the heir to the imperial throne. Even at this stage his pallid looks, his introversion and his obsession with toy soldiers made him seem less than ideal. Yet for a number of years she lavished affection on him as if he were her own son, even on occasions risking her own health to nurse him through bouts of illness.

Meanwhile Elizabeth basked in the general rejoicing at her removal of the Germans and settled back down to a life of pleasure. Her favourite pastime remained dancing, specially masquerades with fancy dress when she often encouraged cross-dressing. Her own speciality was to appear as an ordinary Dutch sailor, which gave her the opportunity to show off her foot-work and her legs. Indeed she was something of a foot fetishist for there were numerous stories of people being required to tickle her feet. The prudish British ambassador George Macartney described her as 'abandoning herself to every excess of intemperance and lubricity.'

Elizabeth was also extremely extravagant and insisted that her courtiers followed her lead. As she never liked to wear the same dress twice and changed frequently throughout the day she amassed a vast collection of dresses. She was lavish in entertainment and expected others to be the same. Foreign chefs were hired at great cost to produce ever more lavish dishes. Her lover's brother Cyril Razumovsky who, like other favourites, had been very generously treated by her and made Hetman of the Cossacks was said to have imported 100,000 bottles of French wine. The more ostentatiously extravagant that her courtiers were, the more Elizabeth liked them. And to add further to the cost of her entertainments was the fact that while St Petersburg was once more the capital she liked to shift the court to Moscow from time to time and all the paraphernalia for entertainment had to be carted backwards and forwards.

The other special area of extravagance was in her building programme. She employed the Italian architect Dominico Rastrelli to enlarge or rebuild almost every royal palace. Her special love was Tsarskoe Selo where he built for her the Catherine Palace, named after her mother, with a brilliant blue façade over 100 metres long. She ordered 25,000 lime trees for her avenues. Nearby were the Grotto Pavilion, a concert hall on an island, the Mon Bijou Hunting Lodge and yet another Hermitage with a sixty-four-column façade. In St Petersburg itself she rebuilt the Summer Palace and the Winter Palace, at the same time greatly extending Peterhof. In addition she built several theatres including a temporary ice one on the frozen Neva and greatly increased the popularity of public concerts, plays, opera and ballet, the last of which was to become lastingly associated with the Romanovs.

For most of her reign she left the government in the hands of the capable team which had helped bring her to power, Bestuzhev the son of Empress Anna's one-time lover ran foreign affairs and the two brothers Shuvalov, Peter and Andrew dealt with most of the rest. Peter Shuvalov in particular carried through some significant tax reforms, shifting some of the burden to indirect taxes and abolishing internal customs dues which had been harmful to business. He kept the army up to a strength of 30,000, well trained and properly equipped, in addition inventing a new Howitzer gun which was to prove of value during the war against Prussia. However the huge cost of this rearmament and the building projects continued to weigh down on the peasant taxpayer so that there was a considerable increase in the number of serf rebellions, albeit they were easily suppressed. She had the fort of St Dimitri built at Rostov-on-Don to cow the Cossacks and ackowledged the influx of Serb asylum-seekers by creating a district of New Serbia.

As part of their strategy for retaining power the Shuvalovs provided a handsome nephew, Ivan Shuvalov, as an additional lover for Elizabeth. To counter this influence her amiably compliant husband/lover Razumovsky procured another toy-boy, Nikita Beketov. Elizabeth was reportedly unfazed even when confronted with all three lovers at the same time, but her general over-indulgence was undoubtedly beginning to undermine her health.

Neither her promiscuity nor her levels of conspicuous consumption seemed to her at odds with her pious adulation of the Orthodox Church. She encouraged the forcible conversion of Jews and Muslims to Christianity, threatening to deport all Jews who refused. Even as she grew less fit she still made regular pilgrimages on foot to some of the monasteries and holy sites like Troitse many miles outside Moscow. There was also her epic pilgrimage to the holy sites of Kiev when it was said that she covered many of the 750 miles there on foot, at the same time bravely nursing her nephew Peter who had contracted smallpox. Yet as she grew too gross to dance she indulged in endless card games.

Meanwhile Elizabeth had at least theoretically safeguarded the succession of the Romanov dynasty. When her nephew Peter came of age in 1745 she found a princess for him to marry, surprisingly a German one, Sophia of Anhalt-Zerbst, later given the Russian name of Catherine as a token of her conversion to the Orthodox Church. Elizabeth organised a lavish wedding ceremony and supervised the bedding of the young couple afterwards. Nine years later when Peter was in his mid-twenties and by which time Catherine had almost certainly consoled herself with alternative lovers, they produced an heir, the Grand Duke Paul. Thus even if the German-born Peter continued in his wayward adulation of Prussian drill movements there was the potential for Elizabeth to skip a generation and leave Russia to a prince who was at least born in Russia though perhaps seriously deficient in Russian genes.

Apart from a half-hearted effort to reform the legal code and to reduce capital punishment the relationship between Elizabeth and her ministers was fairly free from controversy until Russia's entry into the Seven Years War in 1756.

Bestuzhev pleased her by being anti-Prussian, but not quite enough, particularly when he was wrong-footed by the British who despite earlier promises sided *with* instead of *against* the Prussians. Her army captured Memel (now Klaipeda on the coast of Lithuania) and impressively beat the Prussians at Grossjaegerhof. She was not happy with the subsequent retreat, which looked like treachery but was more likely due to the usual Russian problem of poor supplies over long distances. So she sacked her field marshal, one of her old favourites Stephen Apraxin, then Bestuzhev as well. There was a further indecisive battle at Zorndorf with heavy losses and she sacked another general. His replacement, Count Peter Saltykov, scored a truly remarkable victory over Frederick of Prussia himself at Kunersdorf. King Frederick reportedly contemplated taking his own life and the Russians stood at the gates of Berlin ready to finish off Prussia. Thus in her one serious intervention in government affairs Elizabeth had shown remarkable determination, if not an obsession to destroy the upstart Prussian king. She had in effect masterminded the most impressive feat of Russian arms since Poltava in the year of her birth.

Yet in this moment of triumph her health was deteriorating rapidly. Her official heir, her nephew Peter, had barely hidden his distaste for the war against his hero Frederick of Prussia and his mother-in-law, Joanna, was believed by some to have passed on state secrets to help the Prussian war effort. Elizabeth, whose legs were so swollen that she could barely walk, suffered a stroke in her church at Tsarskoe Selo. Within a few days she was dead and power was in the hands of a man who would throw away all the benefits of her remarkable victories. Elizabeth was fifty-three.

1 Tsar Mikhail, who became the first Romanov Tsar at the age of sixteen

2 Tsar Alexei, father of Peter the Great

3 Peter the Great striking one of the *Streltsi*, or musketeers, many of whom he tortured and executed after their mutiny in 1698

4 Peter the Great at the age of fifty, about three years before he died

5 Peter the Great and his wife Catherine sailing on the *Neva*. He encouraged all his courtiers to sail by building St Petersburg with no main bridges. Note the drop keel borrowed from the Dutch

6 The Empress Catherine the Great in her later years when she had begun to put on weight

7 Catherine's son, the volatile Tsar Paul who was murdered in 1801

8 Tsar Alexander I, who used the Russian winter to help defeat Napoleon in 1812

9 Tsar Nicholas I, Alexander's brother, who suffered a humiliating defeat in the Crimea

10 The coronation of Alexander II in Moscow in 1855. He emancipated the serfs six years later but was murdered in 1881

11 The conservative Tsar Alexander III, a huge man who personally lifted his family and others from the wreckage of the royal train in 1888

12 Nicholas II, the last tsar, in full naval uniform. Note the resemblance to his cousin George V of Great Britain

13 The haemophiliac young Tsarevitch Alexis in guards uniform

14 Gregori Rasputin, the peasant mystic and serial womaniser, whose help with the Tsarevich Nicholas and Alexandra came to rely too heavily upon, with disastrous consequences

15 The last tsarina, Alexandra, wearing the uniform of her own Regiment of Lancers

16 Young Jewish victims of a pogrom in the Ukraine, part of the ethnic cleansing programme begun under Alexander III

VII

PETER III
THE DRILL MASTER

' … so hastilly dismissed as a mere cretin'
R.N. Bain, *Peter III, Emperor of Russia*

'18th century Russian autocrats were surrounded by men and women
who told them what they wanted to hear'

Lincoln, *The Romanovs*

Peter was in his early thirties when he succeeded to the throne in 1761
and did not attempt to hide his delight at his Aunt Elizabeth's death. He
was the grandson of Peter the Great through his mother Anna, the late
Empress's sister, who had died soon after his birth in Kiel in 1728. His father
Charles Duke of Holstein-Gottorp was a sufficiently senior offshoot of the
Swedish royal family to have aspirations of grandeur, which were never fulfilled. He neglected his son and died when the boy was ten, leaving him in
the clutches of some particularly sadistic tutors whose behaviour verged on
child abuse. When he made a mistake he was made to kneel for hours on
hard peas. Whether it was they who were guilty of moulding his character
or whether it was partly due to heredity and earlier neglect it is hard to say.
But as we have seen, by the time that Elizabeth rescued him he proved incapable of responding to kinder treatment. He was tall and fair-haired but not
very robust and prone to occasional convulsions so that he was ill coordinated in his movements. He wanted to hide away with his vast army of toy
soldiers who were made to do manoeuvres with Germanic precision that
in real life he could probably never have managed. According to his wife's
diaries he court-martialled and executed a rat for eating two of his guards.

Despite soon being aware that he would probably in due course become Emperor of Russia Peter did not want to learn the Russian language and only acquired a half grasp of it over the ensuing years. Similarly he resisted conversion to the Orthodox Church and only did so for the sake of appearances and a huge bribe from Elizabeth – 300,000 roubles – while still preferring the plainer Lutheran rites of his childhood. Nor did he respond to any other aspect of education other than his obsession with things military and an occasional tune on the violin. He was made first a sergeant, then a colonel in the Preobrazhensky Regiment and that, combined with his titles of Grand Duke of Russia and Duke of Holstein, enabled him to wear a variety of exotic uniforms and medals to assuage his vanity.

Just before Peter's move from Kiel to St Petersburg Frederick II King of Prussia had dramatically defeated the Austrians in three battles and conquered Silesia. This seems to have made a huge impression on the boy who was fourteen years younger than Frederick and from this time onwards idolised him without any apparent concern for the effect on Russia. He hated the Danes for snatching Schleswig from his Holstein ancestors. At the same time he still seemed to prefer his Swedish ancestors to his Russian ones, for when a new offer came to make him the heir to the Swedish throne he was very resentful that Elizabeth turned it down on his behalf.

By the time he was sixteen Elizabeth was beginning to realise that he could not be moulded into the kind of tsar that she wanted to succeed her, so she set about finding him a wife so that he might produce an heir to whom, assuming she lived to a reasonable age, she could hand over the throne direct. Her choice was a German princess – Sophia of Anhalt-Zerbst – surprising to some extent, but a Bourbon princess had already turned down Peter, so Elizabeth's room for manoeuvre was limited. Sophia's father was a general in the Prussian army and her mother Joanna linked to the same Holstein and Swedish royal family as Peter, so Sophia was his second cousin. Sophia obligingly converted to the Orthodox Church and was renamed Catherine before the young couple married in 1745. Despite an extravagant wedding and ritual bedding supervised by Elizabeth herself the plan after this went disastrously wrong. It was to be nine years before a child was produced in 1754 meaning that the chances of his being an adult before the Empress died were very slim.

The reasons for Peter being so slow to produce an heir lie at the heart of his relationship with his bride Catherine, and were to play a major

part in the history of the Romanov dynasty for the next two generations. Just before his marriage, while on pilgrimage to Kiev with Empress
Elizabeth, he had caught smallpox. Elizabeth herself helped to nurse him
back to health despite the risk of infection to herself, but he was left
bald and badly pockmarked. Given the fact that even before this he had
not been desperately attractive this made things even worse. Moreover,
Peter's behaviour remained extremely immature and toy soldiers were
still his main interest; his sense of humour offended nearly everyone; he
drank too much and could be extremely uncouth. When in a temper he
was known to thrash his hunting dogs or hang them up by the tail.

After the marriage Elizabeth was so concerned by Peter's failure to
adapt to his new position that she isolated the couple from many of
his less savoury associates and installed two minders – a couple called
Choglokov – who were meant to control his behaviour and prevent
unauthorised contacts. In particular, Catherine's mother Joanna was
bundled off back to Berlin suspected, probably correctly, of being a
Prussian spy.

Initially, too, Peter was little interested in the opposite sex and apparently impotent until he had a minor operation seven years after his
marriage. By this time he was twenty-four. Meanwhile Catherine had
grown tired of waiting and was fearful that she would take the blame
for their joint sterility so she acquired a lover, Sergius Saltykov, soon
afterwards suffering a miscarriage. It was Saltykov who seems to have
persuaded a drunken Peter to undergo the operation so that he would
not ask questions about Catherine's pregnancy. At about the same time
Peter was provided with a temporary mistress, the wife of a painter called
Groot, to test the effectiveness of the operation. She did not even have
a miscarriage but the affair did at least seem to make Peter marginally
more interested in sex. There is some suggestion that the Choglokovs,
perhaps at the instigation of Elizabeth were now briefed that Catherine
must produce a child and as long as Peter could be convinced that he
was the father nothing else mattered.

Thus at long last the Grand Duke Paul was born in 1754. Peter drank
himself into oblivion and it seems he never again consorted with his
wife. After experimenting with a few women he eventually selected a
mistress, the uninspiring Elizabeth Vorontsova, who did not make him
feel inferior and was willing to share his drinking habits. Catherine was
now redundant and sent away from court with a 100,000 rouble pay-off,

deprived of her baby and dropped even by her lover Saltykov. The baby Paul was so petted by the Empress that in due course he was to turn out just as unsuitable for tsardom as his official father.

In due course Catherine found a new lover, Stanislaus Poniatowski, of whose existence Peter was well aware, as was Catherine of her husband's mistress Vorontsova. Their mutual tolerance was strained when Catherine had her second child who Peter was inclined to disown until it was pointed out to him that his resultant public humiliation would do his reputation as a Grand Duke no favours. This time the baby was a daughter, Anna, who was to die as a child, but Peter acted as if he were her father, put on his favourite uniform and ordered fireworks both at Peterhof and Kiel.

Meanwhile the war against Prussia had started and Catherine's ostracism became more pronounced since she was, after all, the daughter of a Prussian field marshal and even her husband's Germanic prejudices were well known. As a Pole, Poniatowski also came under suspicion and was extradited. However, he was soon replaced by Gregori Orlov, a middle class but ambitious guards officer who entertained her at his home on Vasilievski Island, St Petersburg. This resulted in a third successful pregnancy which meant that Catherine was out of action during the crucial weeks of Elizabeth's final illness and thus could not respond to the plotters who wanted the succession to go straight to Paul with Catherine as Regent.

So Peter became Emperor in January 1762 and his mistress's father was Chief Minister. Wearing the uniform of a Preobrazhensky officer he more or less looked the part and was greeted by the troops. Surprisingly he was much more conscientious in his duties than Elizabeth, rising early in the morning and feverishly charging round the various government departments to see what was going on. Immediately he set about some not unintelligent reforms such as the reduction in the salt tax, improvements in religious toleration and increased policing of the streets. For the time being the secret police were abolished. The aristocrats were delighted to be freed from compulsory service and allowed, for the first time, to travel abroad. The top 20 per cent or so who owned more than 100 serfs could therefore afford to become a leisured, westernised clique. Factory owners were now prevented from buying serfs and most of the serfs on church estates were transferred to the Crown, which could in turn grant them to the privileged class of landowners.

However Peter's great love was still the military and he was now able to play with real soldiers instead of just toys. Nearly every day he spent hours drilling the regiments and though he might have gained some popularity by reducing the use of the knout he soon lost it by insisting on Prussian drill movements and a more Germanic style of uniform. To make things worse he made it clear that he now preferred his own Holstein Guards to the long pampered Preobrazhensky.

One of Peter's other first actions as Emperor was to arrange a peace treaty with his idol Frederick II of Prussia who had been brought to his knees by Elizabeth and could easily have been forced to hand over East Prussia to the Russians. Instead, he was now allowed very lenient terms and was therefore able to resume his meteoric expansion of Prussia. Peter kept a bust of Frederick, whom he referred to as 'the king my master', in his bedroom and often openly admitted that he would rather have been like his own father an officer in Frederick's army than the ruler of all Russia. He even sometimes appeared on parade in Prussian uniform. To accentuate his preference for Germans Peter imported a number of old Holstein friends and relations to join in his somewhat juvenile court antics, playing the violin in his own orchestra at the Oranienbaum, drinking heavily, smoking and indoor scrummages, a sort of male bonding that seemed to reassure him about his masculinity.

Despite all this Peter was much more conscientious than Elizabeth had been in supervising the minutiae of government affairs, frenetically visiting factories, the imperial mint, harbours and army barracks. A kind of hyperactive insomniac, he could never be still. The one area he neglected was in traditional court ceremonies, which he probably felt were un-European and old-fashioned and which offended his still basically Lutheran attitude to the Church.

Meanwhile Catherine was once more ostracised, for she was pregnant again by her lover Orlov and in due course produced a son, Alexis. When the new Winter Palace was completed she was allowed to move into one wing while Peter, their son Paul and Peter's mistress Elizabeth Vorontsova were in another. Yet this *ménage a trois* sometimes showed signs of cracking and despite regular insults Catherine became increasingly confident that she was more popular than her ranting husband or his dowdy mistress. Catherine also won friends by her ostentatious weeping at the tomb of Elizabeth and by her obviously much greater respect for the Russian Church compared with her husband. For his part, he instituted a rash reorganisation of the Church that transferred its property to the State and turned priests into State-paid functionaries. This and his typically Lutheran disapproval of icons and fancy ecclesiastical robes added fuel to the fire.

So as Peter became increasingly unpopular the stock of Catherine continued to rise. In the summer of 1762, after signing an alliance with Prussia, he planned a joint conquest of Austria. At the same time he ridiculously sent an army of 40,000 men into Prussia to attack the Danes as they were in control of a small portion of his birthplace, Holstein. Already irritated by his preference for Germans his Russian officers were alarmed at the idea of a new war on the same side as their former enemy. Catherine's lover Gregori Orlov, his brothers and other fellow officers now began, with her connivance and probably financial support, to stir up a mutiny amongst the guards regiments. Count Nikita Panin, a former failed candidate as toy-boy for Empress Elizabeth (he allegedly fell asleep at the wrong moment), was now the tutor of the Tsarevich Paul and seems to have been the mastermind behind the plot. On 9 July 1762 Catherine made an early morning dash to the Ismailovsky barracks where she received support from the troops and their commander Cyril Razumovsky. This was followed by a visit to the Semenovsky barracks where she was again welcomed as the new Empress. By 9 a.m. that morning she was in the Kazan Cathedral being blessed by the Archbishop, soon afterwards processing to the Winter Palace where she held up the infant Grand Duke Paul to the cheering crowds. For once the Preobrazhensky were the last to join in the coup but did so now, discarding their new German uniforms.

Despite having been warned by his friend King Frederick that a coup was imminent, Peter refused to believe it and was busy at Peterhof preparing for his departure to the Austrian front. When he heard the news from St Petersburg he panicked. His ministers Peter Shuvalov, Vorontsov and Trubetskoy were sent off to investigate but never returned. Old Marshall Munnich advised sending in the troops, particularly the Holstein Regiment, but Peter hesitated and instead boarded his yacht with a view to taking over the fortress island of Kronstadt. He was too slow: Catherine had already sent a force to persuade the Kronstadt garrison to side with her, so they refused Peter permission to land. At this point he apparently fainted and had to sail back to Oranienbaum. There he wrote a grovelling letter to his wife offering to share power with her.

By this time she was en route to Peterhof at the Sergeievsky Monastery and was confident enough of success to refuse. He followed up with an even more abject letter offering to abdicate so long as he and his mistress could retire to Holstein. Even this was not accepted but Peter had to sign away his throne, was stripped of his medals and uniform and locked up in Ropsha under the custody of Alexis Orlov. He asked for his violin, his pet poodle and his doctor. In Ropsha a week later, allegedly in the course of some scuffle with Prince Theodore Baryatinsky, Peter was fatally injured. His death was reported to Catherine of whose reactions there is no reliable report, but she forgave the culprits and announced publicly that Peter had died of natural causes, a colic attack.

Peter was only thirty-four, had reigned for less than a year and had been so shy that he had unwisely postponed his coronation, something that might have strengthened the loyalty of his subjects, till it was too late. As Frederick of Prussia put it 'he allowed himself to be overthrown like a child being sent to bed.'

If the suggestions that Peter was sterile were true then he was in fact the last of the Romanovs, but the aura of the dynasty had now become so strong and the Russians were such a conservative race, that it was the image that mattered more than the reality. The spiritual inheritance counted for more than mere genes.

VIII

CATHERINE II THE GREAT

'I instinctively recoil, for she frightens me'
Chevalier d'Eon

Catherine had achieved power by a coup d'etat based on the support of a few politicians and two regiments of the guards, very much in the same way as Sofia and Elizabeth in earlier years. So her position was far from secure and this was made worse by the fact that she was not a Romanov or even a Russian by birth but a German and if there was an identifiable mood in the country it was anti-German. So she needed to work hard to establish a wider power base.

She had been born Sophia Augusta Frederica thirty-three years earlier in the East Prussian town of Stettin, later known as Szezcin at the mouth of the Oder in what is now Poland. Her father Christian Augustus was the fairly impoverished co-heir of Anhalt-Zerbst, whose principality was so small that he had to earn his living as a general in the Prussian army and was not able to marry until he was middle-aged. Thus, at the time of her birth in May 1729 he was the garrison commander at Stettin. Her mother Joanna of Holstein-Gottorp was twenty-seven years younger and came from a branch of the German dynasty that had taken over the Crown of Sweden, so she was related to the father of Sophia's future husband the Grand Duke Peter of Russia.

Sophia, known as a child by the nickname of Figchen, grew up first in Stettin where she was allowed to wander the streets, then in the small town of Zerbst, south-west of Berlin. Early on she developed a strong independent streak, perhaps because her mother largely ignored her and her father was away with the army. With a highly intelligent French governess, Babet Cardel, she learned French as well as German and acquired a lifelong interest in reading with a preference for serious works rather than mere fiction. Convinced that she was unattractive she concentrated on honing her wit and powers of manipulation rather than relying on physical beauty, although in due course she grew into a tall and impressive, if not conventionally pretty, woman.

As a potential bride for the heir to Russia she was far from the first choice, but as other options were ruled out she appeared as a compromise candidate. She did have one special attraction in Elizabeth's eyes for she was the niece of the Empress's long dead fiancé and bore some resemblance to him. King Frederick of Prussia was particularly pleased at the idea of the daughter of one of his subordinates becoming a future empress of Russia and her mother Joanna acting as a useful informant on affairs in Russia. Thus at the age of fifteen Sophia was removed from Zerbst and taken via Berlin to St Petersburg. She had met her second cousin the Grand Duke Peter five years earlier in Kiel and then he had made a relatively good impression. But sadly, though a year older, he had not matured as rapidly as she had. He seemed to regard his removal from Kiel to Russia more as a punishment whereas for her it was a great opportunity. He was now introverted, petulant and interested only in playing with his toy soldiers. Nor did he show any particular interest in her attractions and reduced her to tears by remarking unkindly that he preferred a Fraulein Korf.

Sophia nevertheless stuck to her task and dutifully converted to the Russian Orthodox Church after which she was renamed Catherine (the name Sophia still had unfortunate undertones due to the regency of Peter the Great's half-sister Sofia) and soon afterwards was made a grand duchess. Her marriage to Peter in 1745 was to last, at least in theory, for sixteen years during much of which their relationship was either acrimonious or non-existent. Peter styled himself Duke of Holstein but continued to play with toy soldiers, puppets or his violin, drank heavily and indulged in petty pranks with his male friends. The Empress Elizabeth took various measures to try to make them behave like a normal couple but to no effect. Peter was given Menshikov's old palace at Oranienbaum and 5,000 real soldiers to drill.

After seven years of almost certainly unconsummated marriage Catherine took her first lover Sergei Saltykov who was introduced to her, perhaps on orders from the top, during a hare hunt on an island in the Neva. She had two miscarriages, which at least proved her fertility. Peter had the operation that ended his impotence and he was provided with a mistress whom he notably failed to make pregnant. The Empress and her advisers probably therefore connived at Catherine's continued affair with Saltykov despite the fact that her marriage was at long last consummated, so that no one would really know the paternity of the baby Grand Duke Paul who was born in September 1754. After a twelve-hour labour the baby was taken from her and she hardly saw it for the next few months. The treatment of Catherine afterwards both by her husband and the Empress suggests that they suspected Saltykov, who was promptly despatched to Sweden to keep him out of the way.

Catherine was to spend the next eight years in limbo, largely ignored by Peter who acquired a mistress; shunned by the Empress; and consoled briefly by the Polish diplomat Stanislaus Poniatovski, who was probably the father of her daughter Anna. Sadly for her he was declared *persona non grata* during the political crisis of 1758 and he was replaced as her third or fourth lover by Gregori Orlov, a guards officer who was one of the heroes of the victory over Prussia at Kunersdorf where he had been wounded three times.

For Catherine in 1762, as for Elizabeth three decades earlier and for Sofia a decade even before that, there was a stark choice between spending the rest of her life as a neglected outcast or risking death in an attempted coup that could, if successful, bring immense power and wealth. Her initial support came from two distinctly different quarters: on the one hand there was Nikita Panin who hated Peter III's pro-Prussian policy and in an idealistic way wanted to replace him with his young heir the Grand Duke Paul. In the same camp was the still teenaged but articulate Princess Dashkova (the sister of Peter's mistress), who played a key role in organising the coup. The other group in the conspiracy were guards officers like the Orlov brothers, particularly Gregori Orlov, Catherine's new lover, whose personal ambition brought him to see the prospect of his mistress becoming the ruler of Russia and sharing that power with him. It was his popularity as an officer that would be an essential catalyst to motivate the troops to take action. For Catherine it was a question of balancing the two different strands of support and at the same time presenting herself as the saviour of Russia from the perils of a thankless war and from the hated presence of so many Germans in the capital.

There is no doubt that Catherine, once the neglected daughter of a petty German prince, was driven by a huge ambition fuelled by the disappointment of what should have been a wonderful marriage but had in fact been a disaster. Through her wide reading she was also fully aware of the opportunities that her position could afford her if she took the risk of dethroning her husband. Her deep-seated vanity had also been scarred by her humiliating failure to win over a man even as pathetic in so many ways as Peter. Together, this ambition and vanity were to continue to drive her for the next thirty-four years and achieve the kind of success which traditionally earned monarchs the title of 'Great' but involves consequential suffering for many millions of people.

Thus the nearly bloodless coup went ahead and Peter's resistance collapsed almost immediately. Though the Preobzhensky Guards were for once late in joining the other two regiments, the Ismailovsky and Semenovsky had quickly rallied to Catherine's cause and, as during previous coups, the tsarist establishment fell like a pack of cards. Her propaganda sheets had already been printed ready for distribution in the streets of Moscow and St Petersburg. For the Orlovs to have Peter III alive, even in the Schlusselburg, would have been asking for trouble, so though Catherine may have had no prior knowledge of any plan to murder her husband, such a fate was almost implicit in what she had already undertaken. Nevertheless, her introduction to power as both usurper and murderess was inauspicious, especially considering that as a German ironically pushed to the fore by anti-German feeling she had several disadvantages. She acted quickly, announcing the death of Peter as due to a fit of colic and distributing a bonus to the guards. She pardoned Alexis Orlov and the other gaolers of Peter and promoted Gregori Orlov to the rank of Adjutant General and Count with an apartment in the Winter Palace and a diamond-studded sword. But on Panin's advice she very wisely decided not to marry him, even when he took mistresses to try to make her jealous and physically abused her for recalcitrance. One of Orlov's juniors, Sergeant Gregori Potemkin, was promoted to lieutenant though his further meteoric rise was to have to wait for another few years.

The Russia she took over had a population of around 20 million of whom half a million, or 2½ per cent, were theoretically so-called nobles or *dvorianin*, hereditary landlords, who since her husband's reign no longer had to undertake compulsory service for the State and were soon to be exempt from all direct taxes. However, of that half-million only about 75,000 came from families who owned more than 100 serfs and could therefore be described as wealthy, some of them such as the Yusupovs obscenely wealthy for they reputedly had as many as 20,000 serfs. Such families could afford to build huge palaces, run private orchestras or theatres and lay on huge banquets with the most exotic of fare. The remainder, particularly the 150,000 who owned fewer than ten serfs, needed to supplement their incomes either by developing commercial sidelines or becoming State servants. So though there was no longer a compulsory officer class, there was a pool of semi-leisured, educated men motivated to become professional soldiers, seamen or civil servants. In addition, as Catherine encouraged French instead of Russian as the language of the Court, there developed an increasing cultural gap between the ruling elite and the mass of peasants. The rich could hire French chefs, dancing masters, hairdressers and musicians, wore diamond buttons and generally indulged in conspicuous consumption.

Meanwhile the only other living ex-tsar, the wretched Ivan VI, was conveniently eliminated as a potential threat to Catherine's position. There was in fact a half-baked plot to rescue him from Schlusselburg as a preliminary to his reinstatement, but this automatically triggered his murder by the fortress guards who had orders to kill him at the merest hint of such a plot. By this time Ivan was in his early twenties but reduced almost to a vegetable by years of solitary confinement.

Right away Catherine distanced herself from the lighter weight members of her support group and committed herself to a frenetic work schedule that was beyond their comprehension, rising at 5 a.m. and putting in a twelve to fifteen hour day. With Panin as Chief Adviser she recalled the veteran Bestuzhev, yet retained Vorontsov from her husband's council. The volatile Princess Dashkova was made Director of the Academy of Sciences to keep her busy. The Orlovs on the other hand had no particular interest in the detail of government and their arrogant behaviour in their new ranks soon worked to their disadvantage. So in due course Catherine was able to demonstrate to Gregori Orlov, who had fathered two children with her, that she could survive without him. Despite her early rising and long hours of work she was still ready in the evenings for cards, banquets, theatre or lovers.

Whereas her husband Peter III had totally neglected the public relations value of a good coronation at the Uspenski Sobor, Catherine immediately set about making the most of hers. It gave her a good opportunity to demonstrate her orthodox credentials and thus win the support of the clergy and of the Moscow crowds. In fact she made a point of treating Moscow as half a capital city again, which won useful friends for her there.

Catherine's next big ambition was at least to be perceived as a great liberal reformer and in 1765 she began the huge task of writing a specification for the reform of the legal codes of Russia. The *Nakaz*, though avowedly copied from various existing tracts, took her around two hours a day for two years. At the same time she made a point of contacting fashionable philosophers in Western Europe, especially Diderot whose financial problems she solved by paying for his library but not taking delivery, and Voltaire who was so flattered by her attentions that he gave her the soubriquet 'Great'. Her letters to these men and others were used to help promote her image as an enlightened despot even though the reform of the law rapidly became bogged down in detail and was never put into effect. In reality Catherine's main aim was to strengthen her own autocracy by quashing any spirit of resistance amongst the nobility. This in turn meant a reinforcement of serfdom so that the landowners realised that their survival as a privileged class depended on the Empress's army being available to stamp out any peasant rebellion. As Catherine handed over more territory, some of it newly conquered, to favoured officers and courtiers so the number of serfs increased. They and their families came to represent more than 60 per cent of the population. Landowners were given the right to send recalcitrant serfs to Siberia as impounded convicts and to knout those who complained about their conditions. The one reform she actually carried through which fits her enlightened image was the abolition of torture, but she did not outlaw the use of the knout by landlords against serfs.

Meanwhile, in 1764 Catherine had made an alliance with Frederick of Prussia so that between them they could control events in Poland. With a Russian army hovering in the background her old lover Count Poniatovski was elected King Stanislaw II Augustus (1764-95), a puppet king with the support of the two powerful neighbours, particularly Russia. He was destined to be the last king of Poland as his kingdom disintegrated over the next three decades. Its decline accelerated after 1768 when the Turks became so alarmed at Russian acquisitiveness in Poland that they declared war. The Russians under Golitsyn captured Khotin on the Dniester, but Catherine was not satisfied with his pace and replaced him with the abler generals Nikita Rumyantsev and Peter Panin, brother of her key mentor. In addition she had the Baltic fleet refitted and by 1769 was able to send it for the first time past Denmark and via Gibraltar to the Aegean. Under the overall command of Alexis Orlov but with two British admirals helping him, Elphinstone and Greig, it defeated a larger Turkish fleet off Chios at Chesme Bay. It was the most significant naval victory for the Russians since Peter the Great won Hango against the Swedes more than half a century earlier.

At about the same time Rumyantsev defeated the Turks on land at Fokshani and Kagul, thus conquering Moldavia. Soon afterwards in 1771 came the first inroads by the Russians into Turkish territories, which had Christian minorities – one of the justifications for her actions. In addition General Dolgoruky conquered the Crimea, which had for so long been a base for Tartar depredations and the slave trade.

At this point Catherine was being so dangerously successful that, had she continued, she might have stirred up some major retaliation by the other main powers. Frederick II took some of the heat out of the situation by suggesting in 1772 that Prussia, Russia and Austria should each take a slice of Poland for themselves. In return Catherine would halt her attacks on the Turks. This resulted in Russia taking over the Belarus or White Russian area, an additional population of nearly 2 million who were ethnically mainly Russian, so not an unreasonable adjustment of the western frontier. This partition was ratified by the pliant Polish diet and peace was finally made with the Turks in 1774, with Gregori Orlov acting as the initial negotiator, when General Suvorov cowed the Turks with two victories, Kirsova and Kozludj. This gave Russia control of the Caucasus and the right to sail ships into the Black Sea while the Crimea was allowed independent status from the Turks, and its Tartar khans would no longer be a threat as slave traffickers.

All this apparent success had nevertheless come at a considerable cost. Food supplies were low and taxation heavy. Since the introduction of paper money in 1769 inflation had been considerable. The foul conditions on the Turkish front had resulted in a plague that spread rapidly northwards to Kiev and Moscow causing well over 100,000 deaths by the start of 1772. It was one of Gregori Orlov's last effective commissions to tackle the spread of contagion in the slums of Moscow itself, and even then it was probably the onset of winter that froze the progress of the germs.

The other way in which the victories cost the ordinary people of Russia was the further expansion of serfdom. For example, General Rumyantsev was rewarded for his victory with 5,000 serfs, a number equal to the casualties he had inflicted on the Turks. This and similar awards that went to Catherine's other successful soldiers and ex-lovers, together with a spread of serfdom into the Ukraine, meant an overall very substantial increase which combined with the tightly enforced laws against escape made life considerably harsher for several millions.

In addition to the financial burdens placed on the peasants by such an expensive war, the fact that so many were drafted to the front led to unrest, which became serious in 1773. Various groups of disaffected Cossacks escaped serfs, Old Believers and Asiatic nomads came together under the charismatic leadership of Emelyan Pugachev. He based himself in the Orenburg region on the Ural River just north of Kazakhstan where a sparsely spread population of around 700,000 was policed by a garrison of 7,000 split between two dozen forts. It typified an empire extended over a vast area with a large and grievously oppressed agrarian class to which Pugachev could appeal. He announced that he was the Empress's husband Peter III and had miraculously escaped the murder scene at Ropsha, just like the false Dimitris of the Time of Troubles. This was coupled with the brilliant propaganda story that Catherine had wanted to murder Peter because he was about to give the serfs their freedom and she was determined to stop that happening. To expand the charade the ingenious Pugachev had a courtier called Orlov and an heir called Paul. With an army of 15,000 men, by the winter of 1773/4 Pugachev was within a week's march of Moscow and there was considerable panic, some suggesting that Catherine should hand power over to her son Paul who was now nearly twenty and theoretically had more right to the throne than she.

Once peace had been organised on the frontier with Turkey Catherine was able to send Panin and Suvurov with a large army to subdue Pugachev's rebellion. Orenburg was besieged and many of Pugachev's supporters deserted him. He was captured and brought in a cage to Moscow where he was eventually executed in 1775. Gallows were set up in most of the rebel villages to hang at least one local leader in each place but Catherine wisely showed mercy to most of the other rebels. For their help against Pugachev the Don Cossacks were rewarded with special status as an elite fighting force that they were to retain right up to the Revolution.

Meanwhile in 1769 Catherine was in her forties and her son Paul, now in his twenties, was beginning to cause problems. He had initially been very close to her after the death of his supposed father when he was only eight. But by the age of twelve he had begun to brood about the rumours of her involvement in Peter's murder. He was seized by a jealous hatred of Gregori Orlov, his mother's lover and the brother of the man blamed most for his father's extremely suspicious death. The news that Pugachev was actually claiming to be his father must have been additionally unsettling for a boy brought up in a claustrophobic and unnatural atmosphere. Partly to regain the boy's favour and partly to test out his future capacity to produce an heir, Catherine had organised a trial mistress for him when he was still only fourteen and was reassured by the production of a bastard. It was hardly a normal childhood and in due course Paul began to have nightmares in which he dreamed he would suffer the same kind of fate as his father.

At the same time Catherine was beginning to tire of Orlov both as a lover and as any kind of adviser, for his abilities were limited. His preliminary negotiations with the Turks had been uninspiring and on his recall he found that she had taken a replacement lover – a young guards officer, Alexei Vasilchikov. Orlov was initially furious but was placated with a bribe of 200,000 roubles and an additional 10,000 serfs, so he retired to Gatchina. Vasilchikov lasted a much shorter time and received a proportionately smaller pay-off: 15,000 roubles and 100 serfs became the standard reward. Countess Bruce and Countess Protasova became the main procurers – *Les Eprouveuses* – of young male lovers, often road-testing them beforehand and having them checked for any venereal infection before allotting them an apartment in the Winter Palace.

There was an interruption in the series of run-of-the-mill lovers when Gregori Potemkin came to the fore. Born around 1740 in Smolensk he had studied Greek and theology at Moscow University, then served as a young cavalry sergeant under the Orlovs at the time of the coup against Peter III at whose murder at Ropsha he was present. As a result he was promoted from sergeant to lieutenant and rewarded with a small estate. He was made protector of ethnic minorities in 1768 and later fought in the Turkish campaigns. He was tall, thin, a brilliant mimic and witty conversationalist but he does not seem to have attracted Catherine's serious attention until 1774, perhaps just because he had disappeared from the court.

This disappearance seems to have been triggered by his loss of an eye after a fight with the Orlovs, coupled with the fact that he may already have been in love with Catherine and was jealous. As a result he felt that his half-blindness meant his career as a potential lover was over, particularly when he saw more handsome competitors like Vasilchikov entering the royal apartments. He was anyway an extremely complex character, prone to almost manic depression and to take breaks from his military career to indulge in long monastic retreats. At this point he entered the Alexander Nevsky Monastery as a monk and was only persuaded to leave when Catherine sent Countess Bruce with an invitation for him to return as the Empress's favourite. He cast aside his monastic garb, shaved off his beard and was installed in the Winter Palace.

Despite an age gap of ten years – Potemkin was thirty-four, Catherine forty-four, and both were now inclined to fat – their tempestuous relationship lasted for the next seventeen years and may have been legitimised by a secret marriage. Potemkin became her virtual Chief Minister and military supremo for that entire period, even though after the first couple of years he had to procure a number of younger lovers to keep her happy while he consoled himself with a succession of mistresses. Both Panin and Gregori Orlov waited in vain for his fall, and Orlov died in 1783 disappointed and deranged when he was still only in his mid-forties.

Meanwhile Catherine's interest turned from conquest to ostentation. She delighted in massive banquets where she could entertain nearly 1,000 guests at one time, appearing bedecked with medals and orders, but more often these days wearing bulky dresses in the kaftan style which disguised her increasing weight. She had built several lesser hermitages for the amusement of her 'Bamboo Kingdom' and began the best-known one, the neo-classical Hermitage next to the Winter Palace in 1764 with Vallin de la Mothe as architect.

She now set about buying artwork in bulk from the West, including the entire collection of 200 old masters that had belonged to Sir Robert Walpole, so that she could amass a huge collection in a short time. She did however encourage native Russian painters such as Dmitri Levitski. De la Mothe was also responsible for a new bridge over one of the St Petersburg canals in the area called New Holland, what Talbot Rice calls 'one of architecture's most beautiful creations.' She also built the Smolny Institute for the training of upper class young women, and had her favourite architect the Scot Charles Cameron extend the pavilions at Tsarskoe Selo including the exotic Cameron Gallery, Greek Rooms, Chinese Rooms, and Agate Rooms with their polychrome marble and jasper, and a study made of pure silver. At Oranienbaum another Italian, Rinaldi, built the exotic Chinese Palace for weekend picnic parties. She began a palace at Pavlovsk for her son, handing over the Anichkov Palace to Potemkin. To this, in St Petersburg she added a huge programme of building new government offices to impress visiting Europeans. She even planned to rebuild the Kremlin in Moscow but in the end only contributed the new Senate House and the Bolshoe Ballet founded in 1776. Yet perhaps the most significant of all her artistic projects was the Bronze Horseman, the equestrian statue by Falconet of Peter the Great whose mission she had aimed to complete. Beneath the rearing horse was the inscription 'PETRUS PRIMUS, CATERINA SECUNDA', emphasising the link between their careers.

The peak of ostentation was reserved for the weddings of her son the Grand Duke Paul. His increasing paranoia and general tendency to disapprove of everything she did tended to make her think of skipping a generation and therefore she needed him to produce a son. His first marriage to a German princess from Hesse in 1776 sadly ended within months when she died in childbirth. A replacement princess was soon found in Wurttemburg and, as she was a niece of King Frederick II of Prussia, Paul went to meet her in Berlin. As a result of this, just like his father, he became an avid admirer of the Prussian King and everything he stood for. Renamed in the Orthodox way as Maria, his new wife proved a devoted support despite his varying moods and they eventually had ten children. Most importantly they had a son. Alexander was born in 1777 and provided Catherine, at least in her own mind, with a potential heir who could bypass Paul. Significantly the second son christened Konstantin (Constantine) presaged her ultimate ambition, to conquer Constantinople (Istanbul) for the Orthodox faith and create a second dynastic empire for the Romanovs in the ashes of Turkey. With these ideas in mind the two boys were removed from their parents, just as Paul had been from his, and trained by Catherine's nominees to provide the next generation of rulers for Russia. Little Konstantin was even taught Greek by a Greek nurse as preparation for his future role. But for a bout of measles he would have been taken on the great trip to the Black Sea in 1786 to see the edge of his future kingdom.

The years of peace were also devoted to the reform of local government in which Potemkin's help was invaluable. Catherine had followed up her early interest in legal reform at least, by encouraging more students to study law in Western universities and to lay the basis for contract law, particularly for the benefit of commerce. She also strengthened the role of the Senate as the ultimate arbiter of law, seeing the throne as bound by law, once it was established. She developed local government by dividing the whole country into around 100 provinces or *gubernii* of 200-300,000 people, with each of these in turn divided into ten districts or *uezdi*. Each province had a governor responsible to the Senate and was backed by a board that dealt with tax collection, trade and law and order. Catherine also implemented a similar system for the big cities, but she notably failed to pursue her idea of a charter for peasants.

One of the benefits of her conquests in the south was the acquisition of large areas of fertile soil that were severely under-populated and had previously been too dangerous to settle. Even in 1783 there had still been slave raids removing as many as 20,000 to be sold on the Turkish markets. Catherine encouraged migration into this temperate area both by Russians, Germans and Christian asylum seekers from the Turkish provinces like Montenegro and Serbia. The result was a massive increase in agricultural production that could offset the difficulties of agriculture further north and sustain a much larger population. In addition with the freeing of navigation through the Black Sea, Russia could become a serious grain exporter. This process was given further momentum when Russia finally annexed the Crimea in 1786 and under Potemkin's guidance began the construction of new harbours and cities such as Sebastopol. Then the Georgian king asked for his nation to become a protectorate of Russia, the prelude, as usual, to its being annexed in the next reign.

As part of the celebration for these achievements Potemkin, now titled Governor of New Russia, masterminded a spectacular royal tour of the south for Catherine. It began with a three-week trip to Smolensk and Kiev on monster sledges with 500 horses laid on at each staging post. Then when the snow was gone the party proceeded down the Dnieper in seven huge luxury galleys with each stopping place organised so that there were crowds of smiling peasants and at least the frontages of smart new buildings. Finally they reached Sebastopol, which had been a vast and rapid construction project almost like Peter's on the Neva and already there were forty new warships in the harbour.

Also contributing to Russia's economic growth was the development of industry, which Catherine encouraged. This included serf-owned cottage enterprises producing textiles, metalwork and luxury items. The development of copper smelting and iron and steel production also advanced steadily in the Urals area, but clearly technological improvement was often inhibited by the low or non-existent cost of serf labour which removed the motivation to mechanise.

Catherine's other great area of reform was in education. She had founded a magazine based on the London *Spectator* and called *Vsyakaya vsichina (This and That)* which was aimed at broadening the horizons of the upper and middle class and to which she contributed her own didactic articles under the pen name of Babushka (Granny). She encouraged the translation and printing of foreign texts as well as independent research in science, technology and agriculture. In 1764 she had founded the first of many orphanages designed to turn foundlings into useful members of society, particularly soldiers. Then came her Smolny Institute, which at least in a small way addressed the education of women. Finally in 1786 she introduced a system of free education at both primary and secondary level geared to turning out useful citizens.

During Catherine's last ten years in power she remained as active as ever and even at sixty was still having young men supplied to her, despite growing obesity and lack of teeth. She undertook further expansion both in Polish and Turkish territory that was to result in an overall increase in population of 50 per cent during the course of her reign, and because so much of the new land was fertile steppe it meant that the population could thereafter grow even faster. Her second war against the Ottoman Empire begun in 1787, under the overall command of Potemkin, resulted after victories by Suvorov in moving the Russian frontier right down to the Dniester and later the founding in 1794 of the new city of Odesa. Potemkin was at the peak of his career supervising the war and the construction projects for new towns. He was made first a count, then a prince. In 1783 Catherine had begun building the Tauride Palace for him, its name reflecting his drive into Turkish territory, but in 1791 at the age of only fifty-two he died. There is no doubt that she was genuinely deeply distressed despite the fact that both of them had resorted to other lovers in recent years. She wrote 'my pupil, my friend, almost my idol died in Moldavia ... now I have got no one left on whom I can rely.' Sadly one of the replacement toy-boys, the unscrupulous Platon Zubov, was forty years her junior and developed an unhealthy influence over her, perhaps the only one of her lovers ever to make her look stupid.

Very much still out in the cold was Catherine's son the Grand Duke Paul who was thirty-seven when Potemkin died. He was increasingly paranoid and cantankerous, losing touch with his three sons Alexander, now fourteen, Konstantin twelve, and Nicholas five, as their education had been forcibly taken over by their grandmother. Paul remained prophetically convinced that he would be murdered and replaced by his son. Yet Catherine gave no sign of instructing a change in the succession.

Meanwhile news of the French Revolution had swept through Russia with its terrifying implications, particularly when Louis XVI was executed in 1793. The once supposedly liberal Catherine now became very conservative, backing the alliance that declared war on the French in 1792. Suvorov was to go to Italy with an army to stop the riot, but Catherine did not live long enough to realise that she, along with the other powers of Europe, had stirred up a hornet's nest and that twenty years later Russia was to suffer dearly for interfering. In the meantime she began a policy of censorship and repression to halt the spread of revolutionary ideas at home.

The second two partitions of Poland in 1793 and 1795 were presented as a logical continuation of Russia reabsorbing the ethnic Russians who had all once owed allegiance to the old princedom of Kiev. In fact, while this might have been true with the first partition which brought in White Russians, it was much less true of the second and third after Suvorov had invaded Poland in 1793 and cowed Catherine's former lover King Stanislaw Augustus into submission. This resulted in the absorption of Polish Ukraine and Lithuania including Courland and Vilnius. Thus Russia took in large numbers of Lithuanians, the Lutherans of Courland and 3 million more Poles who were Catholic, ethnically different, were to remain deeply resentful and thus prove a source of trouble for the future. Catherine had to suppress the resistance of the gallant Polish leader Tadeusz Kosciuszko. Since the Poles had massacred the Russian garrison of Warsaw the Russians took their revenge – Kosciuszko was dragged off as a prisoner to St Petersburg, leaving the Poles with a lasting hatred of their conquerors. Indeed, Catherine referred to the Poles as 'the Jacobins of the East.' 121,000 Polish peasants were transferred as serfs from their Polish landlords to the Russian conquerors and the last king of Poland, Catherine's one-time lover, was allowed to spend his last miserable years in the comfort of the Hermitage.

These partitions also meant the absorption of a large number of Jews who also in their own way caused dissension in Russia. Catherine accepted their usefulness but had no liking for them and developed an anti-Semitic strategy, confining them to the Pale in the south and west.

Catherine was by this time sixty-seven and although still energetic was seriously overweight and suffered two strokes during 1796, the second one fatal. Once the 'Messalina' or 'whore-empress of the north' or the wise, creative 'Semiramis' she had a complex character driven by her early disappointments. She had written 'I came to Russia a poor girl but I gave them the Ukraine, Azov and the Crimea.' She had actually been an enormously effective empire builder and had doubled the size of Russia with an extra 250 million square miles of land and at least another 20 million people.

Yet what benefit this brought to anyone except Catherine herself is hard to see. If she had done it to justify the existence of an autocratic system it simply made the system much harder for her successors to modify: it made the powder keg upon which their throne rested larger and inherently more unstable. It added to the precedent set by Peter the Great that any good emperor should feel obliged to make the empire bigger than it had been under his predecessors. Russia became an even more complex multi-ethnic state riven with potential racial and religious conflict and subjugated nationalisms. At the same time, to support this expansionist state some two-thirds of the population were relegated for the foreseeable future to a semi-servile status against which sooner or later they must react. This was made worse by the fact that she financed her wars by printing paper money, which led to rampant inflation. In addition, by conscripting so many peasants into the army she reduced the agricultural workforce over large areas and deepened rural poverty. Similarly her vast building works and the extravagance that she encouraged amongst her courtiers added further to the oppression of the serfs. Only a handful of landowners, like Darya Saltykova who tortured some of her serfs to death, were ever punished and some serfs had to sell their daughters on the Ivanovo wench market.

Russia still has never quite recovered from Peter and Catherine the Great.

IX

THE EMPEROR PAUL
THE SERGEANT MAJOR

'My advisers want to lead me by the nose but unfortunately I have
not got one'

Attributed to the Emperor Paul

'Not only was he a weak character, he had no character at all'

De Corberon

Until the very moment of his mother's death in 1796 Grand Duke
Paul, now forty-two, must have been dreading that she would skip a
generation and pass the crown to his son Alexander who was nineteen,
attractive, newly married to a German princess and had been trained by
her for the job. Paul himself was uncharismatic with a flat face and high-
pitched voice. In his youth he may have suffered from rickets. In many
ways his character was like that of his nominal father, Peter III, whose
murder he blamed on his mother, and on whose death he should in reality have been proclaimed the new emperor. This may support the theory
that Peter actually was his real father as opposed to Catherine's lover
Saltykov as most people close to him at the time seem to have assumed.

Not only had Catherine usurped Paul's throne for thirty-six years but
also she had studiously ignored or openly despised him and then had
taken away his sons, so he hated her as much as she apparently hated
him. It is not surprising that one of his first reforms when he came to
power was to make the succession to the Russian throne dependent on
primogeniture, not on the predecessor's choice as introduced by Peter
the Great.

Genetically speaking Paul's make-up is clearly uncertain, but he was undeniably at least 50 per cent German if his father was Saltykov; 75 per cent with a dash of Lithuanian if his father was Peter III. He had spent most of the previous few years isolated in his country estate at Gatchina which suited Catherine as even at the age of fourteen it had irritated her when he was cheered by the Moscow crowds. His first marriage in 1773 to Wilhelmina of Hesse-Darmstadt, renamed Natalia, had been a failure, for she despised him and soon took a lover – Andrei Razumovsky. However the problem was solved when she died in childbirth two years later. Meanwhile he had suffered a further humiliation from his mother when she failed to make him Deputy Chief of the Preobrazhensky Guard, as was the custom, and instead bestowed the honour on her lover Potemkin.

Paul's second wife Maria Fedorovna, formerly Sophia, a Wurttemberg princess born (in 1759) like Catherine in Stettin, was much more devoted and they soon produced four sons. Though Catherine still failed to give him any experience of government she did allow them to go on a successful tour of Europe in 1781. It was while on this tour that Paul became impatient with his mother's architect Cameron who had been slow and expensive in his development of Paul's new palace at Pavlovsk, near Tsarskoe Selo. He switched the work to his Italian architect Vincenzo Brenna who turned it into an exotic classical dwelling packed with images of freemasonry and military drill and surrounded by lavishly landscaped pleasure gardens.

He lived happily enough at Gatchina, Orlov's old palace, which he also had remodelled and where his close friend the naval officer Sergei Pleshcheev introduced him to freemasonry, which became one of his passions. He shared this with his old tutor Nikita Panin, but Panin was part of Catherine's circle and could only risk occasional visits to his old pupil. Fired by the ideals of freemasonry Paul became quite liberal in his thinking, providing schools and hospitals for his 6,000 serfs round Gatchina, trying to improve conditions and encourage the development of small businesses. Since they were mostly Lutheran Finns he even provided them with a Lutheran church.

His other great passion he copied from the father whom he had hardly known; a love of military drill movements and smart uniforms. He had fallen under the spell of Frederick of Prussia during a brief visit to Berlin to meet his new wife and from then onwards became like

Peter III obsessed with the virtues of Prussian militarism. He had a barracks built at Gatchina to house his private regiment of 2,000 men and drilled them regularly with the help of his obsessive drill-master Aleksei Arakcheev. Their Prussian-style uniforms were so tight-fitting that they could barely move, let alone fight. He was so obsessive about the details of their buttons and badges, their specially plaited hair and their precision drilling that he would order savage punishments for any man who failed to do everything to his satisfaction. Once he moved as Emperor into St Petersburg his attention to detail became even more frenetic, the parades ever larger and more complicated. Officers who made mistakes were instantly sent to Siberia and the men flogged.

Once in power Paul did make some effort to apply his ideas for the improvement of conditions for the serfs on a bigger scale. He ordered the number of days they had to work on their master's land to be limited to three per week, thus leaving the other three for their own. He also restored the right of serfs to petition the emperor over the heads of their lords and eliminated some of the abuses perpetrated by landowners on their serfs. But by contrast he continued the policy of his predecessors in handing over many royal estates to his favourites, thus increasing still more the numbers in private serfdom. He also allowed factory owners to buy serfs and he added to the tax burdens of the peasants. So any good he may have intended was probably negated by his other actions.

His generally totalitarian approach led to a steady growth in bureaucracy and to numerous petty regulations, which irritated the population and restricted progress. As with military affairs all breaches of discipline were met with instant dismissal or worse.

In foreign affairs Paul sought automatically to reverse most of his mother's policies of which he had disapproved on principle. He wanted to end expansion, avoid war, and possibly give away some of the acquisitions she had made. However, he had little choice as an autocrat but to agree initially with her anti-French stance. Illogically his main concern was with the Order of Knights of St John based in Malta, for as a freemason he had been delighted to be given the post of their Grand Master, even though the Order was of course Catholic. Seeing himself as a crusading hero he sent an army under the elderly and previously out-of-favour General Suvorov to Italy where he won remarkable victories, even capturing Milan in 1799 and Corfu the year after. But he fell out first with the Austrian allies and then the British who had captured his beloved Malta and refused to give it back. Napoleon on the other hand offered to give Malta to Paul, so he indulged in an extraordinary volte-face, now believing Napoleon to be the saviour of Europe, not its nemesis.

Naively Paul now thought Napoleon would help him to conquer Turkey and destroy the British, so the two emperors would share the world between them. He suddenly switched from being anti-expansionist to aggressive acquisitiveness and in 1801 annexed Georgia, which had sought protection against Persia during the reign of his mother but whose royal dynasty he now deposed. He began planning an attack on British India. A force of 23,000 Cossacks under Vasily Orlov was sent to Bokhara ready to invade Afghanistan, but suffered so many casualties before it began its advance that the attack on India was postponed.

In the meantime Paul made the serious error of offending the Russian aristocracy on whose support his rule depended. Without actually changing the law that service in the army was no longer compulsory, he indicated that it was an unavoidable requirement for any who did not want to be disgraced. Similarly without actually abolishing the nobles' immunity from taxes, he began to ask for voluntary taxes with again the proviso that those who did not volunteer would be penalised by demotion. To make these threats even more unpopular he hinted that demotion would mean that the ex-nobles were no longer immune from physical punishment and like serfs could be subjected again to the knout, nostril-piercing or red hot irons.

Thus with extraordinary insensitivity Paul proceeded to alienate the people on whose support his survival depended, the officers of his army in particular and the officer class in general, who all now faced unspeakable punishments for petty mistakes or refusing to serve and pay taxes. On top of this he tried to Prussianise the guards as his father had done. He was repeating the quite avoidable self-destruction undertaken by his father three decades earlier. Even the good will of his normally all-forgiving wife was stretched to breaking point, first by an obsession with one of her ladies-in-waiting Catherine (Yekaterina) Nelidova, then an affair with Anna Lupokhina aged nineteen.

The nephew of his old tutor, another Nikita Panin who had just been sacked from his post as Vice Chancellor and exiled to his estates, led the coup against Paul. His key helper was Count Peter Pahlen the military governor of St Petersburg who obtained the compliance of the Grand

Duke Alexander for his father's removal from power. He also coordinated the group of officers who carried out the plot. These included Platon Zubov, Catherine's final paramour, together with his two brothers and Count Leon Bennigsen, a fellow guards officer. After a heavy evening's drinking the group entered the Mikhailovsky Castle unopposed and murdered the Emperor in his own bedroom. The official announcement said that he had died of apoplexy and there was little effort to contradict it. Paul was still only forty-seven and had been in power barely five years.

X

ALEXANDER I
THE BLESSED

'The coxcomb tsar
The autocrat of waltzes and of war
Now half dissolving to a liberal thaw
But hardening back whene'er the morning's raw'
Lord Byron

'... to rule over his people on the throne conferred on him by God'
Manifesto of Alexander I

'It is impossible even for a genius to deal with these problems'
Alexander I in a letter to Kolubei

Of all the Romanov tsars Alexander was in many ways the least superficially eccentric and therefore also the least predictable. He was twenty-four when the coup took place that resulted in the murder of his father and his own sudden elevation to the throne. It is certain that he had given at least his tacit approval to the plot, albeit he probably had not foreseen the subsequent murder or perhaps had simply not faced up to its inevitability. His father's behaviour towards him and the risks Paul was taking with the Russian nation seemed at the time to justify him condoning the coup, but he had not expected to be tainted with his father's violent end and was to feel guilty about it for many years to come.

Genetically speaking, if his paternal grandfather was Saltykov then Alexander had no Romanov blood, but he could be termed 25 per cent Russian and 75 per cent German. If Peter III was his real grandfather, then he was a Romanov but had an even higher proportion of German genes, more like 85 per cent with a touch of Lithuanian.

It is easy to see why Empress Catherine, Alexander's grandmother, had doted on the boy. He was fair-haired, blue-eyed, and eventually tall, handsome and charming. Yet his upbringing, like that of many other grand dukes, had been peculiar. Snatched away from his father and mother at an early age he had been subjected by his grandmother to the kind of training she thought was appropriate for her successor. Since at that time Catherine was still very much in liberal mode this meant the hiring of a Swiss intellectual called La Harpe who bombarded the seven-year-old child in French with long monologues about republican values. As a result he became fluent in French and English but could hardly speak Russian. Other basic aspects of his education were totally neglected. His head was filled with the latest liberal ideas from France, which were hardly relevant to the antiquated system of serfdom that dominated the Russian economy. Then at the age of fifteen his education was abruptly terminated as Catherine had decided he should marry.

His marriage to the German princess Louisa of Baden, who in the usual way converted to Orthodoxy and was rechristened Elizabeth (Elisavyeta), made his own relationship with his parents even worse than it had been before. Neither they nor he were consulted about the choice of bride, and Paul took it as yet another signal that his mother was about to bypass him in the succession and hand the throne over to young Alexander. Neither did this endear Elizabeth to her new mother-in-law, the Grand Duchess Maria. To make matters worse the Empress gave Alexander a more generous allowance than she did to Paul, making him even more jealous of his son and paranoid about the prospect of losing his right to the throne. With Paul made to stay outside St Petersburg on his estate at Gatchina and Alexander encouraged to make his home in the capital it just made matters worse.

Despite all the pressures the teenage couple seem to have been supremely happy in the first years of their marriage. There was also eventually something of a rapprochement between father and son when in 1795, at the age of seventeen, Alexander was at last allowed to go and stay with his parents at Gatchina. Here Alexander developed an unexpected admiration for his father when he saw him in action, drilling his immaculate private army. This was to inaugurate a kind of split personality in Alexander who up to this point had been saturated with pacifist, liberal ideas and now found himself equally enamoured with the glamour of fine uniforms and well-executed military drill. It was also here that Alexander acquired his lasting admiration for Alexei Arakcheev, the sadistic drillmaster of Gatchina who later became his great artillery expert, minister of war and the organiser of his secret police.

Alexander also found that his father shared some of his ideas, for both of them disliked Catherine's policy of chopping up Poland. But on his return to St Petersburg he had to hide his new feelings from his very perceptive grandmother, thus being forced to acquire some acting skill which was to feature for the remainder of his life. At the same time he leaves the impression that he was one of those people who is enthusiastic about the ideas of the last person he spoke to, but the enthusiasm might not survive the next encounter with some impressive new personality having totally different ideas.

Alexander was nineteen in 1797 when Catherine died and despite all Grand Duke Paul's forebodings it was he and not his son who inherited the throne. Thus for the first time in his life he had control over the prospects of Alexander and his young wife. Surprisingly he approached this new opportunity in two contradictory ways. On the one hand he treated the boy badly, thinking of him as being soft and badly spoilt by his grandmother, so now needing tough discipline. On the other he passed a law of primogeniture so that the tsar could no longer nominate his own successor, but the throne went automatically to the eldest male heir. This meant that Alexander, unlike his father, never had any fear of being disinherited. When he was bawled out and humiliated for minor mistakes on the parade ground Alexander would come increasingly to hate his father, yet at the same time knew that the moment his father was out of the way he would take over the throne. Emperor Paul can only be described as very naive or arrogant for not spotting the potential danger of such a situation. Similarly Empress Maria did herself and her husband no favours by bullying her daughter-in-law the young Grand Duchess Elizabeth to whom Alexander was at this time still very close.

As we have seen, Emperor Paul not only alienated his own potential successor but his parade ground brutality won him numerous enemies amongst the officer class. To compound this he embarked on an erratic foreign policy that frightened most politically aware Russians. His sudden change of heart to become an ally of Napoleon, his annexation of Georgia and his starting a war to conquer India appeared dangerous enough to motivate the plotters who carried out the coup of 1801 and who had convinced the susceptible Alexander that it was the right thing to do.

As a result, at the age of twenty-four Alexander became Emperor of Russia. The Mikhailovsy Castle, favoured as Paul's main residence, was abandoned in favour of the Winter Palace. The only person who objected to Alexander's succession was his own mother who was shocked by her husband's murder and illogically thought that she should succeed him herself. Alexander ignored this as he did demands for the punishment of the conspirators. Panin was still too useful for his diplomatic skill, Bennigsen as a general. Pahlen was sent into comfortable exile in Courland and Nikita Zubov to his country estates. Certainly Alexander did not punish himself, though there was a lasting sense of guilt which future enemies like Napoleon were occasionally to exploit.

For the time being Alexander set about reversing his father's least popular policies. He immediately stopped the Cossack army under Orlov from its projected attack on India and he gave up Paul's anti-English policy. Treaties were signed with Britain and France so that prospects for peace in Europe seemed to be good. He even made friends with Prussia, of which like his father and grandfather he became a great admirer, mainly as a result of the charms of Queen Louise of Prussia with whom he spent a lot of time during a week at Memel (now Klaipeda in Lithuania) in 1802.

At the same time as he was organising peaceful relations throughout Europe Alexander was also pursuing his liberal ideas at home. The security police were disbanded and local government, which his father had inhibited, was restored. The Sovereign Council was replaced by a Permanent Council of twelve members. Just as his grandmother had done forty years earlier he established a law commission to review the entire legal system in Russia. At the same time he appointed four liberal friends to consider the more general aspects of reform, including even the dreaded problem of serfdom. In theory at least he had embarked on a plan that would revolutionise Russia from the top. Yet the only practical measure to help the serfs, the 1803 order that they could be emancipated for cash, led to only tiny numbers gaining their freedom.

Alexander's toleration of France did not last for long. The turning point seemed to be the murder of the royalist Duc d'Enghien, which caused horror in Russia, the same sort of revulsion as a decade earlier after the execution of Louis XVI. Alexander's letter of admonishment to Napoleon evoked the caustic reply that Alexander's guilt for the murder of his own father left him in no position to complain. So Alexander put a plan to the British that they would jointly destroy Napoleon and as its reward Russia would receive British money, together with the rest of Poland, Moldavia, Constantinople and Malta. It was an absurdly greedy plan and Pitt the British Prime Minister ignored most of it. At this point Napoleon altered his plans from a proposed invasion of England to an attack on Austria and Germany. As a result the Austrians were caught not quite ready and badly defeated at Ulm. Alexander foolishly came to their aid and forced his wise old general, Mikhail Kutuzov, against his better judgement, to join the Austrians in facing Napoleon at Austerlitz. Napoleon though badly outnumbered won a brilliant victory and the two emperors, Russian and Austrian, were driven humiliated from the field, Alexander reportedly in tears. It had been one of his worst errors of judgement and as so often with him it had been done to please the person he had last talked to.

Prussia and Austria both made peace with Napoleon, but the Prussians were not happy for long and this time it was they who allied with Russia for a proposed retaliation against Napoleon. Just like the Austrians they were badly defeated at Jena and Auerstadt. Napoleon entered Berlin in October 1806. The Russians themselves were in turn defeated at Eylau and Friedland (now Pravdinsk near Kaliningrad) under Bennigsen the following year.

Meanwhile Alexander's personal life had become rather messy. He had been married to Elizabeth for nearly fifteen years and the gloss had begun to wear off. She produced two baby daughters in 1799 and 1806 but both died young and there seemed no prospect of further pregnancies. Elizabeth was fragile and prone to migraines, so Alexander was regularly seeking sexual solace elsewhere. This came to a head when Maria Naryshkina became his semi-official mistress for fifteen years, bore him several healthy children, flaunted her success in front of the Empress and even curried favour with her vengeful mother-in-law. To add to Elizabeth's misery at this neglect and humiliation there was the intense and some said almost incestuous relationship of Alexander with his sister Catherine, now the Duchess of Wurttemberg but having a Russian base at Tver. She also went out of her way to exacerbate Elizabeth's jealousy, at the same time trying to push Alexander in the direction of reform.

Alexander's military position was also becoming precarious because half his army was away in the south fighting Turkey. The defeats at Austerlitz and Friedland convinced him that his relatively poorly equipped and under-trained troops could not withstand the French. In June 1807, therefore, he met Napoleon face-to-face in an elaborately staged conference on a raft at Tilsit (now Sovetsk near Kaliningrad) on the river Niemen. As previously with Francis of Austria and Louise of Prussia Alexander proved an easy prey to a charismatic flatterer and he became an instant admirer of Napoleon. He allegedly swore that he hated the British and they proceeded to divide up the world between them, with Russia in particular to be allowed to conquer Turkey. The only part of Napoleon's plan to which he objected was the destruction of Prussia.

While the euphoria of Tilsit still lasted Alexander, the emperor who had once been so proud of his anti-imperialist credentials succumbed to greed and conquered Finland from Sweden in March 1808, thus adding a large additional area of non-Russians to the Empire, albeit leaving the Finns for the time being as a largely self-governing grand duchy. By now he was beginning to feel nervous about his association with the hyper-active Napoleon, especially when the latter's former minister Talleyrand wrote to warn him that he thought Napoleon had now overreached himself and would eventually lead France to destruction. So when he again met Napoleon at Erfurt west of Leipzig his conversations were much less sincere. Napoleon said he could keep Finland, Wallachia and Moldavia but had gone cool on Constantinople.

Meanwhile the Austrians rebelled against their subjection, attacked Napoleon again and were once more disastrously defeated at Wagram in 1809. Alexander yet again faced a situation where he had no real allies in Europe if he chose to resist Napoleon.

Between 1809-11 a variety of relatively minor but cumulatively significant disagreements began to drive a wedge between Alexander and Napoleon. First there was a misunderstanding about the possible plan for Napoleon to marry Anna, the fifteen-year-old sister of Alexander. Letters from both sides discarding the plan crossed in the mail and both sides took offence, especially Alexander when Napoleon went on to marry Marie Louise of Austria instead. In addition Russia was alarmed at Napoleon's expansion of the new Duchy of Warsaw. The costs of war had been very high and the Russian economy was struggling with resultant inflation, made worse by the decline in trade due to Napoleon's embargo system against British trade. Then in 1810 Alexander annoyed Napoleon by relaxing the trade embargoes. Napoleon in turn angered Alexander by his annexation the next year of Holland, the Hanseatic cities on the Baltic, and worst of all Oldenburg which had been held by relations of his wife's.

Meanwhile Russia's readiness for a major war was at least marginally better. The reforms of Mikhail Speransky had much improved the civil service and ensured that promotion was based on ability not rank. Financial management was tidied up and departments rationalised, all sensible adjustments which Speransky paid for with his career when he became so unpopular that Alexander had to send him into exile in Perm. At the same time the obsessive Arakcheev had organised rearmament, so the army was better equipped. At long last also there was peace again with the Turks so that Bessarabia, the northern half of Moldavia with its mainly Rumanian population, was annexed and most of the forces there could be recalled to the western front. Russian aggression was also proceeding in other parts of the world: in 1812 they had put up Fort Rossiya in California, trying to create a fur colony where they could also grow crops. They even built a fort in Hawaii, Fort Elizabeth, as they began to flex their muscles in the northern Pacific.

Napoleon crossed the Niemen at Rykonti in June 1812 when Alexander was only 60 miles away at Vilnius. Tolstoy in *War and Peace* describes brilliantly the ball given by General Bennigsen, a Baltic German, at his palace in Vilnius the night news came of the invasion: 'The longer the Emperor remained in Vilnius the less did everybody – tired of waiting – prepare for the war. All the efforts of those who surrounded the sovereign seemed directed merely to making him spend his time pleasantly and forget that war was impending.'

Napoleon ignored protests about the invasion and with an army over half a million strong headed eastwards. The Russians were able to muster less than half that number under the Commander-in-Chief, Barclay de Tolly, who retreated steadily, leaving first Vilnius, then Smolensk in French hands. Alexander had been begged by his ministers to stay away from the front line and reluctantly obeyed, returning first to Moscow, then St Petersburg where he spent the rest of the invasion period in his small palace on Kamenny Island. Barclay de Tolly was replaced by the older but more popular Kutuzov. In his late-sixties, obese and one-eyed, he inspired greater loyalty amongst the troops whose patriotic fervour gradually grew as they realised that Russia was fighting for survival. Yet he maintained de Tolly's strategy of controlled retreat and avoiding pitched battle, waiting for the weather and Napoleon's stretched supply lines to take their effect.

Compelled to make some kind of stand to try to save Moscow Kutuzov faced Napoleon at Borodino. Both sides lost around 50,000 men, the Russians slightly more than the French, but they could replace their losses whereas the French, 600 miles from base, could not and their losses included nearly fifty generals. Kutuzov then held a meeting at Fili, which made the decision not to defend the city itself. Napoleon, having viewed the city from Sparrow Hill, entered Moscow unopposed but found much of it empty of people and on fire – no one knows whether the burning was deliberate. He offered an armistice three times but now it was his turn to be ignored. On 17 October he began his retreat harried all the way back to the Niemen by Kutuzov's guerrilla detachments.

Tolstoy's *War and Peace* gives dramatic descriptions of the retreat:

> The French army melted away at the uniform rate of a mathematical progression ... The crowd fled at a continually increasing speed and all its energy was directed at reaching its goal. It fled like a wounded animal and it was impossible to stand in its path ... When the bridges broke all carried on by vis inertiae pressed forward into boats and into ice-covered water and did not surrender.

By 14 December when Napoleon reached safety his army of 575,000 was reduced to 30,000 survivors.

It was at this point that Alexander found God. As usual he was easily influenced by any new personalities who appeared at court and suited his mood. This time it was two young courtiers who in different ways had undergone sudden conversions. Prince Alexander Golitsyn was a former playboy who had invented a new mystical version of Christianity. Rodion Koshelev was a guards officer who had become involved in freemasonry and esoteric cults. Between them they convinced Alexander that Russia had been saved, not by Kutuzov or the winter, but by God and that it was now his mission to save the rest of Europe.

Having at long last been allowed to return near the front Alexander met Kutuzov at Vilnius. He somewhat unfairly faulted him for not following up his success more rapidly and criticised the troops who had just fought their way through 600 miles of snow and mud for their sloppy uniforms. Tolstoy again gives a vivid description of the Emperor in his green Semenovsky uniform, fresh from St Petersburg as he gradually ousted the untidy old man who had beaten Napoleon and then took over personal command for the next stage of the war. With the reluctant Kutuzov he headed towards Silesia with 110,000 troops and was spared the bother of dismissing him when the old man died. There followed a series of wasteful battles: Lutzen, Bautzen, Dresden and Kulm which between them produced no clear result, but Alexander should be given credit for the coordination of the allies which led to the decisive defeat of Napoleon at Leipzig. Even in the heat of battle it was he himself who went to rally the Cossacks so that they overcame the French cavalry.

Whereas his royal colleagues would have been content just to push the French back into France Alexander took the lead in demanding the deposition of Napoleon as the condition for peace. Thus he pressed on over the Rhine and had perhaps his finest hour when he entered Paris as a hero, welcomed as a liberator even by most of the French. Initially too he was welcomed as a hero in Britain, but his tactless interference in British party politics and his offhandedness with the Prince Regent soon spoiled his image. Oddly, after insisting on Napoleon's destruction he was subsequently lenient and must share the blame for leaving the door open for the great man's escape from Elba. By the time of Waterloo he was no longer the leading light of Europe and found himself sidelined by Wellington. In addition, he had offended his allies by his greedy demands to take over the rest of Poland, though he was allowed to keep a large extra slice round Warsaw.

It was during this relative period of frustration, when he was no longer the centre of attention, that Alexander first met Baroness Juliana von Krudener who was the next personality to become dominant in his life. Born in Riga she was at this time about fifty but with a strong and attractive personality, though her very brief marriage had ended twenty years earlier in acrimony. In 1803 she had written a lurid autobiographical novel *Valerie*, had then seen the light amongst the Moravian Brethren and practiced converting numerous St Petersburg young men before she tackled the dispirited Emperor on his way home from Vienna at Heilbron. She took three hours to convince him that she was in direct communication with God and that his mission was to form a Holy Alliance that would bring peace and Christianity to the whole world. Like most of his fads it lasted for a couple of years before he tired of her. But for a short period 1820-1 he threatened to intervene against the liberal cause in a number of revolutions in other parts of Europe.

Meanwhile the spread of liberal ideas that Alexander and his grandmother Catherine had done much to encourage had taken real root amongst the Russian intelligentsia (this is a Russian word that was coined at about this time and was later borrowed by the English language). In particular those officers who had fought in France and Germany had become aware of how much worse conditions were in Russia compared to those countries. In 1820 there was a mutiny amongst the Semenovsky which echoed what was happening in other parts of Europe and which Alexander stamped out with severity, disbanding the regiment. Now the secret police force was revived under Arakcheev and heavy censorship imposed on all dissident literature. This was the year that the young aristocratic poet Alexander Pushkin (1799-1837) was removed from his civil service post, sent into exile and wrote his first major success *Ruslan and Lyudmilla*. So in Russia it was not so much the oppressed masses that were rebelling against autocracy as the well-born intelligentsia. Arakcheev's spies began to infiltrate the army and thousands of suspected liberals were sent off to Siberia. The intelligentsia responded by joining secret societies such as *Soyuz Spasaniya* (Union of Public Good), which had been founded in 1816 with the abolition of serfdom amongst its aims. Freemasonry was banned but new secret groups sprang up.

As usual there were two sides to Alexander's policies. Surprisingly in the new territories to the west, Poland and Finland, he introduced parliamentary constitutions at a time when he dare not even think of one in Russia itself. He founded three new universities to add to the three in Russia that already existed, but did not really fund them properly. His only new initiative on serfdom was an experiment organised by Arakcheev at Gruzino. The idea was to cut the cost of employing serfs in the army by building little houses for them and their families near the barracks and giving them land to work on nearby. In fact the serfs chosen disliked the new houses compared with their own self-built cottages and resented the enforced movement of their families. Alexander's other main initiative at this time was driven by his new appreciation of the Bible of which he had become an avid reader since the days of Juliana von Krudener. He now recognised the multi-ethnic nature of his empire by having the Bible translated and printed in more than a dozen languages: Slavonic, modern Russian, French, German, Finnish, Estonian, Latvian, Lithuanian, Polish, Armenian, Georgian, Kalmyk and Tartar. It was all part of his plan to unite Catholic, Orthodox, and even Muslim.

Alexander was also obsessed with the external image of his empire and was lavish in his building projects. So much of Moscow had been burned in 1812 that it was an opportunity to recreate it as a grander city and he laid out the gardens to the west of the Kremlin. In St Petersburg he completed the Kazan Cathedral, filled it with 100 captured French eagles, captured Persian banners and the ashes of Kutuzov so that it became a shrine for Russian nationalism. At immense expense he also finished the huge St Isaac's Cathedral, the third largest domed building in the world. The Winter Palace Square had two new monuments to celebrate 1812 and with its connecting open spaces it was possible to hold military displays with 100,000 troops, an absurd and extravagant method of boosting corporate self-esteem. At the same time, Alexander was meticulous in planning regulations for every aspect of the capital's buildings apart from the slums, creating a wonderful panorama of waterside façades, immaculate cast-iron railings and coordinated colour schemes.

Nothing though was going to stop the momentum of the groups looking for radical reform. Rumours arrived of a dissident group in the southern army stationed in Taganrog and the Crimea. It was led by a group of officers including Lieutenant Konrad Ryleev, Colonel Paul Pestel, Colonel Prince Sergei Trubetskoy and Prince Evgenie Obolenski. Their coup was planned for early in 1826.

Suddenly however there had to be a change of plan. Nine years earlier in 1816 in a flurry of religious devotion Alexander had cast aside his long-term mistress Maria Naryshkina and returned to his long-suffering wife Elizabeth. The death of his over-affectionate sister Catherine and the departure of the prophet Baroness Krudener also meant that Elizabeth had less competition for his attentions. But they still had no living children so there was some concern about the succession, particularly when Alexander began to show signs of ill health. He had apparently often toyed with the idea of abdication, but this was perhaps just the permanent ennui of a man who had reached the peak of his career before he was thirty. The problem was that the eldest of his three surviving brothers, Konstantin, had for years indicated that he would refuse to take over the throne and more recently had caused controversy by marrying morganatically a Catholic Polish countess (he had deserted his first wife) on the understanding that he would renounce his inheritance, which he did in 1822.

Meanwhile, their younger brother Nicholas and his wife Grand Duchess Alexandra had produced a son in 1818, so through him the longer term succession of the Romanovs was assured. Nicholas was already Alexander's first choice as successor but this new arrival simply confirmed it. Nicholas and his wife were apparently astonished at their potential promotion. Archbishop Filaret of Moscow countersigned the deed. However, the documents which confirmed that Nicholas, not Konstantin would be the next emperor were kept secret from the general public and most senior officials, leaving potential for major confusion.

In late 1825 on medical advice Alexander set off with Elizabeth from the cold of St Petersburg to the warmth of the far south. It was in vain for a few weeks later after a short illness he died in the seaside town of Taganrog, ironically the very place where news of the potential army mutiny was just being uncovered. He was only forty-eight and had been Emperor for twenty-four years, exactly half of his life. He died just a matter of weeks before the date of the coup that was being planned to dethrone him and replace him with Prince Trubetskoi as a temporary dictator until Russia could be proclaimed a constitutional monarchy.

He had spent vast sums of money on warfare, only a portion of it on defence, but had also been hugely extravagant in building so the national debt had risen dramatically as had the requirements of taxation just to pay the interest, but he did not live to face the consequences.

XI

NICHOLAS I
THE GENDARME OF EUROPE

'Here there is order, there is strict unconditional legality, no impertinent claims to know all the answers, no contradiction … '

Nicholas I

Alexander's strange obsession with secrecy led to a chaotic transition of power after his death in 1825. His junior brother Nicholas was in St Petersburg and knew that he was supposed to inherit the throne, but no one else there knew it. So they set in motion the accession of Grand Duke Konstantin, who was the senior brother and, as far as they knew, the official heir. Konstantin had been living for some years in Warsaw as Governor General of Poland and was there when he received the request to return to St Petersburg to take over the Imperial Crown, a request which he at once refused. In this ridiculous and quite unnecessary crisis Nicholas in St Petersburg swore an oath of obedience to Konstantin, and Konstantin in Warsaw did the same to Nicholas, so the paperwork crossed in the mail. The whole situation was made more delicate by the fact that Nicholas had made himself highly unpopular in St Petersburg by acting the brutish colonel on the parade ground, just like his father and grandfather. Severe flogging for parade ground misdemeanours was not uncommon. Konstantin was marginally more popular because although his behaviour had been much the same it was ten years since he had left the capital and memories were short.

To add even further to the instability Nicholas received news from spies in Taganrog about the plot that had been hatched by officers in the southern army to dethrone Alexander. It was quite clear that the plot would transfer its attentions to whoever became the next tsar and that there were groups of plotters in Moscow and St Petersburg being coordinated to create a revolution that would end the autocratic rule of the Romanovs and possibly, if the views of the southern officers like Colonel Pestel were taken into account, replace them with a republic.

At least once the secret documents proclaiming Alexander's choice of successor were unveiled Nicholas was able to sort out the situation with Konstantin, who was anyway adamant in not wanting the Crown. But he was sufficiently sensitive to realise his unpopularity with many of the officer class and could see that his hopes could be dashed by a mutiny, so he quickly set a date of 14 December for his official accession and oath taking.

Meanwhile the plotters, henceforth known as the Decembrists, realised that they had an unexpected period of weakness working in their favour and should act against Nicholas before his accession was fully sanctioned by the oath taking on 14 December. The St Petersburg members of the plot included Ryleev, Evgeni Obolensky and Trubetskoy as it main leaders. They must have realised that their plans were inadequate but with patriotic fervour decided that they must risk everything, beat the deadline and fulfil their oaths to kill Nicholas before his official installation as Tsar. In this however, they failed, for though they gathered in the Senate Square by 8 a.m. on the 14th, Nicholas took the oath an hour earlier, thus depriving them of one crucial element of psychological advantage. The crowd of mutineers swelled to nearly 3,000 shouting 'Konstantin and Constitution': it became a cynical joke in St Petersburg that the lower ranks amongst the rebels were so ignorant that they thought Constitution was the name of Konstantin's wife. As it turned out support for Konstantin was irrelevant for not only was he himself totally unwilling to take over, but he was anyway just as reactionary an autocrat as his brother Nicholas.

In this crisis Nicholas summoned the Preobrazhensky Guards under Prince Alexis Orlov to surround the square. He sent several mediators including his younger brother the Grand Duke Mikhail to try to get the rebels to disperse. Then according to reports he twice ordered the men to open fire on the mutineers and twice cancelled it before eventually giving them the go-ahead. Some seventy to eighty were killed and the potential revolution was quickly suppressed both in St Petersburg and elsewhere in Russia. Of nearly 600 officers who were arrested and interrogated five including Colonel Paul Pestel (who had been one of the most radical, 'a fiend from hell' according to Nicholas), were condemned to death and around 100 were sentenced to penal servitude in Siberia. Nicholas protested feelings of guilt about the deaths in the square and the executions afterwards, but given his character it is hard to believe that he felt guilty for long. Arrangements were soon made for his elaborate coronation in the Uspensky Sobor, Moscow.

In retrospect the remarkable feature of the Decembrists was that so many were colonels and princes willing to die to win a parliamentary constitution. They were not middle class, let alone downtrodden peasants, but basically aristocrats with a conscience. Amongst this group was Alexander Pushkin, Russia's greatest poet. Descended from an old aristocratic family and a negro favourite of Peter the Great's he had been exiled under Alexander for his poem *Ode to Liberty*, but surprisingly was allowed to return by Nicholas and produced his greatest works over the next twelve years before being shot in a duel in 1837. Nicholas tried to keep him under control and censored much of his work including the play *Boris Godunov*. His fellow poet the brilliant Mikhail Lermontov, a dashing hussar officer descended from a Scot called Learmont, wrote a poem about his friend's death which referred to 'the greedy crowd about the throne, the executioners of freedom'. He was arrested and sent to a Caucasus garrison, came back, insulted the Tsar's daughter Maria and was sentenced to exile again only to be killed like Pushkin in a duel four years later at the age of twenty-seven.

In the longer term the Decembrists did undoubtedly inspire future revolutionaries, for example the Muscovite thinker Alexander Herzen who, like Pushkin, was of half-legitimate aristocratic birth. He moved further to the Left than most of the Decembrists and was a pioneer Russian socialist imprisoned by Nicholas's regime in 1834. Subsequently he headed for Paris, then London from where he organised revolutionary propaganda to be smuggled into Russia.

The new emperor was twenty-nine, nearly nineteen years younger that his eldest brother, so unlike him had been born after his father Paul became the Emperor. As the third healthy son he had not been expected to inherit so he had been brought up for soldiering with a sadistic tutor de Lamsdorff who did not spare the rod, but succeeded in giving him very little broad education. He thus grew up according to the Prussian model followed by so many of his ancestors, obsessed with parade-ground uniforms and drill movements, quick to punish severely any lapse from perfection. In genetic terms, like his brother he was around 80 per cent German and like him married to one. He was less intelligent, less sensitive and less complicated. He was tall, good-looking, blue-eyed like his brother, low-browed but big-chinned, and had a permanent expression of coldness and gloom with what Herzen described as 'wintry eyes.' Yet his height, military posture, parade-ground voice and total conviction in his own mission combined to give this unpromising man a charisma that was acknowledged even by those who secretly despised him. His charm captivated British crowds when he visited Ascot in 1844. Nor is there any doubt about his personal courage, for he faced the mutineers without fear in the December crisis, again mixed with the mob during the cholera crisis of 1831, and never fussed about bodyguards despite the ever-present threat of assassination. He genuinely believed that he had been destined to accept a mission from the Almighty and that the task was a painful burden not a source for personal pleasure. 'I have been born to suffer', he wrote, and that is perhaps why he expected others to suffer in the same cause.

The one leisure activity he seems to have enjoyed was music, for he played the horn in the palace quartet and sponsored a series of concerts by Lizst when he visited St Petersburg. He also gave his blessing in 1836 to the first genuinely Russian opera, Mikhail Glinka's (1804-57) production originally entitled *Ivan Susanin* which told the story of how a humble Russian peasant saved the life of the first Romanov Tsar back in 1613. Nicholas simply asked for the title to be changed to *A Life for the Tsar*. This piece, together with Glinka's *Ruslan and Lyudmilla* that came out eleven years later and was based on Pushkin's text, pioneered the development of a school of major Russian composers.

Apart from the parade ground, and perhaps music, Nicholas's only other joy was his family. In 1814, at the age of eighteen, he had met the Prussian Princess Charlotte in Berlin and as usual with potential German brides she was converted to Orthodoxy and renamed Alexandra for their marriage two years later. They produced a son Alexander in 1818, which was one of the factors that persuaded his uncle Alexander to make Nicholas his heir, thus securing the Romanov dynasty. Then came three daughters and in the early years of his marriage Nicholas seems to have been warm and relatively considerate. He was so much in awe of his Prussian in-laws that it made him an even greater admirer of German militarism than he had been before.

Much to his frustration Alexander did not allow him to join the army until the Napoleonic wars were over, but he did so in 1818 and was soon promoted to Inspector General of Engineers. This appointment gave him plenty of opportunity to conduct the sort of massive ceremonial parade that became his passion and could even reduce him to tears of joy. Yet any carelessness or breach of absolute discipline by those he called his 'beloved soldiers' was met with the harshest punishment. He cared little for pain or suffering inflicted on men or animals under his command.

Once in power he soon resumed his favourite parade-ground activities with even larger army groups at his disposal. He took the opportunity to replace breeches with trousers, rearranged the configuration of tunic buttons and introduced the exclusive and compulsory black moustache for all soldiers. His brother Kontsantin had once complained that there was nothing worse for an army than war since it led to so much dirtying of the uniforms and it is likely that Nicholas's thinking was very similar. Civilians were allowed neither black moustaches nor beards or grey hats.

Russia therefore became more than ever a state run to support its army. Compulsory military service for twenty-five years was the norm for those serfs out of each family who were picked to go and fight. If they were married, their wives were allowed to remarry after three years on the assumption that they would never come back. Often the sons of conscripts were thrust into military orphanages and reared for soldiering. Flogging was a normal punishment and it was not unusual for soldiers running the gauntlet to receive well over 1,000 blows.

Almost immediately Russia was involved in two wars, which gave Nicholas a perhaps exaggerated admiration for his army's capabilities if not of his own, for he was horrified by the slaughter and disease of the front line and never again took personal command of his armies. The first was in the Caucasus where Persia, in 1828, had chosen to attack just at the time of Alexander's death. It resulted in a fairly easy victory that brought Russia the additional provinces of Erivan (Yerevan) and Naxcivan south of Georgia, 20 million roubles compensation and the sole right to have a fleet on the Caspian Sea. It also brought a substantial influx of Christian Armenians, victims of Turkish harassment seeking asylum under the Russian umbrella. Yet the Caucasus was to remain a constant problem for the Romanovs, requiring around 200,000 troops to man the numerous forts along extended communications like the Georgia Highway. It also added to the Muslim population of Russia, even though as the Christian Armenians moved into Russia the Muslim Circassians moved out in large numbers – around 200,000. It also highlighted the immense difficulty and expense of trying to subdue maverick mini-nationalities like the Chechen who had declared an anti-Russian jihad as early as 1785.

The second war was against the Turks where Nicholas took over Wallachia and Moldavia again, and stopped when within easy reach of Constantinople. Then he changed tack in 1832 to help save the Turks from the invasion of Mehmet Ali – as the Turks put it 'a drowning man clings to a serpent'. From this Russia gained a special dispensation to send warships through the Dardanelles thus causing alarm throughout Europe. Great Britain in particular developed an anti-Russian paranoia that envisaged Russia taking over Turkey, Persia, Afghanistan and even threatening India. It was the success of Nicholas in these early days that made him seem a greater threat to the rest of Europe than he ever really was and at the same time gave him a higher opinion of his army's strength than it ever really deserved. These two misconceptions were to prove his undoing nearly twenty years later.

Given his single-minded approach to the preservation of autocracy it is not surprising that Nicholas wanted to be involved in every detail of government and apart from obstinacy his greatest weakness was reluctance to delegate. He was constantly travelling around his empire, inspecting troops or other government activities and constantly interfering. His obsession with preserving the tsarist authority was intensified by news of the series of revolutions that shook Europe in 1830. One of these was in his territory of Warsaw where, despite a garrison of 16,000 troops, his brother Konstantin seems to have lost his nerve and was driven out of the city and died during the cholera epidemic brought on by the war that followed. This all gave Nicholas the excuse for ruthless suppression of the Poles: the abolition of their parliament, the virtual elimination of their national culture, and the sidelining of their language. He was trying forcibly to change the Poles into Russians and this persecution also affected the large Jewish population of Poland. Ironically the recapture of Warsaw was achieved by his youngest brother Mikhail, well known as a boor, who according to gossip had headed off to inspect the troops on his own wedding night.

The half-French, Polish-born Frederick Chopin had just given his debut recital in Warsaw in 1830 and now not surprisingly chose to forge his career elsewhere.

This same policy of Russification was also applied to the Ukrainians, the second biggest ethnic minority in Russia at that time. Taras Shevchenko the great Ukrainian poet and painter, who joined a secret society to promote Ukrainian freedom, was sentenced to serve as a private in a distant garrison for ten years, forbidden either to write or paint. Yet that other significant minority – the Baltic Germans – were treated much less severely because they were staunch supporters of the Emperor and provided so many able officers and bureaucrats. The same applied to some extent to the Finns who kept out of trouble in 1830 and retained the privileges granted by their conqueror Alexander I.

As part of his overall strategy of homogenising the people of his empire Nicholas also clamped down on religious differences and regarded the Orthodox Church as a major prop of autocracy. The concepts of unquestioning obedience to God and Tsar went well together. Again the largest single religious minority were the Catholics in Poland and the Ukraine, so he did his best to encourage conversion. Some 5 million Jews suffered for the same reason as did the Old Believers. With characteristic ruthlessness Nicholas appointed a cavalry officer to run the Holy Synod and set about rooting out non-conformist sects. Old Believer marriages were declared invalid. Their churches were shut down, the bells confiscated, the leaders sent to Siberia and their children drafted into the army. The Irgiz monasteries were dissolved. Muslim enclaves in the Caucasus and elsewhere were attacked whenever convenient. Tolstoy as ever has left a brilliant account of the downfall of the Chechen Muslim leader Hadji Murat in 1852. 'Poland and the Caucasus are Russia's two ulcers … we need at least a hundred thousand men in each of these territories.' Yet the Romanovs always wanted more ulcers to justify their existence.

The education system was also modified to help the task of homogenisation and the education minister Sergius Uvarov was therefore one of the more important members of Nicholas's entourage. Basically schools were required to clone supporters of the autocracy. There was strict class division, so that upper-class schools produced good officers, middle-class schools produced engineers or merchants, while peasant schools produced people who were programmed to stay as peasants. Universities were increased in size but restricted to teaching useful technical subjects and discouraged from anything dangerous like politics or philosophy.

In his efforts to centralise the State Nicholas reduced any contribution made to decision-making by the Senate and was his own Chief Minister, with all others reporting to him direct. Since reform was not on the agenda and public criticism of the government and civil service was made illegal there was an inevitable growth in inefficiency, since mistakes were not uncovered unless the Emperor happened to make one of his surprise inspections. Any political dissidents were weeded out by a new body, the Third Section of Chancery, which was in effect a secret police force and initially under the control of Count Benkendorf, the nearest thing he had to a senior minister. One early sinister example of the culling of dissidents was the case of the writer Peter Chadayev who dared to attack the influence of the Orthodox Church. He was silenced in 1836 by being certified as a lunatic by tame doctors, a trick that was much later to be copied by the Communists.

The one rational improvement presided over by Nicholas at long last was a codification of Russian law which had been attempted but never completed by his predecessors. Naturally it excluded any liberal concepts. Nicholas may have appreciated that serfdom was evil but equally regarded it as the essential foundation of his own authority. He passed a law that let serfs buy land in 1842 but it was of no great practical significance since only about 24,000 out of 10 million were ever able to do so. Two years later he sailed off incognito under the alias Count Orlov to London where he tried to explain his policies to a mystified Queen Victoria.

The one area where Nicholas was less conservative than his own advisers was in transport for he did encourage the first railways. Naturally the first line in 1835 was between two royal residences, St Petersburg and Tsarskoe Tselo, but for the second line seven years later he used his power as an autocrat to eliminate landowner protests by simply drawing a straight line from the capital to Moscow. Industry was anyway beginning at last to expand in Russia and by this time there were around half a million factory workers

In 1848 Nicholas had the third of his revolutionary shocks when Europe was once more the scene of widespread liberal rebellions. The Russians on the whole were too cowed to participate. One notable exception was the Petrashevsky group of socialists, the most famous of whom was the future novelist Feodor Dostoyevsky (1821-81). A doctor's son from Moscow, he had attended St Petersburg Engineering College before qualifying as a junior officer. Then in 1849 he published the short story *Poor Folk*, which won him instant notoriety and, along with fourteen others from the group, he was sentenced to death. Teasingly Nicholas left it to the very last minute, when the blindfolds were on, before reducing the sentence to penal servitude in Siberia, but the impression on the writer was predictably devastating. He was imprisoned in Omsk till 1854 and produced his first great novel the *House of the Dead* in 1860 by which time Nicholas was dead. Rather luckier than Dostoyevsky was another writer, the Ukrainian Nikolai Gogol (1809-52) who surprisingly got away with his comedy *The Inspector General* in 1836 which satirised the corruption and incompetence of local government officials in the provinces, but that year he chose exile in Italy, perhaps thus evading punishment. It was there in 1842 that he began to write his *Dead Souls*, a savage indictment of the evils of serfdom. Yet in almost every other sphere of life the news of the wave of revolutions throughout Europe in 1848 impelled Nicholas to intensify censorship, clamp down on student activity, make education even more narrow and encourage atavistic slogans like 'For faith, tsar and fatherland.'

In Russia itself, 1848 saw another acute shortage of food followed by an outbreak of cholera that cost around 150,000 lives, 30,000 in St Petersburg alone. Then since Nicholas had no revolution to suppress at home he offered his services to his fellow autocrats in Berlin and Vienna, earning himself the nickname 'The Gendarme of Europe' or as Tennyson put it 'The icy Muscovite.'

When he heard of the revolution in Paris that toppled King Louis Philippe he is reputed to have shouted 'Saddle your horses, gentlemen', but this naturally came to nothing. His brother-in-law the King of Prussia rejected his help and earned his disapproval for being so slow to get rid of the Berlin revolutionaries, giving them a constitution instead, so there was a dangerously lasting estrangement in the family. The Emperor Franz Joseph in Vienna was however glad to accept help and Nicholas sent an army of 170,000 to suppress the Hungarian nationalists who were led by Kossuth. Once more the Russian army scored a victory when faced with a relatively soft target, Nicholas accentuated his image as a reactionary bully, and won no friends, not even the Austrian emperor whose skin he had helped to save. The same applied to the Turkish sultan who asked for Nicholas's help to keep order in Wallachia and southern Moldavia.

Thus Nicholas approached the final self-inflicted crisis of his reign. By 1850 he was in his mid-fifties but still healthy and energetic though clearly suffering from nervous strain. His brothers were now dead, Konstantin from cholera back in 1832, more recently the Grand Duke Mikhail whose obsessions as a parade-ground martinet and whose brutal punishment of malingerers had become too extreme even for Nicholas. Luckily for Nicholas, Mikhail had a stroke while inspecting the troops in 1849 so it was one less problem. On the other hand, since the 1840s his own private life had become much more complicated. Having been faithful to his wife Empress Alexandra till his late forties he had a mid-life crisis and began an affair with a Valerie Nelidova whom in due course he made his official mistress, humiliating his wife by having Nelidova installed in court as a lady-in-waiting. One of his aides, Count Peter Kleinmichel, was ordered to adopt the consequential bastards and this continued when Nicholas replaced Valerie Nelidova with a new mistress Kutuzova.

The final crisis began in 1850 when the French Catholics challenged the Greek Orthodox clergy for control of the holy sites in Jerusalem. This arcane dispute rumbled on until 1852 when the Turks, upset by the pushy behaviour of the Russian envoy, settled in favour of the French. Nicholas who hated the French as revolutionaries and also hated Catholics because of Poland had backed the Greek Orthodox cause. He was especially incensed at the rebuff because of the help he had given to the Turks and the long-standing primacy of the Orthodox Church amongst the various sects which had bases in Jerusalem. It also challenged Russia's self-appointed role as champion of the 12 million Christians estimated still to be living inside the Turkish Empire. So since Nicholas was well used to having the Turks accede to his demands he gave them an ultimatum to reverse their decision about Jerusalem or face yet another attack by his army. Naturally he never expected them to refuse.

But history had moved on. The Turks were still weak yet the French and British had both indicated their support for them while even the Austrians seemed sympathetic and the Prussians apathetic. The superpowers of the period simply did not want to see the destruction of Turkey nor the domination of the eastern Mediterranean by Russia that would have followed.

At this point there was still no need for a war, let alone a war involving several superpowers but gradually the tension was racked up. In June

1853 the British and French sent fleets to the eastern Mediterranean to display solidarity with the Turks. The next month, on orders from Nicholas who did not bother to consult any of his ministers, the Russian army crossed the Pruth and once more occupied Moldavia, technically still Turkish territory. The Turks showed no sign of backing down and, faced with this unexpected intransigence, Nicholas started to look for a peaceful solution that would save his face. The British and French failed to oblige and in October the Turks declared war on the invading Russians. Nicholas responded by sending his Black Sea fleet to destroy a Turkish fleet off Sinope. The British Prime Minister Lord Aberdeen sensibly held back from joining the war but accusations of cowardice forced him to change his mind.

Suddenly Nicholas found himself without friends. His traditional allies the Prussian king, his brother-in-law, and the Austrian Kaiser (whose empire he had helped save just seven years earlier), both held back, the latter even demanding that he withdraw from the Danube provinces. There now appeared to be no dignified means with which he could avoid facing a joint attack by the French and British.

Doubtless at this point, though mildly alarmed, Nicholas had faith that the army to which he had devoted his life would beat off all enemies. But even the Turks managed to defeat his troops in Moldavia and he lost control of the Danube estuary. Not convinced that Nicholas had seen the error of his ways, the British and French wanted to teach him a lesson. So they began to implement a clumsy and ill-organised land-sea attack on the Crimea, the home of Russia's Black Sea Fleet. They did not even check that the waters of Sebastopol were too shallow for their ships and there were numerous failings in training, leadership and supplies.

Despite the incompetence of the invaders the following autumn the Russian army suffered three successive defeats, on the river Alma in September, Balaclava in October and Inkerman in November. Nicholas had tried out his secret new weapon – the floating mine – in the Baltic but in the Black Sea his wooden ships had shown their vulnerability to the new shell guns of the allies. His one minor success was to beat a British flotilla in the Far East off Kamchatka. Despite numerous failings, the British had their new Enfield rifles with the modified minnie whereas the Russians had antiquated flintlock muskets. The Russian troops fighting in what was theoretically home territory had run out of supplies. Their munitions factories were woefully inadequate for a modern war, the small serf-run factories could not even produce enough uniforms, and there was still no railway to the Crimea or even a good road, so the troops faced long marches in the harsh winter just to get to the Crimea. Out of an army totalling 1.8 million Nicholas could only deploy a sixth of that in the south and a mere 100,000 to try to save Sebastopol from a smaller-sized force of the allies, who themselves were suffering from poor supply lines, incompetent leadership and disease. Casualties were out of all proportion due to cold and disease. The new outer works of Sebastopol created by the brilliant engineer Todleben would not be enough.

The Russian leadership under Prince Alexander Menshikov relied on sheer Russian pugnacity, the massed bayonet charge and suicidal bravery. The brighter staff officers had all been weeded out after the Decembrist plots and initiative had been discouraged. Junior officers such as young Leo Tolstoy who served in the Sebastopol garrison were not prepared for proper wars. NCOs were badly trained except in parade ground manoeuvres.

As the winter of 1854/5 began Nicholas still feigned confidence that 'Generals January and February' would defeat the Westerners. Yet he must have been mortified by the humiliating defeats of his generals and the huge losses of his army (around 70,000 casualties at this point), many due to hypothermia on the forced marches southwards or cholera in the appalling conditions of the Crimea. He was still posing as 'a martyr of our holy faith', ignoring the fact that it was he who had started the war and it was his administration that had left his army so ill-equipped to cope. He was apparently gripped by a death wish when 'General February' still showed no signs of saving Sebastopol. Having foolishly worn full-dress uniform for a January wedding he caught a severe chill, and then insisted on attending the send-off for a new batch of troops heading for the front, in bitterly cold weather. As he faced up to the dreadful possibilities of a humiliating peace treaty he met 'General February' rather than survive. With typical regard for military protocol he apologised to the Tsarevich Alexander for 'not handing over the command in good order' and died at the beginning of March, thus evading the worst consequences of his actions and the public acknowledgement of his failure. He was fifty-eight and had in effect lost much that he and his predecessors had made huge efforts to acquire.

XII

ALEXANDER II
THE RELUCTANT LIBERATOR

'I have seen our mother Russia and I have learned to love and respect her even more'

Alexander as Tsarevich

'Alexander … ordered them to lock him up in solitary confinement cell. He stayed in it for more than an hour, attempting thereby to sense the state of mind of those he had imprisoned there'

Alexander Solzhenitsyn, *Gulag Archipelago*

Alexander II (ruled 1855-81) was thirty-six and though he was in theory well trained for the job, he took over at the worst possible time. For a state whose main source of pride was its army to have suffered three successive defeats on its own soil at the hands of a foreign army thousands of miles from its own bases was a huge humiliation. Nor was it a humiliation that Alexander could or would simply blame on his father, for he had himself been a devoted admirer of the Russian army for nearly thirty years.

At the age of six Alexander had been given a military tutor, Captain Karl Merder, and begun parade-ground training to which he became just as addicted as his father and grandfather had been. Genetically he was half-Prussian on his mother's side and another 40 per cent German on his father's side, so a maximum of around 10 per cent genuinely Russian genes. When he was seven his uncle Alexander I had died and his father became Emperor, thus making him the new Tsarevich, so from that age he knew that he would be the next emperor. His military training became even more intense, so much so that it seems to have undermined his health, earning the disapproval of his Spartan-minded father, who was anyway shocked by his lack of persistence in military studies. Four years later he paid his first visit to Berlin where he was delighted to be made a colonel of the 3rd Uhlans and don Prussian uniform, confirming him in his adulation of Prussian militarism. Certainly he looked the part with his massive moustache and sideburns, glaring despotic eyes and parade-ground posture.

Meanwhile his education had been given a civilian twist, ironically on the insistence of his Prussian mother. She brought in the poet Vasili Zhukovsky to teach him the liberal arts, though in these subjects too he proved an inattentive and lethargic student, even if he does seem to have been reasonably proficient in five languages: Russian, French, German, English and Polish. Captain Merder was so frustrated by his pupil's idleness that when Alexander was fourteen he had a heart attack, dying two years later and causing the Tsarevich genuine grief, for Alexander seems to have been a warmer and more emotional young man than his father considered appropriate in a potential emperor. He had none of the obsessive self-denial of his father and by his late teens was beginning to put on weight. Yet just like his father it was part of his image to sleep on a narrow military camp-bed.

The final stage in Alexander's education was an intensive six-month course in Russian law, government and finance organised by the justice minister Mikhail Speransky. Then, when he was nineteen Alexander was taken on a seven-month tour of the Empire, covering thirty provinces with Zhukovsky as travelling companion. He thus saw more of peasant life than any previous tsarevich and was the first Romanov to visit Siberia. He was introduced to the surviving Decembrist mutineers who had been exiled by his father and was so shocked by their hardships that he sent a letter home asking for them to be remedied. He also met the young socialist exile Herzen in Vyatka both making and succumbing to a favourable impression, though later Herzen was to be one of his most severe critics.

Back in St Petersburg the Tsarevich, now aged twenty, caused his parents deep anxiety, not so much by having an affair with a Polish lady-in-waiting but by wanting to marry her. This was an idea that would have made his father apoplectic and even his mother was saddened at the boy's lack of self-control or sense of duty. So he was packed off on a tour of Europe with a list of potential German princesses. This succeeded in making him forget his Polish lover but only because he fell in love with an almost equally unsuitable German who was not on the list. She was theoretically Princess Marie of Hesse-Darmstadt, but because her mother had been living apart from the Grand Duke for several years everyone knew that he was not her real father and that she was instead the daughter of a lowborn palace retainer. This did not deter Alexander, who at twenty-two was besotted with the pretty young fifteen-year-old and for once stood up to both his parents, threatening to renounce the succession if he did not get his way. Meanwhile he had made the most of his trip round Europe with visits to many of the capital cities including London where he met the newly crowned Queen Victoria who was only two years his junior (she later referred to him as 'weak as water') and his aunt Maria Pavlovna, the queen of Holland.

Thus at the age of twenty-three Alexander married Marie who as usual for German princesses was rechristened in the Orthodox Church, but for once did not have to change her Christian name except to become Maria. They lost their first child, a daughter, but soon went on to provide four sons and a daughter. It was a reasonably happy marriage until 1857 when after fifteen years he was to be tempted away by yet another lady-in-waiting 'the young tigress' Princess Alexandra Dolgorukaya, thirty years his junior and at that time a pupil at the Smolny Institute.

Meanwhile Alexander's training for the throne continued as he often stood in as Regent when his father was away from the capital. He was made chair of a secret committee investigating serfdom or perhaps more correctly discussing the impossibility of abolishing it. He was thirty when the court was stunned by the outbreak of revolutions throughout Europe in 1848 but he approved of the conservative stance of his father and showed at this time no particular signs of liberalism, let alone any serious desire to tackle the deep-rooted problems of Russia. In 1852 he read *A Sportsman's Sketches*, the epoch-making book by Turgenev about peasant misery, which had a profound effect on him and others but like Oblomov, the conscience-stricken anti-hero of the writer Ivan Goncharov, he was too lazy to get out of bed and do anything about it.

Four years after the turmoil of 1848 began the dreadful series of errors by his father that brought about the Crimean War and the defeats that reduced the great martinet to a pathetic old man who no longer wanted to live. To his great annoyance Alexander, who had been on a depressing tour of the front line, insisted that Menshikov should be dismissed in a vain effort to stem the defeats, so there was acrimony between the dying emperor and his heir.

Though Alexander did not concede defeat immediately after his succession there was nothing he could do to save Sebastopol from falling to the allies in September 1855. By this time casualties were close to 100,000, supplies of ammunition and uniforms almost non-existent, the State was nearly bankrupt and Austria was threatening to join the war on the other side. The Emperor's brother Konstantin suggested a backs-to-the-wall retreat as in 1812, but this was hardly necessary for the allies had no desire to conquer Russia, only to teach it a lesson and that they believed had now been accomplished.

So Alexander gave the go-ahead for peace talks and got off quite lightly. Russia lost Bessarabia to the fledgling state of Moldavia and Wallachia, which not long afterwards became Rumania. It was also forbidden to replace its Black Sea navy and its fortified bases, forbidden to send war-ships through the Straits and it lost one recently captured fortress – Kars in the Caucasus – but its control of Poland was left unchallenged. Though it was humiliating in terms of international prestige the only real loss was the weakening of Russia's aggressive capabilities in the Black Sea.

With the peace negotiations well in hand Alexander could now turn his attention to his coronation, though it was an expense that the treasury could ill afford. Vast sums were spent on redecorating the Kremlin, special pavilions and huge supplies of food for the estimated million coming to Moscow for the event. There was the customary peel of 8,000 bells from the Moscow churches. There was the usual mile-long procession including the thirty golden coaches belonging to the Romanov family and vast numbers of attendants from cossacks to negroes, all bedecked with exotic uniforms and fancy plumes. Everywhere the double-headed eagle proclaimed the corporate identity of the dynasty. Alexander himself came alone in a glass and silver coach pulled by eight white horses and there was a banquet for 3,000 guests. Though his experience in the Crimea had given him an intense dislike of war he nevertheless maintained the family obsession with drill parades and uniforms.

At the same time Alexander was still secretly indulging the usual Romanov penchant for aggressive expansion elsewhere. His governor in Eastern Siberia, Nikolai Muraviev, built a series of illegal forts along the Chinese frontier at the Amur River and by 1857 Alexander was able to claim a new province there from the Chinese. Further acquisitions followed and by 1860 Muraviev was able to found the new city of Vladivostok (Power of the East) on the Pacific Coast. At about the same time Russia had quietly renewed its expansion in the Caucasus with a long-running and genocidal war (1834-59) against the local highlanders under Shamil and a continued exodus of Muslim Circassians to Turkey that left a lasting legacy of hatred.

It was Alexander's character to follow the line of least resistance, to avoid unnecessary confrontation. Thus he was aware that the last decade of his father's rule had seen some 350 outbreaks of peasant violence, something more than double the number in the previous decade. Many of the intelligentsia including some of his own more enlightened relations had therefore been pressing for a reform of serfdom for years. He must also have been aware that mass conscription of serfs had not provided the kind of army that would stand up to professional opponents. Yet he faced implacable opposition from the bulk of serf-owners to reform the aristocracy on whose loyalty and service his power still to some extent depended. Thus in the aftermath of the Crimean disaster he introduced some palliative measures such as the relaxation of censorship, greater freedom for universities, an amnesty for many political prisoners such as the Decembrists, less restraint on foreign travel, a moratorium on conscription and some cancellation of tax arrears, but he hung back from solving the big problem. Instead he appeared bored and lazy, preferring to escape on bear hunting expeditions. The British envoy Grenville wrote, 'He does not give the idea of having much strength either of intellect or character, but looks intelligent and agreeable ... is liked by those around him but blamed for not having the habits of punctuality and quick decision-making that characterised his father.'

It took several events to jerk Alexander out of his torpor. The first was an unexpected alliance between his wife Maria and his mistress Alexandra who forgot their differences and began a joint effort to make him take action. The second was a panic in Lithuania where the nobles were alarmed by the level of serf unrest and decided unilaterally to free all their serfs, but not give them any land. Alexander realised the futility of such a plan and vetoed it, but the incident increased the pressure on him to provide a general solution. In addition, there was an expectation sensed through the diplomatic community that the only way Russia would drag itself into civilised European society was by freeing its serfs. Thus Alexander announced at a St Petersburg Christmas ball in 1857 that it was 'his categorical will' that serfs should be emancipated but should at the same time each be given some land. Naturally this caused horror amongst the landowners who would not only lose their free labour force but also a lot of their land. Great serf owners who were amongst Alexander's closest advisers, like Prince Orlov, of course did nothing to implement the policy.

So the affair rumbled on. His brother Konstantin, who was guilt-ridden for having played a small part in the suppression of Hungary in 1849, was so angry at lack of progress that he had to be sent off to the navy where he made useful improvements. Others of Alexander's nearest relations pressed him to act: his neglected wife Maria, his mother, his mistress Alexandra and his sister-in-law Helen. Alexander's key aide on the serfdom committee, Prince Jacob Rostovtsev, died in 1860 but at least Alexander made a perceptive choice of replacement – Count Victor Panin. Panin himself owned more than 20,000 serfs and was expected to be anti-reform, but since he was overtly going to suffer from the changes was better placed than a poorer man to persuade his fellows to share in this sacrifice. A plan was drafted and though the Council of State voted against many clauses in it, Alexander overruled each objection. After a four-year delay he was now desperate to have the plan in place before the 1861 planting season. It was announced to great rejoicing from every pulpit and village hall. Alexander who had been so slow to grasp the nettle now called it 'the happiest day of my life' and celebrated by buying a new palace at Livadiya in the Crimea where the warm climate would help the health of his ailing wife.

Sadly the rejoicing was in many respects premature. Certainly around 50 million people had been freed from servitude and were no longer subject to arranged marriages, but the ultimate land allocation was far from adequate. The 25 million state peasants, especially those on the imperial family estates, did better than the 21 million private serfs who had less land allotted to them than they had for centuries enjoyed the use of for their personal food supply. Besides, the land was allocated in bulk to each village community, meaning that there was no personal ownership to incentivise investment. On top of that the serfs had to pay for it over a forty-nine-year period. Worst off were the 1.5 million household serfs who were allocated no land at all. What is more, all ex-serfs were still liable to corporal punishment, to conscription and to tax. They had even lost their traditional right to pick up free firewood and timber from the forests. So many were actually worse off in economic terms than they had been before emancipation. The rural population rose from 50 to 79 million over the next 50 years but that simply put more strain on the subsistence level of the majority of peasants.

For the aristocrats the transition to a serf-free society was relatively painless. They had to be more business-like in using their land and hiring labour, but their overall losses were tolerable. The opulent lifestyle of the St Petersburg aristocracy carried on as if nothing had happened, the day starting in the early afternoon and finishing just before dawn. Alexander kept the aristocracy happy with his 'Bals des Palmiers', when palm trees were specially shipped into the Winter Palace from the garden of Tsarskoe Selo and a supper table for fifteen people built round each tree. Alexander knew how to work the crowd: he made a point of circulating for a drink of champagne at one table or something to eat at another. He made sure everyone was impressed by wearing the most exquisite uniforms, for instance, the three-quarter length white tunic with gold flutings and edged with blue Siberian fox, immaculate sky-blue trousers and black boots.

Perhaps still under the influence of his tempestuous affair with Alexandra Dolgorukaya the Emperor had a further short period of reforming zeal. The period 1863-5 saw the reform of the penal code, the freeing of universities, the reduction in censorship and particularly the founding of the *zemstvos*, the nearest thing Russia had to local self-government. These were village councils with the power to build schools, hospitals and other infrastructures, albeit they were often dominated by local landlords and had a very narrow franchise. Generally however bear hunting rather than politics remained Alexander's favourite pursuit.

Stress tended to bring on his asthma, which in turn made it hard for him to sleep and then made him short-tempered. He was at his best not when trying to solve complex problems but in action, for when a devastating fire raged through St Petersburg in 1862 he and his son both worked as ordinary firemen, gave out cash, and chatted to those who had lost their homes. His sister-in-law Helen ran a soup kitchen.

The unexpected revolt of Poland in 1863-4 was the spur to make Alexander abandon his liberal period, especially since the revolt was the ungrateful response to a reform programme that included the abolition of serfdom and the return of numerous Polish exiles from Siberia.

Alexander sent his brother Konstantin to be the new governor in Warsaw, but like his namesake of the previous generation he was regarded as too soft and was dismissed. Potentially the offers of land to Polish serfs were better than to their Russian counterparts, but the underhand motive was to win their approval at the expense of their local aristocracy. The Russian army was nearly driven out of Poland and an attempt to assassinate Konstantin very nearly succeeded. It took an army of 80,000 eventually to restore order and then only because the Poles were divided amongst themselves. Many of the land-owning class were now driven into exile and repression of the Polish nation intensified as it was renamed simply the Ten Provinces of Vistula, regions of Russia. Count Mikhail Muraviev known as 'the hangman of Vilnius' was given extensive powers to weed out opposition and many Catholics were forced to convert to Orthodoxy. There were public executions in Warsaw and a devastating clampdown in Poland and Lithuania that generated deep-seated resentment.

Nevertheless, in industrial terms Poland remained one of the most advanced and prosperous parts of the Empire. With its ruthlessly down-trodden work force that represented only 8 per cent of the Russian total, it managed to produce 25 per cent of the Empire's manufactured goods. The three Baltic States also shared in the dramatic industrial growth, helped by their access to the sea.

Other factors contributed to the hardening of Alexander's attitudes. In 1862 there appeared the first Russian translation of Karl Marx's *Communist Manifesto*. The same year Turgenev's *Fathers and Sons* spread the idea of Nihilism as a credo that all authority should be destroyed. Soon afterwards Chernyshevsky wrote his extremely influential novel *Chto Dyelat?* (*What to do?*) while in prison, yet still managed to get it published. At about the same time there were a series of student riots at the newly freed universities. Most of them were in sympathy with a small but significant peasant rebellion in Bezdna where fifty ex-serfs had been shot and 300 wounded for protesting about the inadequate terms of the emancipation settlement. Herzen published his pamphlet *B Narod* (*To the People*), which later gave its title to the Narodnik opposition movement. Then in the same year came the Tver Address in which thirteen nobles from that area petitioned for an elected parliament. It seemed that all Alexander's imagined liberality had simply given the Russian people a taste for further reform. From now on instead of encouraging reform he would clamp down on it with utter ruthlessness.

At the same time Alexander was boosting his morale with further acquisitions for the Empire in central Asia. Perovsky, his governor in Orenburg, was like many of the ambitious frontier soldiers of this period creating his own little empire and ignoring the plaintive restraining orders that came from distant St Petersburg. He had been building forts beyond the Russian frontier in the Muslim khanate of Khiva. This provoked a reaction from the tribesmen, which gave him the excuse for further aggression that resulted in the capture of Tashkent and Samarkand between 1865 and 1868, and Kokand in 1876. Further additions were to follow later, completing the new Russian province of Turkestan by 1882.

As ever the Russians massaged their military egos with defeats of backward nations and acquired unhealthy confidence in their imperial power. Railways were now built from Orenburg to Turkestan and linked with the Transcaucasian line so that Russia could move troops along the frontier with relative rapidity. This now left only Afghanistan as a buffer between Russia and British India, reinforcing the paranoia that had gripped the British a few decades earlier. Together with unauthorised Russian expansion beyond the Caspian by von Kauffmann and in north-east China by Admiral Putyatin and General Ignatiev, this constituted a further major expansion of the Russian Empire, mopping up new ethnic and religious groups which would later cause problems. The only retreat was in America where the Alaskan colonies were sold off to the United States in 1867 for $7,200,000.

So by 1870 Alexander was shaking off the sense of failure that followed the Crimean War and could ignore the treaty by which he had promised not to rebuild the Black Sea fleet. His minister of war, the talented Dmitri Milyutin, had conducted a series of drastic reforms in the army, which at least theoretically addressed the problems of supply, medical care and quality of officer training that had led to the disasters in the Crimea. After 1874 this included a new form of conscription by lot that allowed for six years compulsory service followed by eight years in the reserve. Therefore, with renewed confidence Alexander resumed the diplomatic initiative by forming the Three Emperor League (*Dreikaiserbund*) with Germany and Austria.

However little credit Alexander could take for this expansion of the Empire and however great the official discouragement for such moves, it is hard to believe that he was not secretly pleased. Yet as he approached his fiftieth year he was beset by another mid-life crisis. In 1865 his eldest son, the gifted and charming Tsarevich Nicholas had died of consumption after falling from his horse near Nice. Alexander had to readjust his thoughts on the succession as the less intelligent, less tractable Grand Duke Alexander became the new heir. A marriage was arranged for him with his dead brother's Danish fiancée and took place soon afterwards.

In 1866, when Alexander was forty-eight, he survived the first of a series of assassination attempts, this one in the St Petersburg Summer Gardens by a student called Karakozov who objected to the poor terms of peasant emancipation. His life was only saved because an ordinary bystander deflected the killer's pistol. The event emphasised both the insecurity of the Emperor in his own capital and the lack of residual respect left by his reforming activities. From this moment police surveillance had to be increased dramatically and Alexander could never feel totally secure. Two other events in his personal life helped shape the Emperor's state of mind. The first that same year was the beginning of his last great love affair. Maria, the mother of his eight children, had once again been discarded as too prim and religious, while Alexandra Dolgorukaya was now replaced by her distant cousin Catherine Dolgorukaya as his mistress. He seemed to enjoy renewed happiness in her company: she was allowed to enter the Winter Palace by a secret door; he practiced drawing her in the nude; she became his 'wife before God'; and in due course they had three children who were even acknowledged as Romanovs. The other event soon afterwards in 1868 was the birth of his grandson Nicholas, a son for the Tsarevich and his Danish wife Maria, which secured the future for the dynasty.

Meanwhile the intellectual ferment and creativity continued almost unabated despite the heavy censorship and increased police presence. In 1866 Tolstoy had produced his *War and Peace*, the political content of which was fairly well disguised, and Dostoyevsky his *Crime and Punishment* which seemed at least superficially quite conservative yet drew attention vividly to the extreme poverty and disillusionment of the St Petersburg slums. In the 1870s the city had the highest mortality rate of any city in Europe and cholera and typhus were rampant due to the almost total absence of sanitation – it was estimated that there were 30,000 tons of garbage and excrement littering the back streets. Venereal disease was also common. The year 1870 witnessed the first strike by industrial workers in St Petersburg. Four years later came the somewhat disorganised demonstration by the Narodniki in support of the peasants, followed by mass trials. The reformists simply went underground with new groups like *Zemlya i Volya* (Land and Freedom), which organised a mass demonstration by the Kazan Cathedral in 1876. There was a second assassination attempt against the Emperor, this time by a dissident Pole, and Dmitri Tolstoy presided over ever-increasing repression as education minister. Yet even the most unlikely art forms were harnessed to express insidious criticism of the regime. In 1874 came the first performance of Mussorgsky's opera *Boris Godunov* with its anti-autocracy under-tones; Borodin was working on *Prince Igor* and Rimsky-Korsakov had left the navy to become a music teacher in St Petersburg. The premiere of Tchaikovsky's *Swan Lake* was in Moscow in 1878.

Alongside the new socialism and liberalism there was also a new nationalism. Pan-Slavism was ultimately the fault of the Romanovs, who had toyed with the idea of supporting the oppressed Christian popula-tions of the Turkish Empire to provide a cause that might take peoples' minds off reform. In the 1870s however, it became a mass movement with almost hysterical overtones that Alexander rightly regarded as dangerous. Yet, as so often, he was unable to control the forces that he had helped to unleash. One of his own favourite generals, Chernayev, took charge of the Serbian army without authority but with encouragement from the Tsarevich. He soon had 1,000 Russian officers volunteering to join him as the Serbs were identified as fellow Slavs struggling for their freedom against the infidel. There was great enthusiasm for the causes of Bosnia Herzegovina and Bulgaria, as like Serbia they moved to shake off Turkish rule. With nearly half the urban population now able to read, the reports of the Bulgarian atrocities at the hands of the Turks caused widespread public emotion. Even the peasants supported the movement because of their sympathy for persecuted members of the Orthodox Church. Despite his misgivings, in 1876 Alexander could not withstand the tide of public opinion. His own family pressed him to accept the idea at a con-ference in the Livadiya Palace in the Crimea. His brothers and son told him aggressively that Constantinople was the proper capital of Russia. His wife as president of the Red Cross together with other emotional ladies pressed him to rally to the red, white and blue flag of the Slavs.

Thus, rather against his better judgement, Alexander drifted into war with Turkey again. He issued an ultimatum designed to protect the Slav minorities, but instead of yielding the Turks announced it as a declaration of war. An army of 300,000 men under his brothers the Grand Dukes Konstantin and Nicholas set off to besiege Plevna (Pleven) in northern

Bulgaria while the third brother, Mikhail, moved into the Caucasus. Four of his five sons served in junior positions: Tsarevich Alexander with two corps, Vladimir with one, Alexis with the fleet and Sergei with the guards. Alexander now aged sixty offered to serve as a male nurse. As even one of his critics, Vladimir Cherkassky, put it 'you cannot but love him as a man.' He worked hard, retained his composure, dithered and his hair went white.

As ever, despite the reforms of Milyutin, the Russian army found it hard to operate so far away from its bases and the war progressed slowly. Plevna was only captured at the fourth attempt. There were around 25,000 casualties before the army even reached the front. General Skobelev scored a victory in the Shipka Pass. Mikhail was defeated in the Caucasus. Grand Duke Nicholas was corrupt as well as inefficient though he did eventually reach Adrianople, just 60 miles short of the target, Constantinople. Now once again there was huge alarm throughout Europe that Russia was once more thrusting towards the Mediterranean. Even in Australia there was serious panic about an impending Russian invasion and forts were built to protect Sydney. In Britain the music hall chorus of *By jingo* ... provided the language with a new word and the fleet was put in readiness for another Crimean war. When Grand Duke Nicholas saw the British warships near the Hellespont he hung back from the final assault on Constantinople, contented himself with one small suburb, San Stefano and made peace.

In this first treaty Russia won major concessions from Turkey, including the creation of an enlarged Bulgaria under Russian protection, but when the British fleet off Constantinople indicated the allies' serious displeasure Alexander prudently backed down. The replacement treaty accepted by other European powers was much less favourable to the Pan-Slav concept. Bulgaria was to be much smaller and Bosnia Herzegovina was handed over to the protection of Austria instead of Russia. The Serb rebellion had failed. It was a huge anti-climax for the Russian public and Alexander was openly blamed for his lack of courage, even by his own son who was especially bitter about the alleged venality of his uncle Nicholas, the commander-in-chief. According to Disraeli the Russian minister confessed that 'they had lost 100,000 men and spent 100 millions of roubles for nothing.'

In 1880 after the death of Tsarina Maria from tuberculosis, with indecent haste Alexander married his long-term mistress Catherine, now Princess Yurievskaya, much to the disgust of his heir Tsarevich Alexander who openly expressed a disapproval also felt by many others. She flaunted her youth, her power over 'Emperor Sasha', her previously secret children and her fondness for liberal ideas. Her sexual vitality was blamed for the Emperor's increasing signs of exhaustion and his asthma – he was coughing, sleeping poorly and drinking too much. One of her protégés, the Armenian Michael Loris-Melikov, was made the new Chief Minister with almost dictatorial powers and used them to create a much more liberal atmosphere, even bringing forward a plan for constitutional monarchy. Yet this was the year that saw the first performance of Tchaikovsky's *1812 Festival Overture*, which opens with the tune of *God preserve thy people* and had been commissioned to celebrate the Emperor's silver jubilee and to erase the memory of recent military mediocrity with a stirring reminder of long gone successes.

Sadly though, the number of assassination plots had continued to escalate: the third in Paris alongside Napoleon III; another involving the blowing up of the royal train; another a bomb in the Winter Palace itself. Alexander spent more time in the seclusion of Gatchina, which had extra high walls and was more easily guarded. Loris-Melikov was targeted too as were several other ministers. Count Peter Tolstoy's policy of purging revolutionaries from the universities had simply created a larger task force of dedicated opponents. Trepov, the unpopular governor of St Petersburg who had flouted the new law to flog an agitator, was wounded in a murder attempt and the culprit daringly acquitted by a St Petersburg jury. There was virtually martial law in Russia's three main cities and tsardom was beginning to look shaky.

Despite all these warnings in February 1881 police cover was relatively relaxed and there was no proper check on Alexander's route back from a February Sunday parade. Yet he always wore a bulletproof vest in public and had given up cigars in case someone gave him one filled with gunpowder. The People's Will made their base in a fake cheese shop at 56 Malaya Sadovaya Street and equipped four members with a nitro-glycerine grenade (one that would almost certainly kill the bomber as well as the intended victim) each. Alexander chose a different route along the Catherine Embankment but the suicide bombers shifted their stance. They allowed him to pass the first bomber in case Alexander turned back. The second bomber threw his grenade but missed, instead killing several Cossack guards. Alexander stopped his carriage to help the wounded, got out and was hit by the third bomber. He died in the Winter Palace a few hours later in the arms of his new wife, surrounded by his family including a little boy in a sailor suit – his grandson Nicholas. As so often in Alexander's life, good intentions had been his undoing.

As well as his first family, of whom six out of eight children survived him, Alexander also left his second wife Princess Catherine Yurievskaya (1847-1922) as a very young widow with three young children: George (1872-1913), Olga (1873-1925) and Catherine (1878-1959). The widow moved first to the Petit Palais Rose but found her imperial status challenged and emigrated to live in the Avenue Kleber, Paris and the Villa George in Nice. Whereas very few spare Romanovs survived in previous generations, the numbers were now getting out of hand.

XIII

ALEXANDER III
SASHA THE BULLDOG

'As wax before the fire every revolutionary struggle will melt before the man tsar who fulfills the law of Christ'

Tolstoy

Alexander III (ruled 1881-97) was born in 1845, the second and least talented of the children of Alexander II and his wife Maria. He had even less Russian blood than his predecessor since each generation of his male ancestors had one after the other taken a German wife. But he also had less blue blood than the others for his Darmstadt grandfather was an unnamed lover of the Grand Duchess who had long since been deserted by the Grand Duke. His huge height was typical of the family but his massive strength was not – it was rumoured that he could bend horseshoes and pokers – even less so his fidelity, for he was probably the first tsar since Alexis to refrain from adultery. Yet from an early age this huge man had a fear of horses.

From the start Alexander had been brought up in the shadow of his clever and charming elder brother, Nicholas. They had shared tutors: the usual Romanov mix of military, General Zinoviev, and civilian, the right-wing lawyer Pobedonostsev who taught him to despise the liberal minded including his uncle Konstantin whose gentle policies had failed in Poland. Then in 1865 when he was twenty, came the event that would totally alter his prospects. While on tour in France Nicholas fell off a horse near Nice and died of tuberculosis or meningitis soon afterwards. Alexander suddenly became the Tsarevitch and one whose simple brain had mainly absorbed the reactionary views of the anti-Semitic Pobedonostsev.

Not only did Alexander take over his brother's role as the emperor-in-waiting, but he even took over his fiancée, Princess Dagmar Sophie Frederica of Denmark whom he married the following year. She had as usual converted to Orthodoxy and changed her name to Maria. Though she was neither very beautiful nor intelligent it seems to have been a genuine love-match, which he never betrayed. Tchaikovsky was commissioned to produce a new *Festival Overture* for the reception at the Winter Palace and was paid with a pair of cuff links. Within two years the couple produced a son Nicholas. He sadly was to inherit their combined lack of brainpower and all the difficulties that his father's reactionary regime left unsolved.

For the next dozen years Alexander made his home in the Anichkov Palace. He was fond of music and played the trombone himself. A conscientious worker and early riser he was never fond of the hyperactive social life of St Petersburg, which interfered with his sleep pattern. Unlike his father he did not really enjoy dressing up, but preferred cheap, simple clothing. In his impatience to shorten the inevitable balls he would quietly send home one member of the orchestra after another till only one was left and his guests were obliged to leave.

Like many of his fellows, but unlike his father, Alexander was greatly attracted to the Pan-Slav fashion that gripped the capital in the 1870s. He had his first serious confrontation with his father in the autumn of 1876 when the royal family and its advisers met at their new summer palace at Livadiya in the Crimea, where orangeries had been planted for the now ailing Empress Maria. This was just after the disappointing failure of the Serbian rising despite the number of Russian soldiers who had gone to help the Serbs with encouragement from the Tsarevich. At thirty-one young Alexander, even with a collection of parade-ground uniforms, had never seen active service and was extremely keen that Russia should declare war against Turkey.

Young Alexander was therefore one of the key family members who pushed the reluctant Emperor into the attacks that followed and was himself sent to the front in charge of two corps where he found out the harsh reality of modern warfare in action on the river Lom. Though his timidity when near horses was noted by onlookers his behaviour otherwise seems to have been brave enough, but he was furious with the generals in charge. He was extremely unhappy with the conduct of the war by his three uncles, particularly corrupt Grand Duke Nicholas and the slightly supine way in which his father surrendered most of its gains due to pressure from the British and Austrians. He returned home in such a disgruntled mood that his father even threatened him with arrest.

The next confrontation came four years later in 1880 when he was thirty-five. Alexander had just lost his much-neglected mother Maria. He found himself seriously at odds with his father who had taken the opportunity to marry his attractive young mistress Catherine Dolgorukaya and was threatening to turn their illegitimate children into grand dukes. Not least amongst his worries about this liaison was the more liberal turn in his father's thinking and the fact that he was once more drafting a constitution, a concept quite alien to the ultra-conservative Tsarevich.

It is not unreasonable to suggest therefore that his father's murder came to Alexander as more of a relief than a disaster. Given his training by Pobedonostsev it came naturally to him to insist on savage punishment for the murderers. Five of those implicated were publicly executed in Semenovskoe Square. Similarly he responded with alacrity to the suggestion that Jews – he always called them Yids – were behind the plot. It was also in his character to burn the documents in which his father had been about to put forward a liberal constitution and to sack the ministers who had backed this proposal.

It was also natural for Alexander III not to think of making concessions in the aftermath of the murder, but to clamp down even more intensively on all opposition to autocracy. His reaction to the terror campaign waged by the opposition was not to try to win popularity but to show that terror was ineffective by refusing to make any concessions. He shut himself and his family away from harm by moving them from the Anichkov to the Winter Palace, where their sole exercise for the time being was in its tiny back garden. He then moved home for most of the time to Gatchina 40 miles south of St Petersburg, a castle of 600 rooms but with a protective moat and a high wall round the estate that could be patrolled night and day by his guards. There he could dress like a peasant, with baggy trousers and a *muzhik* blouse, cut down on unnecessary candles and soap, wash in cold water, eat his favourite meal of cabbage and gruel and avoid society as much as possible. When he did appear in public it was in an armour-plated carriage so heavy that the horses soon died from exhaustion; wherever he went the secret police hovered around. There was a rapid increase in the size of the *Okhrana* (literally bodyguard) with officers working under cover, vigilantes and encouragement of informers.

With Pobedonostsev, sometimes called the Black Tsar, installed as his Chief Minister Alexander set about his new policy of 'Russia for the Russians' with a special targeting of the Jews who he considered could be blamed for four things: the death of Jesus, the death of Alexander II, collapsing the stock market and the wretched peace brokered in 1878 by the British Jew, Benjamin Disraeli. His grandfather, Nicholas I, had cleared all the Jews out of St Petersburg, Kiev and Sebastopol, had made Jews liable for military service and outlawed many Jewish customs. His father had continued along mainly anti-Semitic lines and in 1871 there had been the first Odesa *pogrom*. Alexander now made sure that he did not need to borrow any more money from the Rothschilds before he and Pobedonostsev set a target for the ethnic cleansing of Russia's 6 million Jews: a third should be made to emigrate, a third to die and a third be assimilated. Massacres in Kirovo, Kiev and Warsaw followed with lesser *pogroms* elsewhere in the Pale area first defined by Catherine the Great and which was now even more closely restricted. Around 225,000 Jews emigrated to Western Europe or the United States. No Hebrew books could be published and all Jewish schools were closed. Jews were kept out of professions like the law and medicine. Alexander's brother, the psychotic homosexual Grand Duke Sergei, began to evict thousands of Jews from Moscow to the Pale.

Jews were not the only victims. The oppression of the Poles continued but now for the first time the Finns were also deprived of their privileges and forced to use Russian. Similarly many Germans, particularly those from the Baltic States, found themselves demoted or compelled to adopt Russian surnames if they wanted to keep their careers. Once more the army uniforms were redesigned, this time to make them look less German. Alexander convinced himself and many others that he was a conscientious ruler by ploughing through mounds of trivial paperwork instead of confronting major problems.

The journalist Mikhail Katkov, whose ranting received ample coverage at times when liberal writing was strictly censored, orchestrated the main propaganda for the racist policy. Alongside this racism there was also a State-sponsored drive against religious unorthodoxy. This applied not just to Jews and Catholics but to German Lutherans in the Baltic provinces, to Old Believers and other fringe sects like the Dukhobors,

Russia's version of the Quakers, many of whom chose to emigrate to Canada rather than give up their beliefs.

In addition to the racist and religious persecution there was also a deliberate clampdown on class mobility. The working or peasant class were to be largely excluded from secondary education to make sure that they could not aspire to middle-class status. University fees were increased to make them prohibitive for the poor and courses were anyway rigidly controlled to prevent intelligent debate. The strange fact was that now Russia was so desperate to Russify all its ethnic minorities it could not even risk training enough teachers of the Russian language in case they also learned to think. Besides, French had for so long been the only polite language acceptable in upper class Russia. Sadly, since such a large and clumsy empire desperately needed well educated, competent administrators it dared not train them properly, for they might learn to question their masters and that was unacceptable.

Now that he was Emperor Alexander had no intention of risking the army in a war: that idea now offended his parsimonious instincts, but he did still want to pursue the Pan-Slav policy of expansion. His solution was therefore to move the attack underground. For example in Bulgaria, where he still resented the fact that Russia had not done better in the 1878 treaty, he infiltrated the area with agents. One trick was to set up special schools to train youngsters as rebels. They stirred up a mutiny in the Bulgarian army and arranged for the kidnapping of the uncooperative Prince Alexander of Battenburg, the Tsar's own distant cousin, who had been installed as ruler.

Similarly, Serbia was flooded with agents posing as icon salesmen but stirring up rebellion without really being able to deliver much effective help. It was a policy that must take at least some of the blame for the fanatical Serbian secret societies one of which, the Black Hand, caused so much trouble in August 1914. It won Alexander few friends, for later he was to say that little Montenegro was the only country that was a genuine ally.

The third main area for agent infiltration was Afghanistan when the Russians took over the city of Merv (now Mary in southern Turkmenistan near the Afghan border), and once more aroused the paranoia of the British, who not unreasonably feared Russian encroachment from Afghanistan into India. This became the period of 'The Great Game' between the two sides and very nearly led to war. Even in the far

North in Norway Russia tried to push the frontier at the expense of her neighbour.

Meanwhile at home, Alexander and his ministers did their utmost to put the clock back. Aristocratic landowners had suffered some minor decline since emancipation, so they had to be boosted. A new bank was founded in 1885 to give them cheap loans and they were given guaranteed majority powers in the *Zemstvos*. So they did not have to sell their lands but could simply pay for extra labour to work on them. The peasants on the other hand were only given access to dearer loans and found themselves restricted by new land managers, the *Zemskii Nachalniki*. Under the emancipation act the freed peasants often had too little land for it to be viable and such as they had was held in common, so there was little incentive to improve production methods and no cheap money to fund such investment. To add to the problems the peasant population was still rising, many were drifting into factory jobs in the towns or heading for Siberia. Peasant distress climaxed with the bad harvests of 1891-2 when there was famine in twenty of Russia's provinces and the government was not properly geared to supplementing the food chain.

The picture in the towns was not much better as there was an industrial recession in the 1880s. High tariffs had tended to protect inefficient industries and added to the cost of living. Workers frequently went on strike but achieved little, especially when they could often be replaced with cheaper child labour. It was not until 1891 that investment levels were raised when Alexander's new technocrat, the former railway executive Sergius Witte, took control. The Trans-Siberian railway was begun as a massive construction project; coal and iron outputs were doubled; industry generally expanded rapidly. Historically it was ironic that in this period Russian industrial expansion was essentially the product of government investment not private capitalism. Yet at this very time the frustrated opposition were beginning to read seriously the *Communist Manifesto* and other tracts that suggested that private capitalism was the root of all evil.

While all this was going on Alexander continued to keep away from the public in Gatchina where he practiced his relatively austere regime, cutting back on candles and hot water. His favourite entertainment was a beer evening where the participants swilled down half-gallon mugs. He enjoyed long walks with the family, often interrupting them to chop down an old tree or dig in a new one. His only two extravagances were the annual purchase of Fabergé eggs, which began in 1882 and his royal yachts, which became status symbols, especially when he sailed to meet all the other European royals at Fredensborg near Copenhagen, his wife's former home. Twenty railway wagons of luggage and 100 servants were loaded onto barges for Kronstadt where they transferred to the yacht *Livadiya* together with one cow for fresh milk. For a brief time the royal family regarded it as an escape from prison and relaxed with picnics down the Baltic. In Denmark Alexander was more his normal self, sharing dubious stories with Bismarck, flirting to his annoyance with Franz Joseph's new mistress Katherine Schratt and sharing Dagmar/Maria's distaste for Kaiser Wilhelm II who they referred to as 'an exhibitionist nuisance'.

One other luxury for Alexander III was his love of music. His favourite opera was Tchaikovsky's *Evgeni Onegin* and he was present at the premiere of the *Sixth Symphony – Pathetique* in 1893, shortly before the composer's death caused probably by drinking unboiled St Petersburg tap water.

If the Emperor was notable as being less ostentatious and extravagant than his predecessors the same could not be said of the rest of his family. In particular his two brothers Vladimir and Alexis were notorious for their champagne lifestyle and were well-known playboys on the Paris nightclub circuit which became 'La tournee des grands ducs.' When in St Petersburg they turned to racing troikas round the gypsy quarter in the early hours of the morning. On his own initiative Vladimir organised an unofficial extra police force known as the Holy Band while Alexis, known for 'slow ships and fast women,' set about doubling the size of the navy. Of his other brothers Grand Duke Sergei continued to make himself unpopular as the reactionary governor of Moscow and a regular visitor to dubious all-male clubs. Paul was banished from the Guards and from court for the more heinous sin of marrying a commoner.

Despite fairly competent security the terrorists still struck. Strelnikov was murdered in Kiev, a bomb was delivered to the Kremlin and there was even some paranoia about dynamite-filled eggs. Alexander, who slept with a pistol under his pillow, accidentally shot one of his own aides who had been rash enough to loosen the Tsar's collar when he seemed to be breathing with difficulty during a nap. Fear of terror became so widespread that Grand Duke Vladimir's private police force the Holy Band made a mockery of security by getting in the way of the professionals.

Whenever the royal train moved there was another look-alike royal train to confuse attackers. So it was still natural in 1888 to blame terrorists when the royal train went off the rails in the Borki Gorge on its way back from the Caucasus, but in fact an inquiry suggested the train had simply been going too fast on a fragile stretch of line. There were two long-term consequences of the crash. The railway investigator Sergius Witte was so impressive that he was rapidly promoted and became the architect of Russia's economic revival. Alexander himself used his huge strength to lever his family out of the wreckage, but his own injuries were later blamed for the kidney problems, which led to his early death six years later. The Empress and other ladies tore up their underskirts to use as bandages for the injured.

Yet though the odd terrorist incident continued, the opposition was regrouping itself all the time in a less violent, more practical form. In 1883 the Marxist thinker Georgi Plekhanov, who had been involved in the Narodnik demonstrations of 1876, founded a new party The League for the Emancipation of Labour, later to become the Russian Social Democratic Workers' party. Young Vladimir Ulyanov, later to be known as Lenin and to take over the mantle of Plekhanov, was expelled from Kazan University in 1887, the year that his brother was executed after a failed murder plot. It was also the same year that the future Polish leader Josef Pilsudski was sentenced to five years in Siberia for his efforts to win freedom for Poland.

As Alexander entered his late forties he still seemed strong and inde-structible, which is why he seems to have paid much less attention to the succession than his predecessors. He had a very low opinion of his eldest son and Nicholas, now in his twenties, was still unmarried. In fact Alexander had recently forbidden him to marry the German princess Alix of Hesse because he was entering an anti-German phase. He had mocked the suggestion that Nicholas should be made chairman of the Trans-Siberian Railway and thought him still too immature to involve in serious politics. He did not mention to him therefore the momentous realignment of Russian foreign policy, which he undertook in what was to be his final year. This meant abandoning the old alliance with the two kaisers, Wilhelm II of Germany and Franz Josef of Austria, with whom relationships had cooled over recent years, and instead he turned to the Republic of France on which the Romanovs had frowned for so many years. This momentous change of direction was to be a major contributory factor in the start of the First World War and consequentially also in the downfall of the dynasty twenty-three years later.

Suddenly in 1894 the Emperor began have nosebleeds and to lose weight, suffer from migraines and lose the strength of his legs. He was suffering from dropsy – nephritis or kidney failure blamed on the Borki crash – and having found that he could not sleep well at his Spala hunting lodge in Poland was sent south where his new yacht the *Polar Star* was anchored off the Livadiya Palace in the Crimea. Nothing could be done to save him and he died aged only forty-nine, too weak in those final days to give any serious brief to his nervous successor. Yet even if he had there is doubt if it would have made any difference. He had been a man trapped in his own reactionary education and the horrendous legacy of Romanov expectation.

Alexander was outlived by his wife Dagmar/Maria (d. 1928); his five brothers: Vladimir (d. 1909), Alexis (d. 1908), Sergei (murdered 1905) and Paul (executed 1919); his sister Marie the Duchess of Edinburgh (d. 1920); his half-siblings, children of his father's second wife, Catherine (d. 1922): George (d. 1913) Olga (d. 1925) and Catherine (d. 1959).

XIV

NICHOLAS II
THE HENPECKED HUSBAND

'I am not prepared to be the tsar. I never wanted to become one'

Nicholas II

Nicholas II (ruled 1894-1917) was twenty-nine when he found himself unexpectedly early in the position that he had dreaded from his early youth. Physically he was much shorter and thinner than his father, shy, diffident and suffering from low self-esteem. He had fine blue eyes and bore a very close resemblance, especially when they were both wearing beards, to his first cousin George, the son of Edward VII of Britain and his wife Alexandra, sister to Nicholas's own mother. He was the least German of all the tsars since Peter II, for his mother was Danish, albeit the Danish royal family did have German antecedents.

Nicholas was born in 1868 on the day of Job, which he later took to be an ill omen. He was not Alexander's eldest son for there had been another Alexander who died in infancy. He was brought up in the Spartan atmosphere of the Anichkov Palace with his two brothers and two sisters, though his best friend was the son of his Danish nanny. There the regime dictated 6 a.m. rises and a long walk to the nearest bathroom. Though his Danish mother doted on him his father remained remote and by his very size awesome, so the little boy became introverted and apparently humourless. He was provided with a Swiss tutor, Danilovich, who is credited with teaching him to disguise his feelings, and an English tutor called Charles Heath who gave him a good command of the English language. To this he soon added passable French and German but in terms of general knowledge his training was very limited and even such as there was he made little effort to absorb.

Then when he was twelve came the harrowing death of his grandfather. In his sailor suit he was brought in to say goodbye to the dying Tsar and kiss his cheek. This clearly had a deep impression, and not one likely to convert him to democracy. His education was rounded off with the reactionary ranting of the now elderly Pobednostsev, so that if there was ever any possibility of a mind open to ideas this was quickly squashed. Nicholas was neither bright enough nor brave enough to question the concept of Russian autocracy, which was dinned into his head at this time.

Once he came of age he found that army life suited him much better and he acquired the same life-long love of the parade ground as his last four predecessors. At eighteen he was made a squadron chief in the Hussars and later transferred to the Preobrazhensky Guards as a colonel. The humdrum training routine of a peacetime army and the camaraderie of summer manoeuvres were perfect for one who did not want difficult decisions or a complicated life. In the evenings there were the gypsy nightclubs from which, according to his diary, he was sometimes brought home seriously the worse for drink. Here he had his first unsuitable love affair with a singer. Then, apparently after she had been given a train ticket to exile, his father arranged an introduction to a slightly more respectable mistress, the ballet dancer Mathilde Kschessinska. This affair was interrupted when he first met Princess Alix of Hesse Darmstadt. She was on a visit to see her unlucky sister Ella, wife of Nicholas's uncle Grand Duke Sergei, the homosexual and anti-Semitic governor of Moscow. Alix, or Tinka as he called her, was only seventeen and as introverted as he was himself, so they hit it off, and did the St Petersburg party circuit together. But as a potential match it found no favour with her grandmother Queen Victoria (Alix's late mother had been Alice, Victoria's daughter), who thought Russia was too dangerous, nor with his parents who for mainly political reasons wanted nothing to do with Queen Victoria.

So in 1890, at the age of twenty-two Nicholas was sent off on a world tour with his brother George in order to keep him away from Alix. The trip took in Egypt, India and Japan where he was the object of a murder attempt by a religious fanatic while riding through the streets of Ossu in a rickshaw. This left him with a minor scar and a lasting contempt for the Japanese – he referred to them as 'monkeys' – which perhaps seriously impaired his judgement fourteen years later. Meanwhile he laid the first stone of the new railway terminal at Vladivostok.

When Nicholas was twenty-five Witte made the suggestion that he should become the chairman of the Trans-Siberian Railway. Alexander still regarded him as seriously immature and laughed at the idea but in due course it was accepted.

Nicholas attended the company's meetings and those of other government departments but remained apparently bored and contributed little. Then with the rest of his family he attended a wedding in Coburg where he once more met Alix and their love affair became serious. She was hesitant, particularly as she resented the compulsion to convert to Orthodoxy, but they spent six pleasant weeks together in England and the relationship blossomed. His parents still disapproved but as Alexander III suddenly began to sicken, the need for a fairly rapid marriage became imperative and the dying Tsar resigned himself when for once Nicholas stood up for something that he really cared about.

Soon afterwards Nicholas was summoned to the Crimea where his father now lay dying. Alix followed him and arrived in Livadiya to be shocked at the extent to which his family treated him as a nonentity. Thus, now that their wedding had at long last been authorised Alix (rechristened Alexandra but known to him as Sunny) set about stiffening her fiancé's spine for the first time. This was a task that was to dominate the twenty-one years of their marriage and contribute substantially to the demise of the dynasty, for, sadly, the issues upon which she was to persuade him to make a stand were so often the wrong ones.

So on his father's death Nicholas aged twenty-nine, with neither much ability for the job nor much training, took over as Emperor of an empire that now had a population of 130-150 million, probably about twice what it had been when his father assumed power, though only about 60 million of them were ethnic Russians. Its land mass stretched 5,000 miles from west to east and 1,000 from north to south and covered 8,750,000 square miles. The population was still largely illiterate and though heavy industry had expanded considerably there was neither much supply nor demand for consumer goods due to general poverty.

The population was also riven with ethnic and religious fault lines. Of the suppressed racial minorities the Poles with about 8 million were still the most vocal and the most bitter but there were also the other Slavonic groupings like the Ukrainians (2 million) and Belarussians (0.5 million) whose languages and customs suppression had damaged but not destroyed. If they had been given better treatment by the Romanovs their ethnic roots were close enough to the Muscovites for them all to have become a homogeneous nation, but the mainstream Russians had been too careless with their own racial identity, their leaders despising even the Russian language, and had thrown away such a possibility. In addition there were over 2 million Finns and about a million each of Georgians, Estonians, Latvians, Lithuanians, all recently repressed.

Around 2 million Jews had already or were just about to escape westwards but there were still around 5 million left stranded in the Pale from Lithuania to Odesa on the Black Sea. They had suffered severe suppression and it was noted years later that the Bolshevik leadership included a high proportion of Jews like Trotsky and Sverdlov who were believed to have been responsible for the execution of the last tsar and his family. To the east there were numerous survivors of the Tartar empires from small rebellious pockets like Chechnya to larger, newly conquered areas like Turkestan and Kazakstan. Some racial minorities like the Circassians had chosen to seek asylum in Turkey while others like the Armenians had come in the opposite direction. Yet as they poked around the Pacific Coast for new harbours the Romonovs were still intent on adding more minorities, for the Chinese of Manchuria were soon under threat and conflict with the Japanese over Korea was just around the corner.

The religious fault lines were just as deep. There were by this time an estimated 14 million Muslims in the Russian Empire and even they were not homogeneous for there were Sufis in Dagestan and Chechnya, Sunni in the Crimea and Shiites in the Caucasus. Then there was the strongly Catholic population of Poland and Lithuania, Lutherans in the other Baltic States, the Armenian and Georgian Churches and numerous minor sects. Again the conservatism of the State-controlled Moscow patriarchate and its long adherence to a half-dead language had made its conversion record very poor despite the huge numbers of vast cathedrals that it built in every provincial city from Helsinki to Vladovostok.

For some days Nicholas, who perhaps had a vague awareness of these problems, brooded on the shores of the Black Sea before at last being persuaded to tackle his unwanted role. He had never questioned his father's policies whilst he was alive and did not do so now when he was dead. Within a week he married Alexandra who soon made her first enemy at court, the Tsar's mother Dagmar, of whose undiminished influence over Nicholas she became increasingly jealous. Now that she was a Russian and a member of the Russian Orthodox Church she became an extreme nationalist for her new nation, a fanatical supporter of her new faith and an ardent proponent of old-fashioned autocracy. She probably therefore gave Nicholas encouragement for the speech that he made in January 1895 announcing commitment to his father's policy of undiminished authority for the Tsar. And though later damned for being German she looked on herself rather as a Hessian and disliked intensely the Prussian regime that had taken over Germany.

One of Nicholas's first major changes was in 1895, to renege on one of the more enlightened promises of his predecessors who had allowed relative freedom to the Finns and had therefore enjoyed something approaching cooperation in return. Nicholas cancelled their freedoms and imposed conscription into the Russian army, which proved both unpopular and unsuccessful. It was no coincidence that four years later the patriotic Finnish composer Sibelius wrote his *Finlandia*.

In May the same year came the first of a series of relatively minor disasters mixed with errors of judgement that cumulatively were to undermine the credibility of Nicholas as the father of his people. Immediately after the coronation in Moscow there was a stampede at the traditional feast provided for the population in Khodynka field. The number of casualties was bad enough (1,389 deaths was the published figure though widely thought to be a deliberate understatement), but even worse was the fact that Nicholas was still persuaded to go to a ball at the French embassy that same evening against his own judgement. His and Alexandra's actions were interpreted as callous and no efforts to visit the injured afterwards would make up for them. The vast number of free commemorative enamel mugs doled out was little compensation.

It did not help the popularity of the new Tsarina who was awkward in company, that she had not mastered the Russian language and was rarely known to smile. She tried to offset her red complexion with brocade and too many diamonds. Her prudish refusal to invite divorcees to her balls meant that they were sparsely attended and stilted affairs and she spent her time fussily redecorating the Alexander Palace at Tsarskoe Selo or consulting quack doctors about her pregnancies. Nor did it help the imperial couple that they had inherited a plethora of grand dukes and duchesses from the previous generation, most of them involved in marital scandal and bringing little credit to the dynasty. Of his four main uncles Alexis was still dabbling with the navy, Sergei was the reactionary governor of Moscow who had mismanaged the coronation banquet,

Vladimir patronised Diaghilev and his ballet while George lived in expensive exile.

While committed to being an autocrat Nicholas had no intention of doing anything but delegating the real work. Unlike most of his predecessors he tended to have prime ministers rather than heads of department reporting direct to him. He was quite conscientious about detail but usually failed to see the bigger picture. So he regularly lost faith quickly in ministers for the wrong reasons, often later because Alexandra found fault with them, so he replaced them with others who were even less suitable. Amongst his poor choices were Sipiagin, his Minister of the Interior until he was assassinated in 1902 and his successor, the psychotic police chief Vyacheslav Plehve. It was under Plehve's management that the infamous *Protocols of the Elders of Zion* was produced – the fictitious account of a Jewish plot to take over the world, to be used as an excuse for further persecution of the Jews. *Pogroms* were reckoned to appeal to most Russians' customary xenophobia and provide a useful distraction from other hardships. Nicholas was certainly anti-Semitic and encouraged this policy. Amongst other ethnic victims were the Finns, Poles, Armenians and the Chinese, for in 1903 Nicholas appointed the aggressive Alekseev as viceroy of Kwantung, the new Russian province on the Amur.

There was also suppression of political dissidents. In his mid-twenties the young lawyer Vladimir Ulyanov, or Lenin by this time, was sent to Siberia for three years in 1895 for his role in running the illegal Union for the Liberation of the Working Class in St Petersburg. Three years later the same fate awaited his younger contemporary Lev Davidovich Bronstein later known as Trotsky, a nineteen-year-old Ukrainian Jew who, after his escape, joined Lenin in London in 1902. The same year that Trotsky was sent to Siberia young Iosif Vissarionovich Dzhugashvili, born in Tiflis (Tbilisi) Georgia two years after Trotsky, and later known as Stalin, was expelled from Tiflis Seminary for preaching Marxism and soon afterwards he too was sent to Siberia.

Meanwhile since nothing had been done to sort out the basic problems of agriculture compounded by a rising population there were bad harvests and food shortages in 1897-98 and 1901, followed in many areas by peasant violence. For example, in Poltava and Kharkov it was particularly serious in 1902. These in turn were followed by waves of strikes, which became more violent in places like Rostov in 1903 and spread rapidly throughout Russia. The terrorists continued their assassination campaigns with Sipiagin Minister of the Interior, Bogolepov the Minister of Education, Grand Duke Sergei, the Tsar's uncle and the vicious Plehve himself, as the most prominent victims. Less violent though just as potentially effective opposition was being developed by new political parties such as the Social Democrats and the Socialist Revolutionary Party. Apparently less of a threat at this time was the meeting of the Russian Marxists in London in 1903 where the party was so divided about its future that it split into two factions, the Menshevik and Bolshevik, small and large. Yet despite all these signs of restlessness Nicholas chose completely to ignore a letter from the septuagenarian Leo Tolstoy warning him that he must change with the times.

The solution to all his problems that appealed most to Nicholas at this time was not to make concessions or undertake reform but to start a war which Russia would surely win and thus distract the people with a glorious victory. The target recommended to him by Plehve and his other minsters was Japan, still regarded as a backward oriental nation and easy to defeat. Besides, Nicholas still had a grudge against the 'monkeys' for the murder attempt back in 1890.

The original plan had been to annex Manchuria, helped by the fact that the Chinese were having the worst of a confrontation with the Japanese and sought Russian help. Witte, the old railway supremo, negotiated a deal for a rail extension that gave Russia access to Mukden (now Shenyang in China), the Liaotung peninsula, Port Arthur and Dalian, the attraction being that Port Arthur unlike Vladivostok was ice-free all year round and a base also for the economic exploitation of Korea. Japan in alarm made an alliance with the British and Witte urged caution. Kaiser Wilhelm muttered about 'the yellow peril' and tried to make Nicholas feel inadequate. It was agreed to withdraw Russian troops but Plehve was for aggression and the withdrawal was delayed. Instead Nicholas himself gave the provocative go-ahead to Russian infiltration of North Korea and timber exploitation on the Yalu River. The Japanese offered to have talks but when this was ignored they responded with an unexpected attack on Russian troops on the Yalu near the Korean border. This resulted in Port Arthur being cut off from Mukden. At the same time Admiral Togo made a surprise attack on the Russian fleet in Port Arthur, which was under the command of Admiral Evgeni Alekseev, believed to be an illegitimate son of Alexander II. The lights were burning brightly, there were no torpedo nets in place and the main guns could not function for lack of grease. Russian ships failed to avoid Japanese mines and Cyril, a cousin of the Emperor's who was serving in the fleet, was one of only eighty survivors from a crew of 500 in one of the ships that was sunk.

The Russians, despite superior numbers (around 250,000), failed to stop the Japanese at Liao-Yang and retreated. The Japanese fought with suicidal bravery, sometimes with suicide bombers, captured Port Arthur in January 1905 and drove the Russians northwards to Harbin. The Japanese had suffered around a quarter of a million casualties and the Russians perhaps the same, for the defence of Port Arthur alone cost 100,000 lives. The Russians might have been able to recover as they had access to reinforcements but even that was difficult as there was still a 25-mile gap in the Trans-Siberian railway where ferries were used in the summer to cross Lake Baikal and the trains ran across the ice in winter. One supply train disappeared without trace when the ice broke. The confidence of the Russians had been shattered anyway and the will to continue had gone.

In the meantime Nicholas had been distracted by events in his own household. In July 1904 Alexandra had at last, after four daughters in five years, produced a son, reason for great rejoicing but some ten weeks later the Tsarevitch was diagnosed as a haemophiliac and regarded as having not long to live. It was thus in the early autumn that Nicholas heard bad news both from Liao-Yang and about his son. At this time also he endorsed the decision to send the Baltic Fleet right round the world to rescue Port Arthur. It set sail in late October 1904, so ill-prepared and nervous that it fired on British trawlers near the Dogger Bank, imagining they were enemy torpedo boasts, an incident for which Nicholas obstinately refused to apologise to the British who would otherwise have let them take the shortcut through the Suez Canal. After a difficult six-month voyage via the Cape of Good Hope the fleet arrived in the Far East in May 1905 too late to save Port Arthur. It was then comprehensively defeated at Tsushima by the Japanese under Admiral Togo, with eight Russian battleships, seven cruisers and six destroyers sunk.

For Russia the losses sustained were far less damaging than for the Japanese and with persistence the Russian army could still have won, but the level of unrest at home was increasing, so when American President Theodore Roosevelt offered to broker a peace Nicholas agreed. It resulted in the loss of the Liaotung peninsula with Port Arthur to Japan. Manchuria went back to the Chinese for the time being. It was a devastating outcome for a regime whose greatest pride was its military.

Meanwhile Nicholas had been hit by a severe domestic crisis. Workers even in the elite Butilov works could barely make ends meet and many were below real subsistence level. A strike at the Putilov factory in January 1905 spread alarmingly and a charismatic priest called Georgi Gapon, who was also organiser of a labour union with police compliance, tried to coordinate a peaceful protest. His connections both with the Church and the police made him seek a compromise that would both satisfy the angriest of the strikers and not excite violent retaliation by the authorities. With a petition signed by 135,000 and a crowd even larger he headed to the Winter Palace to deliver the petition, singing hymns, carrying icons and portraits of Nicholas. Despite the fact that the Tsar was not in the Winter Palace but miles away at Tsarskoe Selo, the police and Cossack guards overreacted and began shooting. The number killed was probably several hundred but the repercussions of this Bloody Sunday massacre were far-reaching, particularly for Nicholas who was blamed despite his absence from the scene. Grand Duke Nicholas volunteered to share the blame as area commander for he had not issued clear orders of engagement to his troops. Spasmodic violence and protest continued throughout the summer, particularly with further bad news from the Far East, the humiliating defeats of Tsushima and Mukden.

In July came the seizure by its own crew of the battleship *Potemkin* in the Black Sea. The mutineers murdered their officers and when they saw that no other ships were joining them sailed it from Odesa to Rumania. There was a further wave of strikes and in October Witte recommended the calling of a representative assembly, the *Duma*. Having vacillated with divergent policies for the previous four months Nicholas at long last agreed. He asked his uncle Grand Duke Nicholas to act as a military dictator but he very sensibly refused.

If Nicholas had been wholehearted and taken the new policy seriously he could probably have saved his dynasty. But he was neither consistent nor strong-minded and a month after he made this decision, his wife was for the first time introduced by a friend to an itinerant holy man known as Rasputin or 'The Debauched'. She was a hypochondriac herself, as proven by her earlier relationship with a Dr Philippe in 1902 and was by this time also seeking any kind of cure for her haemophiliac son Alexis.

The problem was that Rasputin was not just a healer but immediately started to influence Alexandra's mind on other topics such as politics. This gave her the confidence to start undermining her husband's relationship with Witte whom she hated, in spite of or perhaps because he had been such a successful minister and failed to hide his contempt for Nicholas. So in May 1906, when the *Duma* had at last been elected, Witte was dismissed.

Rasputin had been born Gregori Efimovich around 1871 in the village of Pokrovskoe near Tobolsk and belonged to the type of wandering monastic order the *Khlysti*, who were totally reliant on begging for survival, and still highly regarded by many Russians. His receipt of royal patronage might therefore have caused no alarm, but for the fact that he took advantage of his new status to indulge his substantial sexual appetites with a defiant disregard for public opinion. In addition his exploits with so many other women suggested in the absence of any other known reason – and no ordinary Russians knew about the Tsarevich's illness – that his popularity with the Empress Alexandra must also have sexual implications.

From this time onwards, instead of supporting the new constitution and working with the new *Duma* Nicholas did his best to undermine both and thus undid any good that he had achieved by his 1905 decision. On at least two further occasions, the 300th anniversary of the dynasty in 1913 and the outbreak of war in August 1914, he was again to enjoy a mild resurgence in popularity but each time threw the opportunity of survival away.

Just before the opening of the first *Duma*, which had a reasonably wide franchise, Nicholas had sacked Witte the prime minister who had introduced it and had also helped salvage the ruins of his Japanese policy. He now made the mistake of appointing a mediocre reactionary, Ivan Goremykin, as Witte's replacement. The new *Duma*, which met with great excitement first in the St George's Hall of the Winter Palace, then in the Tauride Palace, was quickly deflated by the Emperor's lukewarm address and the antipathy to reform of his ministers. In an atmosphere where peasant violence and strikes were still prevalent it demanded radical change and was given no encouragement. When it asked for legislation about land reform it was palmed off after weeks with a bill for a new laundry at Dorpat University. Meanwhile Nicholas regained his confidence, regretting his surrender to the new constitution and taking note of Alexandra's insistence that he should ignore it. At the same time he was using the Semenovsky Guards and volunteer groups of vigilantes from the aristocracy to suppress the malcontents who were anyway beginning to run out of steam.

Within three months Nicholas appointed a new prime minister, Peter Stolypin, who dissolved the first *Duma* and had it replaced with one elected deviously on a narrower franchise. The result was a group only marginally less radical than the old one but Stolypin was much better able than Goremykin to handle it. He had himself just survived a bomb attack in which one of his children was seriously injured, but wisely mixed repression of terrorists with a more liberal approach to law-making, helped by yet another crafty reduction in the franchise for the election of the third *Duma* in 1907. 'Stolypin's Necktie' accounted for around 500 executions but at the same time he brought in genuine land reforms. These included the new law that ended the communal ownership of peasant land. Instead of uneconomical strips shared out communally, successful peasants, or *kulaks* as they came to be called, could now build up viable farm units in which they could invest for improvement and pass the holdings on to their children.

Some 3 million peasants were able to take advantage of this or other changes that let them sell up and move to Siberia or into cities. It was so successful that it nearly took the wind out of the sails of Lenin and other radicals who disliked the idea of small capitalist farmers and wanted a still dissatisfied peasantry to justify their own version of revolution.

Despite the fact that Nicholas and Alexandra were so preoccupied with their own family problem and so prejudiced against any point of view but their own they must at least have been conscious that the nation they led at this time had many talented and creative people. In 1895 Alexander Popov had invented his own version of wireless telegraphy at just about the same time as Marconi. In 1904 Ivan Pavlov, a pioneering physiologist from Ryazan, won a Nobel Prize for his work on mental reflexes, the same year that Chekhov saw the first night of his play *The Cherry Orchard*. In 1907 Igor Stravinsky from Oranienbaum, a pupil of Rimsky-Korsakov's, had the premiere of his *First Symphony* and three years later combined with Diaghilev for the ballet *The Firebird*. Anna Pavlova had danced the *Dying Swan* for Fokine in 1907 and Vaslav Nijinsky from Kiev led the Ballet Russe in 1909. Marc Chagall a young painter from Vitebsk had his first one-man show in 1914. Maxim Gorky, in exile, was just completing *Childhood*, the first volume of his auto-biographical trilogy. With so much talent and such social energy the Romanovs just needed to stand back and let it happen, but instead they blundered on as if they were indestructible.

The economic performance of Russia improved dramatically over the five-year period of the third *Duma* but Nicholas, urged on by his wife, was not content with success. Alexandra hated Stolypin for two reasons: he was abler and more confident than her husband so she felt he outshone him too much, but even worse Stolypin had the effrontery to complain about Rasputin. By this time Rasputin had been a regular visitor and sometimes long-term guest at Tsarskoe Selo for nearly seven years and had been regarded as indispensable for the survival of the delicate Tsarevitch. Throughout this period he had been involved in numerous drunken orgies and had exploited his hypnotic powers over otherwise respectable women who were fascinated by his strange mixture of other-worldly holiness and unwashed lust. Having just returned from a pilgrimage to Jerusalem, he was urging Alexandra and the Emperor to sack Stolypin when, in September 1911, the prime minister was shot at point blank range, pre-empting the decision.

The new prime minister, Count Vladimir Kokovtsev, was much less able than Stolypin and the fourth *Duma* was no easier to handle than the one before. Alexander Kerensky, the rising star of the Social Revolutionary Party was elected now for the first time and soon grew to be a key figure in the opposition, which became obsessed by the scandals connecting Rasputin with the royal family. Nicholas and Alexandra had kept the illness of their son as a closely guarded secret so any sympathy they might have received on that score was lost, nor could any of the Russian public therefore understand why the Emperor and his wife should tolerate Rasputin's rapes, abuses and acts of indecent exposure which were widely covered in the press. The gap in understanding between ruler and ruled was further exacerbated in 1912, when the Tsarevitch injured himself while on holiday in their Polish hunting lodge at Spala so that Nicholas was even more dependent on his help than usual. So the more the *Duma* attacked Rasputin the more Alexandra nagged Nicholas to dissolve it.

Nor were Nicholas, and more particularly Alexandra, even very popular amongst their own wider family. The prudish and somewhat anti-social temperament of the Empress, her peculiar relationship with

Rasputin and the slightly dim-witted dithering of the Emperor left many of the sixty or so other Romanovs in the capital frustrated and disillusioned, despite the fact that the Tsar's patronage ensured their lavish standard of living. Yet equally their generally parasitic existence was not a very good advertisement for the functional part of the dynasty. Nor did Nicholas make any real effort to curb expenditure, visiting Cowes for instance in his massive yacht the *Standart*, which had cabins as large as the bedrooms in Peterhof.

Nevertheless the year 1913 gave the Romanovs a chance to regain their popularity for it was the 300th anniversary of the dynasty's succession. The celebrations were well-enough managed to bring out modest crowds of rejoicing people in both St Petersburg and Moscow. Notable services took place in the Kazan Cathedral in the capital and the Uspensky in the Kremlin. The royal couple visited Kostroma and other sites associated with the rise of the Romanovs. Once again however, Alexandra could not forgive the *Duma* or the prime minister for their criticism of Rasputin. Kokovtsev was dismissed in January 1914 to be replaced by the even less effective Goremykin for his second term. Yet the *Duma* now turned its hatred to Ivan Shcheglovitov, the right-wing minister of justice, and Nicholas summoned his ministers to Peterhof in July 1914 to inform them that he was going to abolish the *Duma*. Luckily they dissuaded him from such a reactionary step, made all the more dangerous by the fact that a new crisis in the Balkans meant that there was the real possibility of war.

Three days before the cabinet meeting at Peterhof, the Arch Duke Ferdinand had been murdered by a Serb in Sarajevo. Within days the Austrians were demanding the punishment of the Serb culprits and as the threats escalated Nicholas made the foolhardy remark that, 'In no case would Russia remain indifferent to the fate of Serbia.' It was a piece of careless bombast, for Russia had never achieved anything of any moment for the Serbs in the past. The concept of shared ethnic origin and camaraderie was just populist sentimentality considering the way the Romanovs had treated their own Russians, let alone other related ethnic groups that they had absorbed. It was particularly dangerous to contemplate interfering between the Austrians and the Serbs because the Germans were likely to support the Austrians in any conflict. The fact that the French would then in turn support the Russians might be superficially comforting, but only so long as it was confined to diplomatic posturing, not to a real world war. Thus Nicholas did in the end sensibly urge the Serbs to cooperate with Austria.

But it was too late. At the same time as telling the Serbs to cool down Nicholas was also ordering a precautionary mobilisation of troops on the Austrian border. Then after a false report of German movements he extended the mobilisation to the German frontier. This was countermanded when the Germans complained but, after a succession of half decisions, by 30 July the Russian foreign minister, Sazonov, recommended total mobilisation, Nicholas signed it and his chief of staff cut off his phone in case the Tsar changed his mind.

The Germans responded by demanding total demobilisation and since this would have meant a huge loss of face Nicholas ignored them. So on 1 August Germany declared war on Russia. The next day the crowds sang *Te Deums* outside the Winter Palace. Within two weeks of that France and Britain had also joined in the conflict. It was by no means all the fault of Nicholas II but, along with the two other trigger-happy kaisers Wilhelm II and Franz Josef, he had played his part. None of them had properly foreseen the domino effect as one country after another was pulled into a major conflict as a result of half-forgotten treaties and mindless high-level blustering. Treaties that had been devised as a form of deterrent to war ended up having the opposite effect.

Surprisingly the threat of a major war enhanced rather than reduced the popularity of the Tsar and he was able to pose like his ancestor Alexander I as defender of the sacred fatherland. St Petersburg was renamed Petrograd to avoid its Germanic overtones. Even the left-wing leaders of the *Duma* like Kerensky rallied to the call. Amongst the very few serious protestors against war were the former minister Witte, and Rasputin who was at the time in his home village of Pokrovskoe recovering from an attempt on his life. It is reasonable to suggest therefore at this point that the fall of the Romanovs was still not inevitable. If the war had been effectively managed and the interference of a German-born empress had been less obvious all could still have been saved.

By the end of September Nicholas had conscripted 4 million men as the call came from Russia's ally France to create a diversion against the Germans. Initially the mobilisation was remarkably efficient thanks to improvements in the railways and also to the fact that there were sizeable armies already based in Vilnius, Warsaw and Kiev. Ironically much of the significant fighting between the three emperors took place in the territory of the nation their predecessors had chosen to carve up between them, Poland. In the German portion, East Prussia, the Kaiser promised all kinds of improvements, as did Franz Josef in Galicia, the Austrian province and Nicholas in his round Warsaw. To start with the war went well enough for the Russians since they managed to defeat an Austro-Hungarian army that totalled a million men, but it was a different matter when the Germans, under Hindenburg and Ludendorf, turned eastwards to help the Austrians. The Russian army was badly beaten at Tannenberg (now in Poland by Stebark, south of Dansk) in 1914 and then further east in the marshes of the Masurian Lakes. All Poland and most of Lithuania were lost. Within a year Russian casualties amounted to nearly 2 million men.

As ever, Russian organisation proved inadequate for long-distance campaigns: the war office was incompetent and supplies, particularly of ammunition, were short. When the *Duma* was recalled Goremykin was blamed for the disasters, but on Alexandra's advice Nicholas opposed the idea of a coalition government and foolishly adjourned the *Duma*. Meanwhile Alexandra had also taken a dislike to Commander in Chief Grand Duke Nicholas, the Tsar's uncle, who was a more imposing and respected figure, so she felt he outshone her husband. To make matters worse the Grand Duke despised Rasputin and had rashly threatened to hang him if he came to army headquarters. Even the Tsar's mother was so angry about Rasputin that she removed herself to Kiev in protest.

So, against the advice of all his ministers, Nicholas rashly took over from his uncle as Commander in Chief. Not only did this potentially expose him as incompetent in strategy but as he was now away in the *Stavka*, a mobile headquarters train in the forest near Mogilev (now Mahilyow in Belarus), it left a political vacuum in the capital. Thus, since there were no politicians of any calibre left in office, this was regrettably filled by the interfering Empress and her much-hated guru. Goremykin was removed again and the unpopular Sturmer took over as Prime Minister whilst the propaganda campaign against Alexandra and the priest, now generally assumed to be her lover, intensified. This was unfortunate as the Tsarevich had recently had another fall and Nicholas had to take time off to bring him back home for treatment. Alexandra simply scolded her husband, 'Be more severe, dearest', and lamented the loss of Poland since that was a crown that she thought belonged to her beloved Tsarevich. Even the fact that she often slaved away as an ordinary nurse in a military hospital did not salvage her image.

Surprisingly there was a brief improvement in the war effort during 1916. Ammunition supplies were restored, mainly thanks to General Polivanov whose success therefore offended Alexandra so that she got Nicholas to dismiss him. The army under General Alexis Brusilov made reasonable advances against Austria during the summer, though there were a million more casualties. But affairs on the domestic front were worse. There was rampant inflation due to the war and the cost of living had increased three-fold. There were serious food shortages. When the *Duma* was recalled, Sturmer was dismissed to the foreign office and Alexander Protopopov, a member of the Rasputin circle, was made Minister of the Interior. Sturmer did much more harm than good by bringing Rumania into the war with the effect that the Germans easily conquered it and thus outflanked Brusilov's offensive.

One problem at least was ended in December 1916 when Rasputin was murdered by Prince Yusupov, a Romanov relation with at least one Romanov grand duke amongst his accomplices, Dmitri Pavlovich. After poisoning and shooting still had not killed the victim at Yusupov's palace by the Moyka Canal, he was reputedly drowned under the ice of the Malaya Neva. Clearly the plotters expected a real change of policy to follow, but no such change materialised. Nor did it improve relations between the *Duma* and the Empress, while the Emperor was still acting the part of Commander in Chief at Mogilev. Alexander Trepov became briefly Prime Minister only to be replaced soon afterwards by Nicholas Golitsyn.

As 1917 opened there were waves of strikes in the Petrograd factories and the response from Nicholas was that he would use force to suppress them. Naturally this had little effect and it was far from clear that he had sufficient loyal troops remaining to carry it out. Mikhail Rodzianko, the *Duma's* moderate president, warned Nicholas that the country was on the verge of revolution but he ignored advice. Anyway it was too late. On 1 March bread rationing was introduced and the bakeries were soon empty. By 8 March (new style calendar, otherwise 22 Feb) there were over 100,000 workers out on strike and the mood was growing violent, crowds were shouting, 'Down with the German woman.' On 12 March mutineers from the Probrazhensky Guard joined the strikers at Vyborg, an ominous sign. So was the fact that the Petrograd Soviet met once more in the Tauride Palace. Nicholas's message, 'I command that the disorders in the capital be stopped', was hardly realistic and when the Volsky machine gun detachment fired on the crowds things only got worse.

Some of its gunners had joined the mutineers and the only troops still loyal to the Tsar, about 2,000, were isolated in the Winter Palace. They had to evacuate even there when the revolutionaries, who took the Peter and Paul fortress on the other side of the Neva, pointed guns in their direction. The next day Nicholas, who despite the advice of two grand dukes had refused to yield ground on a new constitution, took the train from Mogilev to Petrograd and was stopped half-way at Dno by railway workers on the orders of the *Duma*. Having back-tracked to Pskov he telephoned Rodzianko and offered to reduce the powers of the tsar, so there could be a proper constitutional monarchy with Rodzianko as Prime Minister. It was a huge climb-down for Nicholas who had totally ignored previous suggestions from the despised 'fat Rodzianko.' But now it was too late and the reply came that things had gone too far for such a moderate plan to work. By this time there had been around 1,300 casualties, minuscule compared with the losses during the war: out of an army of 15 million, 7 million had been killed, wounded or captured.

Meanwhile the *Duma* and Petrograd *Soviet* haggled over the formation of a new government. Grand Duke Cyril broke ranks by swearing allegiance to the Provisional Committee, using as his excuse that this was the only way to keep the allegiance of his navy guards. On 15 March the Committee agreed to demand the Tsar's abdication and sent two of their members to meet him at Pskov. Nicholas, still waiting in his train, had just received a note from his top five generals, including Grand Duke Nicholas saying that they too all thought he must abdicate. Initially Nicholas signed a deed of abdication in favour of his son, Emperor Alexis II, with his own brother Grand Duke Mikhail as Regent. A few hours later, when doctors advised him that Alexis's haemophilia was incurable, he replaced it with a new deed handing over the throne to his brother.

Mikhail lived at 110 Milliony Street in Petrograd. When the two *Duma* members who had received Nicholas's abdication in Pskov announced the possibility of his accession to the crowd there were loud protests. Most of the members of the new government were against retaining any form of monarchy, except surprisingly Milyukov and Kerensky, now vice-president of the *Duma* and Minister of Justice. Mikhail was neither very strong physically nor tough mentally and was extremely cautious in response to his brother's telegram asking him to take over. In the end, on advice from Kerensky, Mikhail II abdicated within a day and the Romanov dynasty was over.

The revolution had been relatively bloodless and the Provisional Government under Prince Lvov could not be described as extremist, but ominously a few days after the abdication Lenin, helped by the Germans, made his famous journey in a sealed train from Geneva to Petrograd. He told his followers to prepare for a second revolution that would do away with the Provisional Government. As it turned out he was a little premature and had to beat a temporary retreat to Finland until July, but he was already planning the next stage.

Meanwhile Nicholas asked if he could go back to Mogilev to say goodbye to his troops who were still fighting the war. When Alexandra tried to send him telegrams they were returned with 'Address unknown', and the electricity at Tsarskoe Selo had been turned off. But in due course Mr Colonel or Citizen Romanov came home to Tsarskoe Selo and the royal family were united under a kind of house arrest, which was explained as protective custody in case of murder attempts. Many visitors commented that at this point Nicholas seemed to be much happier now that he was relieved of the awesome problems of decision-making. Alexandra too seemed much more relaxed, simply being an ordinary mother with no more obsessions about politics.

At this point there was no reason to think that the royal couple would not be allowed to live out their retirement peacefully as Tsarskoe Selo. But the new government, first under Prince Lvov as Prime Minister and later under Kerensky, made several crucial mistakes: the most serious being to continue the war against Germany. This in turn led to delays in solving the problem of peasant land distribution and also to neglecting the food supply in a nation already beset by inflation and shortages. In this atmosphere the factory workers soon resumed their unrest and within four months of the abdication the riots and strikes had begun again. The violence of the period known as the July Days ensued. It was in this atmosphere that Kerensky decided to move the royal family out of harm's way to Tobolsk on the far side of the Urals, 700 miles east of Moscow. They left just in time, for the Kronstadt sailors were already planning a march on Tsarskoe Selo.

As it turned out Lenin's attempted take-over in July did not materialise and he had to head back over the border to Finland, but as the war continued conditions deteriorated, the Provisional Government's position became weaker and weaker.

King George V of Britain had offered political asylum to his first cousin the ex-emperor and his family, but at the time there was a smallpox scare and no action was taken. Anyway, at this point Nicholas was still hoping to be allowed to retire to the Livadiya palace in the Crimea. Later George V became alarmed at the potential repercussions of having the Romanovs in London, so the offer of asylum to his 'dear friend Nicky' was withdrawn.

Nicholas and his family were in Tobolsk for ten months until May 1918 but meanwhile the situation had changed radically in Petrograd. In October 1917 the Provisional Government's insistence on continuing the war had brought about its downfall and, under Lenin, the Bolsheviks took over power. The Winter Palace had been stormed: the cruiser *Aurora* had turned its guns on the city and the Provisional Government had been removed. This might, on its own, not have caused any immediate danger for the Romanovs, but the civil war between the Whites and Reds that followed made matters much worse for them. In May 1918 the family were moved from Tobolsk to Ipatiev House in Ekaterinburg to the south west and closer to the Urals. Here as the hardships and bitterness of the civil war were felt over wide areas the treatment of the ex-emperor and his family became markedly more unpleasant. They were subjected to reduced food rations and deliberate humiliations such as total loss of privacy. Then as the possibility arose of them being rescued by a detachment of the White Army, a Cheka squad was sent to execute them, probably on the orders of Lenin himself. Sulphuric acid was poured on the bodies before some or all of them were dropped down a mineshaft. Five of the bodies were later shifted to an unmarked grave in the forest. There was an initial investigation afterwards by Sokolov, a White Russian lawyer, then another by the Bolshevik Bykov, but both agreed that the whole family had been killed. Nearly eighty years later the remains were recovered and what was left of the last emperor was buried beside his forbears in the Cathedral of Peter and Paul in St Petersburg.

EPILOGUE
THE SURVIVORS

'For a period of thirty years from 1876-1904 486 people were executed, in other words about 17 people per year for the whole country ... In a period of sixteen months June 1918 to October 1919 more than sixteen thousand were shot which is to say more than one thousand per month'

Alexander Solzhenitsyn, *The Gulag Archipelago*

'Waves of revolution swept across Russia, each greater and more extraordinary than the last'

Boris Pasternak, *Dr Zhivago*

As on so many previous occasions, when tsars had died in mysterious circumstances, there were rumours that some of the family had survived, and people purporting to be such survivors appeared fairly regularly during the 1920s. Just as the rise of the Romanovs had followed a period when there were look-alike Dimitris and other resurrected candidates for tsardom, so their fall was followed by a succession of unlikely resurrections.

The least likely survivor but, if genuine, the most significant would have been Tsarevich Alexis who would have bled to death with even a minor wound, though there are some who argue that the blood disorder was exaggerated. At least four would-be tsareviches did turn up – one in Siberia, one in Baghdad and a third as a Polish Colonel Goleniewski who defected to the United States in 1964, looking young for his age. He did some work for the CIA and lived on Long Island. There was a rumoured fortune at stake, some said $400,000,000 buried in various banks, but equally there was evidence that Nicholas II had directed any spare cash that he had towards the war effort and that is perhaps more likely. The fourth supposed tsarevich lived in Ireland under the name of Nikolai Chebotarev and died at the age of eighty-three in 1987, allegedly having produced a son from an affair with Princess Marina of Kent.

The best-known and most arduously researched of the claimants to survival was the would-be Tsarevna Anastasia who appeared in Germany in 1920. She claimed to have been rescued by a man called Tchikovsky with whom she had a child. She had a nervous breakdown afterwards before reappearing in Germany when she tried to drown herself in a Berlin canal. She convinced some but not others and eventually settled down under the name of Anna Anderson or Manahan (her husband by this time was a history lecturer John Manahan), dying in Virginia in 1984 at the age of eighty-two. Subsequent DNA analysis suggested conclusively that she was a fake.

There were even some sightings of Nicholas II himself in various parts of the world, but curiously no one made any effort to return as the ex-Empress Alexandra. Besides, bone remnants of Nicholas, Alexandra and three of their daughters were unearthed in Siberia in 1990 and their identities confirmed by DNA. In 2007, Russian archaeologists working in the same area unearthed the remains of two bodies which corresponded with the descriptions of Tsarevich Alexis and the missing fourth daughter. DNA tests were to follow.

The two ablest genuine survivors of the old dynasty were, firstly the Grand Duke Nicholas (1856-1929) who had been restored briefly as commander of the Russian army after the abdication. He escaped after the October Revolution to live in Paris and died there in 1929 still planning to reconquer Russia from the Bolsheviks. The other notable survivor was Cyril, the son of Vladimir, who had been one of the few officers to survive the naval battle of Tsushima with any credit. After escaping to Finland he too settled in France, proclaiming himself the Emperor Cyril in 1924. Sadly, he then became an admirer of Italian fascism and made himself even less credible by encouraging strange salutes and black shirts from his home St Briac in Brittany. When he died in 1928 he passed on his shadowy title to his son Vladimir. His daughter Kira caused some excitement when she married Louis Frederick Hohenzollern, the heir of the ex-Kaiser, and at that time an employee of the Ford Motor Company, later with Lufthansa. But this was really no more than musical chairs amongst the different groups of émigré royals, none of whom were remotely likely to regain power.

Of the other grand dukes, the nearest to the throne Mikhail who had been emperor in theory for a few hours was executed shortly before his brother Nicholas, though his son, George Count Brassov, survived till a car crash in 1931, and his wife till 1952.

The sister of the Empress, Elizabeth or Ella, the saintly widow of Grand Duke Sergei the anti-Semitic governor of Moscow, was thrust along with several other Romanovs down a mineshaft at Alopaevsk in June 1918, and allegedly the sound of hymns was heard for some time afterwards from its depths until rubble was poured down on top of them. Another group of grand dukes and princes was shot at the Peter and Paul fortress, St Petersburg in January 1919. It included Grand Duke Paul (son of Alexander II), Grand Duke Nicholas Mikhailovich together with his brother George and Grand Duke Dimitri Konstantinovich, but in total, of the grand dukes still alive at the time of the revolution, eight out of fifteen survived.

The senior female survivor was Dagmar, the dowager empress Maria, widow of Alexander III. She was looked after by the British whose dowager Queen Alexandra was her sister, but then moved back to Denmark where she died in 1928. Two of her daughters, Xenia and Olga, also survived with their families in London and Canada, so the Romanovs soon multiplied again though none of them seem to have found the alleged Romanov treasure. Xenia was the last of the genuine grand duchesses to die – not till 1960 when she was eighty-four. She outlasted the ex-Tsar's other sister, Olga, who died in her flat in Toronto in 1959. The last genuine grand duke to die was Dmitri who, after service with the British army, had spent some of his time as a champagne salesman and lasted till 1941. Prince Yusupov, the murderer of Rasputin, died in Auteil in Paris in 1967 at the age of eighty-one. Rasputin's daughter Maria appeared in New York in 1938 as a lion tamer.

Amazingly, all of Alexander II's second family survived the revolution other than Boris who had died at birth and George who died before the revolution began. Alexander's one-time mistress and later second wife Princess Catherine Yuirevskaya lived till 1922 in France, her elder daughter Olga till 1925 and her younger Catherine, the would-be opera singer till 1959.

Of the other characters that contributed to the fall of the Romanovs, Kerensky eventually became a lecturer at Stanford University, USA and

Right: 1 St Basil's Cathedral, Moscow, burial place of Anastasia Romanovna's favourite holy man

Below: 2 Tsar Feodor's 40-ton cannon, *Pushka*, cast in 1586

Left: 3 The seven-storey Trinity Tower used as the ceremonial entrance to the Kremlin by the tsars

Below: 4 The Cathedral of the Annunciation where Ivan IV married Anastasia Romanovna in 1547. Alongside is the Great Kremlin Palace built for Nicholas I in 1837

5 The Bolshoe Theatre, Moscow, originally founded by Catherine the Great in 1780, but twice burnt down and rebuilt

6 The Cathedral of Assumption where all the tsars were crowned, with part of the Faceted Palace on the left

Above: 7 The Kremlin wall seen from the Moskva River with the Ivan the Great Bell Tower and Assumption Belfry to the right

Left: 8 The Bronze Horseman, Falconet's statue of Peter the Great erected by Catherine the Great in St Petersburg

Right: 9 The walls of the Peter and Paul Fortress, the first building begun by Peter the Great in his new city, St Petersburg, in 1703. The tower of its cathedral was meant to dominate the skyline and below it was the new burial place for the tsars

Below: 10 The Great Cascade built to celebrate the naval victory over the Swedes. It is 20 miles west of St Petersburg in front of the Peterhof Great Palace, begun by Peter the Great but rebuilt by Elizabeth

11 The superb façade of the Winter Palace begun by Peter the Great but substantially rebuilt by his successors, particularly Catherine. Behind it was her Hermitage, which as an art gallery has now been extended to use most of the Palace. The Palace was used as a base for the Provisional Government in 1917, hence the incident when it was stormed by the Communists in October 1917

12 Part of the Winter Palace interior

Above: 13 The Smolny Convent Cathedral built for Elizabeth in 1748. The Institute was added later as a school for girls by Catherine the Great

Right: 14 The statue of the eccentric Tsar Paul in front of his new palace at Pavlovsk outside St Petersburg. It has been largely rebuilt since its virtual destruction by the Germans in 1941

Left: 15
The Spilt
Blood
Cathedral
built on the
spot where
Alexander
II was
assassinated in
St Petersburg
in 1881

Below: 16
The cruiser
Aurora, a
veteran of
the Japanese
war in 1904
and famous
for firing a
shell at the
Winter Palace
to begin the
October 1917
revolution

died in 1970. Lenin survived an assassination attempt in 1918 but took a severe stroke in 1924, dying when he was only fifty-four. Leon Trotsky was exiled to Central Asia in 1927, later sentenced to death and then in 1940 murdered in Mexico City on the orders of Stalin. Josef Stalin survived them all to be a more successful empire builder than any of the tsars and also a more ruthless one, for his internal reforms alone cost some 10 million lives.

Sadly, what outlived the Romanov dynasty was the obsession that had driven it, which made control of a huge amorphous empire the excuse for ignoring freedoms and bullying those who objected. The Bolsheviks were in their own way just as obsessive as the Romanovs. In the first decade of the twenty-first century, as Vladimir Putin acted in many ways just like a Romanov, there was still a question mark over how well Russia is able to cope with democracy itself, let alone the numerous small states that have emerged or re-emerged since the collapse of the Soviet Union.

PART THREE

A TOUR AROUND THE
EMPIRE OF THE ROMANOVS

THE TOUR

A tour of the vast number of palaces and other buildings left by the Romanovs inevitably leaves a dual impression: on the one hand of unbelievable extravagance and exploitation of a virtually enslaved labour force; on the other an extraordinary heritage of architectural beauty which hardly any other dynasty in world history came near to matching. It also leaves an impression of the large number of nationalities and cultures which the Romanovs absorbed into their empire and attempted but failed to suppress, leaving a litter of now empty Orthodox cathedrals and palaces in nations that have come back to independence since the collapse of the Soviet Union.

This is not meant to be a substitute for conventional guidebooks but simply to relate the history and achievements of the Romanovs to surviving sites and monuments both in the former Russian Empire and other parts of the world.

Overleaf:

Maps

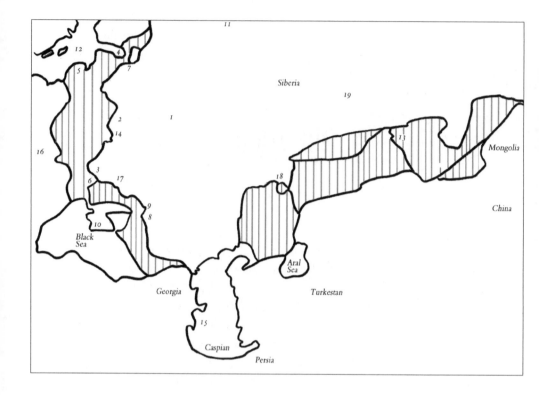

1 RUSSIAN EMPIRE showing additions from Peter to Catherine the Great

1	Moscow	8	Azov	15	Baku
2	Smolensk	9	Taganrog	16	Poland
3	Kiev	10	Sebastopol	17	Ukraine
4	Narva	11	Archangelsk	18	Orenburg
5	Talinn (Reval)	12	Baltic Sea	19	Perm
6	Vilnius	13	Omsk		
7	St Petersburg	14	Minsk		

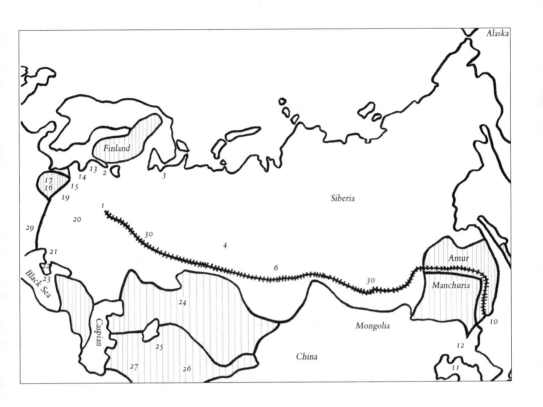

2 RUSSIAN EMPIRE from Catherine the Great to Nicholas II, showing additions 1796–1900

1	Moscow	12	Mukden	23	Sebastopol
2	St Petersburg	13	Tallinn	24	Kazakhstan
3	Archangelsk	14	Riga	25	Turkestan
4	Tobolsk	15	Vilnius	26	Dushanbe
5	Ekaterinburg	16	Poland	27	Mary-Merv
6	Tomsk	17	Warsaw	28	Almaty
7	Kabul	18	Smolensk	29	Bessarabia
8	Yakutsk	19	Minsk	30	Trans-Siberian
9	Okhotsk	20	Kiev		Railway
10	Vladivostok	21	Odesa		
11	Port Arthur	22	Crimea		

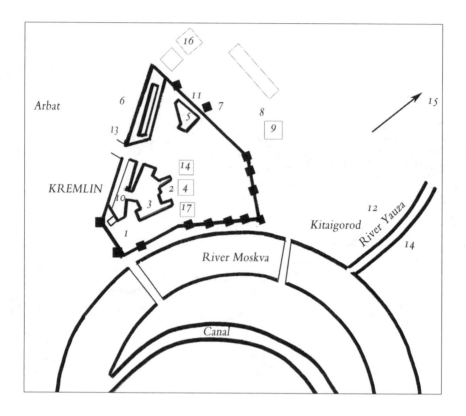

3 PLAN OF HISTORIC MOSCOW

1 State Armoury	8 Lobnoe Mesto	14 Cathedral of the Assumpion
2 Faceted Palace	9 St Basil Cathedral	15 Preobrazhenskoe Palace
3 Great Kremlin Palace	10 Terem Palace	16 Kazan Cathedral
4 Ivan the Great Bell Tower	11 Lenin Mausoleum	17 Cathedral of the Archangel
5 Senate	12 Nemetskaya Sloboda	
6 Arsenal	13 Trinity Tower	
7 Red Square		

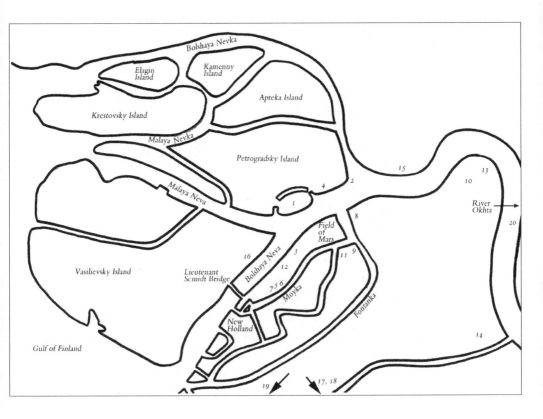

4 PLAN OF HISTORIC ST PETERSBURG

1	Peter and Paul Fortress	8	Summer Palace	15	Finland Station
2	Cruiser *Aurora*	9	Mikhailovsky Palace	16	Menshikov Palace
3	Winter Palace	10	Tauride Palace	17	Chesme
4	Peter the Great's cottage	11	Cathedral of Saviour on spilled blood	18	Route to Tsarsoe Selo
5	The Bronze Horseman	12	Admiralty	19	Route to Peterhof
6	St Isaac's Cathedral	13	Smolny Institute	20	Fort Nienschantz
7	Decembrist's Square	14	Alexander Nevsky Monastery		

RUSSIA (ROSSIYA)

Moscow (Moskva)

Moscow first became prominent under Ivan Kalita (1325-40), shortly before the ancestors of the Romanovs arrived from Lithuania and when the city was able to grow as a taxation centre for the Mongol overlords. It then developed further as an independent state under its own ancient Rurik dynasty, gradually overcoming its neighbours until the death of Ivan the Terrible and Anastasia Romanovna's son Tsar Feodor in 1598 brought the dynasty to an end and resulted in a crisis. This lasted till the first Romanov tsar was appointed in 1613. Moscow remained the capital of an expanding Russia till 1712 when St Petersburg took over, resuming as capital again in 1918 under Lenin. It is now a city of 10 million people.

The **Kremlin (Kreml)**: The original wooden fortress or Kremlin was founded in 1156 at the junction of the Moskva and Neglinnaya rivers, triangular in shape with each of the three sides about 600m in length. It was substantially rebuilt by Ivan III and now has nineteen towers around the perimeter. Among the best known are the **Trinity Tower**, the tallest at seven storeys high and built in 1495. Napoleon marched through it in 1812 when he captured Moscow, and the tsars and their wives normally used it. It was linked by a bridge over the River Neglinnaya, now channelled underground, to the Clumsy Old Woman or Kutafya Tower, the only survivor from the earlier set of towers built to defend the Kremlin.

The Saviour's Tower which dominates one side of Red Square is 79m high and named after an icon of Jesus installed over the gate in 1648 after fancy upper works were added to the tower in 1625 by an English architect brought in by Tsar Mikhail. Everyone entering, including the Tsar, had to raise his hat to the icon. The chimes of the clock have been used to play various patriotic tunes.

The Nicholas Tower was the one through which Moscow was recaptured from the Poles by the Russians in 1612, just before the first Romanov tsar was installed. The Secret Tower or Tainitskaya supposedly had an underground passage leading to the river and also an as-yet-never-recovered cache of books and documents from Ivan IV.

The Beklemishevskaya Tower recalls the execution there of the Boyar rebel Beklemishev by Ivan III to discourage his comrades. This tower was also used as a gaol and torture chamber. Until the late seventeenth century all the bridges across the Moscow River were made of wood as were most houses. In the early Romanov period there was a shift towards at least having brick or stone foundations for aristocratic homes and by this time the predominant stone colour of the Kremlin buildings was white.

The **Patriarch's Palace (Patriarshy Dvoretz)**: The Patriarch Nikon, the ambitious and intolerant Church reformer, who served under Tsar Alexis, rebuilt the palace in 1656. It includes its own Church of the Twelve Apostles. Now a museum, it houses a substantial collection of icons, church robes and the school book of Tsarevich Alexis.

The **Faceted Palace (Granovitaya Palata)**: This is a surviving section of the original tsarist palace built in 1491 for Ivan III and receives its name from the distinctive Italianate stonework. Its main vaulted hall was the throne room and banqueting hall of the tsars. It was exotically repainted in the 1880s. On its south side is the **Red Staircase**, scene of the massacre of Peter the Great's relations by the *Streltsi*. It had been demolished under the Communist regime but Boris Yeltsin had it rebuilt.

Next door is the **Terem Palace (Teremnoe Dvorets)** with its extra two storeys added in 1635 for the first Romanov tsar, Mikhail. It takes its name from the Terem or women's quarters on its top floor, which has a steep red and white chequered roof. Beneath were five luxuriously furnished rooms for the tsar, a council chamber where he met the boyars, an ante-room for foreign ambassadors and other distinguished visitors to wait for an audience, his throne room, his bedroom and a small room for prayer. The elaborate carvings include the double-headed eagle adopted from Byzantium.

Alongside is the **Church of the Deposition of the Robe (Tserkov Rizpolozheniya)** with its single gold dome celebrating the arrival in 1485 of a robe of the Virgin Mary brought from Constantinople and credited with several times saving Moscow from capture by enemies.

The **Great Kremlin Palace (Bolshoy Kremlevsky Dvorets)** with its yellow and white façade was built for Nicholas I in 1837-49 as a new Moscow residence for the emperor and his family. The private rooms were on the ground floor and the state chambers on the first floor include a number of huge ceremonial halls. The white-walled St George's Hall has the names engraved in gold of all those awarded the much-coveted Order of St George.

The **State Armoury (Oruzheynaya Palata)** was used as a factory to produce weapons, icons, gold and silver wear. It was much extended in 1508, then rebuilt under Nicholas I in 1851.Its collection includes the golden carriage given to Catherine the Great by her lover Gregori Orlov and the famous Orlov Diamond that he gave to her for inclusion on her sceptre. There is another carriage sent by Elizabeth or James I of Great Britain to Boris Godunov. The sacred gold crown of Monomakh, sent to Russia from Constantinople in the fourteenth century was used at Romanov coronations until 1682. Catherine the Great's elaborate coronation dress is on display as is a huge collection of her jewellery, her new crown that had 5,000 gems including the later addition of the Shah Diamond given to Nicholas I by Shah Mirza of Persia, the Diamond Throne made in Persia for Tsar Alexis in 1659 and a number of Fabergé eggs.

The **Arsenal** was commissioned by Peter the Great in 1701 but damaged by fire in 1711, delayed while he cancelled all building work in Moscow to concentrate on St Petersburg, then recompleted in 1736. It was badly damaged by Napoleon's troops in 1812 and rebuilt in neo-classical style with a yellow and white façade in 1825 for Alexander I. The huge array of cannons includes a number left behind by Napoleon's retreating forces.

The **Ivan the Great Bell Tower (Kolokolnaya Ivana Velikovo)** named after Grand Prince Ivan Kalita dates from 1505 but was increased in height by Boris Godunov in 1600 to make it the tallest building in Moscow of its time at 81m. The 64-ton largest bell in the Assumption Belfry was rung three times whenever a tsar died. The tent-roofed annex was built for Patriarch Filaret Romanov, father of the first Romanov tsar in 1642. The Tsar Bell, at 200 tons the largest bell in the world was ordered by Tsar Alexei, the second Romanov, but fell from the tower and was broken in the fire of 1701. The bits were recycled for Tsarina Anna but the new bell was damaged by another fire in 1737 before it could be hung.

The **Tsar Cannon-Pushka**, at 40 tons the world's largest, was built for Tsar Feodor I, son of Ivan the Terrible and Anastasia Romanovna, but it proved too heavy to move.

The three Kremlin cathedrals all date from the period of Ivan III and are all of the same fine white stone. The **Cathedral of the Assumption or Dormition (Uspensky Sobor)**, rebuilt under Ivan the Terrible by an Italian after its predecessor had been wrecked by an earthquake is the most important church in Moscow. Modelled on the Dormition Cathedral at Vladimir it was the place of enthronement of the tsars and of burial for the patriarchs. With its five gold cupola towers it contains the Monomakh Throne made especially for Ivan IV and the gilded tsarina's throne with its double-headed eagle used by Anastasia Romanovna. It was looted by Napoleon who used it as a stable in 1812 and the great chandelier was made from melted-down silver recaptured from the French invaders.

Cathedral of the Archangel (Arkhangelsky Sobor) was built by a Venetian architect for Ivan III on the site used for the burial of tsars since the 1340s. All the Muscovite tsars were buried in white stone sarcophagi with bronze covers, but from Peter the Great onwards the royal burial place was moved to St Petersburg, except for Peter II who died from smallpox in Moscow in 1730. The superb frescoes date from the period of Tsar Alexei and the icon factory in the State Armoury. There are historical paintings of tsarist triumphs by Simon Ushakov and full-length portraits of all the early tsars and of their protector the Archangel Mikhail after whom the cathedral is named.

The Cathedral of the Annunciation (Blagoveshchensky Sobor) was also built for Ivan III but by a Russian architect as the private chapel of the tsars next to the palace. It has its distinctive cluster of white towers with golden, onion-shaped cupolas. Here Ivan the Terrible and Anastasia Romanovna were married in 1547. It has an extension built by Ivan IV in 1572 when he wanted to marry for the fourth time but was not allowed to do so in an existing church.

The Senate was first built with its yellow façade for Catherine the Great by her favourite architect, Matvey Kazakov, and had a rotunda symbolising the happiness expected of her enlightened rule. It was partly rebuilt in the late 1790s in neo-classical style for Alexander I and later housed Stalin's military headquarters during the Second World War. One side faces Red Square and looks towards Lenin's Mausoleum.

The **Alexander Gardens (Aleksandrovsky Sad)** were part of the reconstruction project of Alexander I after the fires of 1812, when the Neglinnaya River, once part of the defensive moat of the Kremlin was channelled underground to allow new landscaping as a park. It contains the obelisk put up by Nicholas II in 1913 to mark the 300th anniversary of the Romanov dynasty.

To the east of the Kremlin is **Red Square (Krasnaya Ploshchad)**. The name red suited it in Communist times but the Russian word *Krasnoe* also means beautiful, which may have been the original intention as it began life as a space cleared by Ivan III for use as a market square for pageants and ceremonials. At its northern end is the **State Historical Museum** built in the reign of Nicholas II as was the **Gum Department Store** completed in 1894 which dominates the east side facing the **Lenin Mausoleum**.

Between them is **Kazan Cathedral (Kazansky Sobor)** an exact replica of the original erected in 1637 under Tsar Alexis to house the icon of the Kazan Virgin (also a replica as the original was stolen in 1904), which had inspired the recapture of Moscow from the Poles in 1612. Beside it is the **Resurrection Gate (Voskresenskie Vorota)** with its twin red towers, another replica from the Yeltsin era replacing the original built in 1680 but destroyed in 1931 with its mosaics of St George, the patron saint of Moscow. All tsars visiting Moscow were expected to call first at the chapel here of the Iverian Virgin.

Up the Nikolskaya Ulitsa from here is the **Lubyanka**, built before the revolution as the headquarters of the Rossiya Insurance Company but taken over by the secret police in 1918, first the Cheka, later the K.G.B., and thus the scene of many unpleasant interrogations during the communist era.

To its north are the **Sandunovsky Baths (Sandunovskie Bani)** founded in 1808 by an actor called Sandunov but rebuilt in 1895 with an exotic-ally sculpted façade and ornate interior that can accommodate 2,000 bathers, many for the traditional self-beating with birch twigs and steam bath.

At the southern end of Red Square is the **Lobnoe Mesto**, a platform used for public announcements and public executions. Nearby is the memorial statue of Prince Dmitri Pozharsky and the butcher Kuzma Minin, the two men who led the recapture of Moscow from the Poles in 1612 just before the accession of the first Romanov tsar.

Behind them is **St Basil's Cathedral (Sobor Vasiliya Blazhennovo)** built for Ivan the Terrible in 1561 just after his wife Anastasia's death to celebrate his capture of Kazan. Based on the traditional design of Russian wooden churches it has a multiplicity of gables, tent roofs and twisting onion domes. These were originally in gold but were painted different colours in the 1670s. Anastasia had befriended the wandering holy man or 'holy fool' St Basil after whom the building is commonly named and who was buried here in 1588.

Heading east from Red Square along Ulitsa Varvarka, the main thoroughfare of the old merchant quarter or Zaryade, are several significant buildings. **The Old English Court (Stary anglisky dvor)** was where Ivan the Terrible housed the English explorer Richard Chancellor after his shipwreck in 1553 so in due course it became a trading house for English merchants. It is now a museum reflecting its own original uses.

Beyond it is the **Palace of the Romanov Boyars (Musey-palaty v Zaryade)**, built originally by Nikita Romanov, the brother of Anastasia Romanova and grandfather of the first Romanov tsar. Built on a steep slope leading down to the Moskva River it was the home of the Romanovs until 1613 when Mikhail became Tsar. The double-headed eagle, the family crest, surmounts the gateway. The building was turned into a dynastic museum by Alexander II and houses a fine collection of Romanov memorabilia including the robes of the Patriarch Filaret, father of Tsar Mikhail.

The street also has a number of historic churches: the **Church of St Barbara the Martyr (Varvara)** after whom the street was named was rebuilt in 1796. The **Church of St Maxim the Blessed** paid for by the Novgorod merchants beside the **Old Merchants Chambers (Stary Gostiny Dvor)** with its Corinthian columns dates from 1698.

At the end there is the **Church of St George** built by the merchants of Pskov in 1698 near which are some surviving sections of the old city walls.

The **Church of the Trinity of Nikitniki** is one of Moscow's finest merchant churches, now a museum, built in 1653 in early Romanov times by the merchant Gregori Nikitnikov who died from the plague a couple of years later, just before the superb biblical frescoes were completed. It has five green domes and tiers of gables – *kokoshniki*. Nearby is the seventeenth-century house of the painter Simon Ushakov who worked on the church.

North of the Ulitsa Varvarka is the parallel Ulitsa Ilinka, the main street of the area known as *Kitaigorod* which sounds like China town but is normally believed to mean just a merchant city. It includes the original Stock Exchange of 1873. The **Monastery of the Saviour behind the Icon Stalls** has not survived except for the baroque church with balconies.

The **Monastery of the Epiphany (Bogoyavlenskiy Monastir)** founded in 1296 is the second oldest in Moscow but its fine cathedral built early in Peter's reign (1693-6) is baroque. Of slightly later date and away from its fellows is the church known as **Menshikov's Tower (Menshikova Bashnya)**, an ostentatiously beautiful building paid for by Peter's great lieutenant Alexander Menshikov and in its day boasting the tallest tower in Moscow. Peter himself adopted the new style of Western baroque for his first Moscow church, **The Virgin of Vladimir**, built in 1691-4 following the Westernising fashion of architecture with no onion domes pioneered by his mother and her Naryshkin relations in their churches at Fili, built 1693, and Troitsa Lokhovo in 1708. The last great building Peter planned for Moscow before he became obsessed by St Petersburg was his **Sukharev Tower** built in 1710 like a ship's mast to be part of his new school for navigation.

To the east of Kitaigorod towards the Yauza River is **Maroseika** originally Malorussy, the area for the Little Russians, the name given to the Ukrainians who settled in Moscow after the disruptive war of 1683. Beyond is the **Church of SS Peter and Paul**, the church for the German Lutheran population of this area, the former **Nemetskaya Sloboda** so much frequented by Peter the Great as a teenager, where he met with his long-term mistress Anna Mons and learned many crafts. **The St John's Convent (Ivanovsky)** founded by Ivan the Terrible on a hill, was used as a female prison, housing amongst others Maria the widow of Tsar Vasily in 1610 and Avgusta Tavakonova, allegedly the bastard daughter of the Empress Elizabeth who was kept here in solitary confinement till 1810. The Khokhlovsky Pereulok was also central to the local Ukrainian community, particularly the Cossacks after whose *khokhly* or tufts of hair the district was named. **The Trinity Church in Serebryanki** (silversmiths) was built by the guild that made coins and icon frames for the tsars. The Yauza River was at one time part of the water route from Moscow to the Volga. Near it is the **Church of Nikita beyond the Yauza**, a seventeenth-century Serbian Orthodox monastery owing allegiance to the order of Mount Athos. Similarly the Bulgarian Orthodox Church is based at the **Assumption Church in Gonchary** (ceramicists), so called because of its ceramic tiles and gleaming cupolas dating to the reign of Tsar Alexei.

On the south side of the Moscow River is the area known therefore as **Zamoskovorechye**, a low-lying area lived in by artisans and the rebellious *Streltsi* during Peter the Great's early days until they were suppressed. Here is another church founded by Tsar Alexei, **St Gregory Neokesarisky,** which shared the same brilliant tile maker, Stepan Polubes. The **Church**

of St Nicholas in Pyzhy was built by a regiment of *Streltsi* who were amongst the special victims of Peter the Great's persecution in 1698 as they had been associated with the brutal murder of his mother's close relatives and plotted rebellion against him during his long trip abroad. Nearby is the convent hospital founded in 1908 by the last tsarina's sister Ella or Elizabeth, the **Sisterhood of SS Martha and Mary**. Ella was the widow of Grand Duke Sergei, brother of Alexander III and an anti-Semitic, reactionary governor of Moscow until he was murdered in 1905. Ella herself survived till 1918 when she was thrown down a mineshaft. The **Church of St Clements** was built by Alexei Bestuzhev-Riumin to celebrate the coup that brought the Empress Elizabeth, his one-time lover, to power in 1741. This area also still has some signs of the fact that it was historically much lived in by Islamic traders, mainly Tartars.

The area is crossed by the **Vodootvodny Kanal**, dug in 1783 to prevent the floods caused by the Moscow River when in spate. Near the canal is the **Tretyakov Gallery** founded in 1892 by a millionaire textile manufacturer Pavel Tretyakov whose brother provided a large collection of Russian paintings.

Crossing back to the north side of the Moskva River we come to the area west of the Kremlin known as the **Arbatskaya**, taken from 'Arbat', the Mongol word for a suburb. In early Romanov days this was mainly a district for artisans and junior aristocrats, but gradually later moved up-market and was particularly associated with the arts. It includes the **Pushkin House Museum**, where the poet lived from 1831; the **Skryabin House Museum**, lived in the by the pianist and composer till his death in 1915; the **Shalyapin House Museum** lived in by the ex-Volga dock hand and great operatic singer; and the **Lermontov House Museum**, the small wooden house lived in by the poet from 1829-32 when he was a student.

There is also yet another reconstructed cathedral, this one the massive **Cathedral of Christ the Redeemer (Khram Khrista Spasitelya)** begun in 1839 to celebrate the victories over the French in 1812 and capable of holding 10,000 people. There is also the **Pushkin Museum of Fine Arts** founded in 1898 during the early reign of Nicholas II to house classical sculptures but now displaying major collections of paintings.

To the north is the fifth of the main districts of old Moscow, the **Tverskaya**, named after the road to Tver, which was also a major processional route for the tsars. It also contains two writers' museums

– the **Chekhov House** and the **Gorky House**. The Empress Elizabeth built the first public theatre in Moscow, a wooden one that accommodated 5,000 people. The **Bolshoe Theatre** was originally founded by Catherine the Great in 1780 but since then has twice been rebuilt after fires, the current building dating mainly from 1853. The **Moscow Arts Theatre** was opened in 1898 and famously staged the premieres of Chekhov's *Seagull* and *Cherry Orchard* soon afterwards.

Two hotels date from the same period: the **Hotel National** of 1903 and the **Hotel Metropol** of 1905, both refurbished but retaining their fine original façades and grandeur of pre-revolutionary days. The **House of Unions (Dom Soyuzov)**, a classical mansion built in the 1780s as an aristocratic club, was the venue for Alexander II's famous speech announcing the proposed abolition of serfdom in 1861. It was also later the scene of Lenin's lying in state in 1924 and of Stalin's in 1953.

Moscow Old University (Moskovskiy Universitet) is the oldest in Russia and was founded by Lomonosov in 1755, moving into this building in 1786 after Matvey Kazakov designed it for Catherine the Great. The **Moscow Conservatoire (Moskovskaya Konservatorya)** was founded in 1866 by Nikolai Rubinstein, brother of the pianist and composer Anton. The young Tchaikovsky taught here till 1878.

The **Manege** was built as a massive indoor drill hall in 1817 under Alexander I and later converted to exhibition space. The **Theatre Square (Teatralnaya Ploshchad)**, formally a marshy meadow by the Neglinnaya River, was also used as a military parade ground from 1839-1911.

The Bolshaya Nikitskaya Ulitsa, once the main road to Novgorod, was once lined by palaces of prominent aristocrats and the **Menshikov Palace** with its pale blue façade has survived though it had to be partially rebuilt after the great fire of 1812. The rest of the building dates back to 1775.

Out on its own near the edge of this district is the **Upper Monastery of St Peter (Vysoko Petrovskiy Monastyr)** rebuilt in the seventeenth century by the Naryshkin family to which Peter the Great's mother belonged. It has six churches, one of them the Church of the Icon of the Virgin of Bogolyubvo, dedicated to Peter's three uncles who were all murdered by the *Streltsi* in the mutiny of 1682 when Peter was still a boy.

To the north-west of the city Khodinskaya Ulitsa recalls the dreadful accident which cost so many lives on the eve of the coronation of Nicholas II and Alexandra when at least 1,400 people were crushed due to failures in organisation of the public feast for which the Emperor's uncle Sergei took much of the blame.

Also to the west is the spectacular red, white and gold **Church of Intercession in Fili** built in 1690-3 by Peter the Great's uncle, Lev Naryshkin, all of whose brothers had been murdered by the *Streltsi*. The pew used by Peter survives. It was here that Marshall Kutuzov held his fateful meeting in 1812 when it was decided to abandon Moscow to the French.

To the south of the city near the new University is **Sparrow Hill (Vorobevy gory)**, a wooded ridge from which Napoleon famously wearing his grey greatcoat surveyed Moscow as the fires started to burn in 1812.

Moscow was ringed by six great fortified monasteries, dating back to the period of Tartar attacks. The oldest was **St Daniel's (Danilovsky)** from the thirteenth century. The one with most Romanov connections is the **Novodevichy Convent** founded on a bend in the Moscow River in 1524 to celebrate the capture of Smolensk from the Lithuanians. Peter the Great used it as a prison both for his sister Sofia who was here when plotting the *streltsi* revolt of 1698 but was rewarded by having them hung outside her cell window. Another inmate was Yevdokia Peter's pious first wife. Its cemetery is the burial place for Gogol, Chekhov, Shalyapin, Nikita Khrushchev and Stalin's second wife Svetlana.

The **Donskoy Monastery** was founded by Tsar Feodor, the son of Anastasia Romanova, in 1591. The area round the **Rogozhskoye Cemetery** was given in 1771 to members of the long-persecuted Old Believers so that they could bury those of their members who had died in the recent plague. Catherine the Great lifted the restrictions on their sect and they built two old-style churches here.

The **Church of St John the Warrior (Tserkov Ioanna Voina)**, was one of the Moscow churches built in 1713 under Peter the Great in the new baroque style, which he had developed in St Petersburg. It has a tiered octagonal tower and geometric patterns formed by the roof tiles.

Monasteries Outside Moscow
Nearly 50 miles outside Moscow to the north east there is another massive fortified monastery which played a key role at the beginning of Peter the Great's reign the **Trinity Monastery of St Sergius (Troitse Sergieva Lavra)**. Founded in about 1345 in Sergiev Posad, it became

one of the key religious centres in Russia. It was visited by Ivan the Terrible and Anastasia as part of their honeymoon and it later survived a siege by the Poles in 1610. It was visited and extended by Tsar Alexei and provided a refuge for his son Peter the Great during the *Streltsi* mutiny of 1682. Peter allegedly used one of its towers, the Duck Tower, for shooting at ducks and the palatial tsar's apartments were built by his father, Tsar Alexei who visited the monastery with as many as 500 attendants. Boris Godunov is buried here. The Monks' Refectory was added in 1692, the Gate Church of St John the Baptist by the Stroganovs in 1699 and the magnificent Palace of the Metropolitans in 1778.

Mikhail, the first Romanov tsar, was given the news of his appointment when staying at the **Ipatiev Monastery** at Kostroma to which he and his mother had been exiled and where his mother was made to become a nun. **Kostroma** on the Volga, 200 miles north east of Moscow, grew to be the third largest city in Russia after Moscow itself and nearby Yaroslavl. It had been the original home of the Godunov family who built much of the monastery, which is on the banks of the Kostroma River near where it joins the Volga. In gratitude for his elevation Tsar Mikhail built the **Romanov Chambers** which had to be visited by every new tsar there-after. The city suffered from a huge fire in 1773 but was rebuilt in classical style by Catherine the Great. A **Romanov Museum** was built here in 1913 to celebrate the tercentenary of the dynasty.

Sites Outside Moscow

Moscow is also surrounded by a ring of royal country palaces. Perhaps the oldest was **Kolomenskoe**, 12 miles south of the city, where Ivan the Terrible had started to build and where his wife Anastasia Romanovna died at a tragically young age. The second Romanov tsar, Alexei, added a massive and magnificent wooden palace with barrel-shaped roofs and onion domes which Catherine the Great sadly demolished, though the churches survive – one of them the spectacular **Church of our Lady of Kazan** built in 1650 for Tsar Alexei – as does Tsar Alexei's ceremonial entrance. **Peter the Great's cabin** from his Archangelsk visit was reconstructed here in 1934. There is one pavilion surviving of Alexander I's palace built in 1825.

Also significant historically was the **Preobrazhenskoe Palace**, 3 miles up the Yauza River from Moscow, where Peter the Great spent much of his boyhood in a palace built by his father, Tsar Alexei. Alexei also built a theatre here for his German troop of actors. It was on this estate that Peter first formed his staff and friends into a make-believe regiment which eventually became so highly trained and well-armed that it helped him to seize power and crush the *Streltsi*, surviving in later years as the illustrious Preobrazhensky Guard. Nearby was the village of **Semenov**, which gave its name to the other great new guards regiment under Peter, the Semonovsky. The palace burned down about 1720.

Another favourite country palace of the Tsar Alexei was **Ismailovo**, about 12 miles to the north east across the Yauza River, where in 1683 he set up an experimental farm with trial herb gardens and fruit orchards. According to legend it was in the ponds of this palace that Peter the Great found the old sailing dinghy on which he learned to sail and which became known as 'the father of the Russian navy.' Only the Cathedral and Bridge Tower of the palace survive from this time, now part of a huge country park.

Tsar Peter went to the next stage of building a navy at **Pereslavl** 85 miles north east of Moscow on Lake Pleshcheevo from which galleys could navigate down the Volga.

Tsaritsyno Palace, 6 miles south of Moscow, was the never-finished brainchild of Catherine the Great who liked the Black Mud – Chornaya Gryaz. She did not like the first set of buildings designed for her however and ran out of money so that most of the exotically façaded buildings were never more than shells.

Eighty miles south-west of Moscow is the battlefield of **Borodino**, where Marshall Kutuzov led the Russians against Napoleon in 1812 and both sides fought to a standstill. Approximately 50,000 Russians and nearly as many French were killed, but this was much more damaging for the French than the Russians. Though Napoleon subsequently occupied Moscow it had been deserted so if a victory at all, it was a hollow one and in due course Napoleon had to begin his disastrous winter retreat. There are numerous monuments and a museum.

St Petersburg (Sankt Peterburg)

The name of the city was changed in 1914 to Petrograd to make it sound less German, to Leningrad in 1924 to get rid of the tsarist connotations and in 1991, after a referendum, back to St Petersburg. It was the capital of Russia from 1712 till 1918.

Peter the Great founded his new city in 1703 on an inhospitable, marshy site on the delta of the River Neva and most of it is only about 4ft above sea level. Although originally Russian territory, the area had been taken over by the Swedes in 1617 just after the Romanovs came to power in 1613 and had remained in their hands until Peter finally began to drive back their armies more than eighty years later. They had built the fort of **Nienschanz** at the mouth of the Okhta just above the Neva delta. Whilst it was a spectacularly difficult and unhealthy site upon which to found a new city it at least immediately offered the prospect of good harbour facilities and connections to the other vital waterways of Russia. In addition it was well placed strategically as a base from which to dominate the Gulf of Finland and the eastern Baltic.

The river Neva has five main arms: the Bolshaya (Big) Nevka is the furthest north and has two extra outlets to the sea, the Malaya (small) Nevka and the Srednaya Nevka; south of these three are the Malaya Neva and the Bolshaya Neva separated by the biggest of the islands, Vasilevski Ostrov. Two much smaller arms of the Neva, the rivers Moyka and Fontanka (so called because of the nearby fountains) surrounded what became the central part of the new city in concentric semicircles separated in due course by the manmade Griboyedov Canal. This entire area was prone to serious flooding, as for example in 1824. To the south there was another larger canal the Obvodny.

The fact that here were so many islands and watercourses meant that the digging of foundations for the new city required a massive number of labourers, most of them conscripts or prisoners of war, who lived in dreadful conditions and died in large numbers due to the extremes of temperature – cold in the winter and disease-ridden marshes in the summer.

While the original city had a strong functional basis for imperial expansion and governmental control it also became a monster advertisement for the extraordinary power and wealth of the Romanovs and was peppered with reminders of their victories on land and sea. Yet the sheer vastness of the palaces and government departments gives a clue to the ultimate inefficiency of trying to manipulate such huge numbers of people.

The first buildings erected were those of a new fort on Hare Island (Zayachy Ostrov) near the top corner of the delta, beside Petrogradsky Island (*Ostrov*), thus guarding all three branches of the Neva, and this became the **SS Peter and Paul Fortress (Petropavlovskaya Krepost)** originally with earthen outer walls in the shape of a six-pointed star which were later replaced by stone. The **Peter and Paul Cathedral (Petropavlovsky Sobor)** was given a spectacularly high spire at 122m to dominate the new skyline and was designed by Domenico Trezzini to replace the Kremlin as the burial place for future tsars. Now that the remains of Nicholas II have been recovered from Ekaterinburg all the tsars from Peter himself onwards, except for his grandson Peter II, are buried here with marble sarcophagi. Most of the rest of the fortress is now a historical museum including the notorious prison the Trubetskoi Bastion, which once housed numerous would-be rebels against tsardom and also the members of the Provisional Government after the October Revolution in 1917.

To the north is the **Kronverk**, a moated fort also built in the early stages of the city as part of its northern defences but replaced in 1850 by the **Arsenal**, now a military museum.

To the east and still on the north bank of the Neva is **Peter the Great's Cottage (Domik Petra 1)** the small, now brick-clad but originally wooden house built for Peter in the summer of 1703 so that he could supervise work on the city. Outside it now are two stone lions brought from Manchuria in 1907.

Nearby, as a contrast, is the **Kshesinskaya Mansion** a tile-covered art nouveau mansion built for the ballet dancer mistress of Tsar Nicholas II, Matilde Kshesinska, in 1904. It was used by the Mensheviks in 1917. The **Nakhimov Naval Institute** dates from 1909 and the massive blue-tiled **Mosque (Mecket)** from 1910, paid for by the grateful emir of Bokhara, who had been kept in post after the Russian conquest of his emirate.

Round the corner anchored in the Bolshaya Nevka is the **Cruiser** *Aurora* **(Kreyser Avrora)**, which fought as a brand new ship in 1904 at the disastrous Battle of Tsushima and during the First World War before firing the famous shot across the river to the Winter Palace to set off the October Revolution.

The rest of Petrogradsky Island is mainly art-nouveau period housing favoured by the pre-revolutionary intelligentsia. To its northern end across the small river Karpovka is Aptekarsky Island, in the early days of the city planned as a medicinal herb area. To its north again across the Malaya Nevka is Stone Island (Kamenny Ostrov) once the estate of Peter the Great's Chancellor Gavril Golovkin, but more recently an area for politicians' *dachas*. **Kamenny Ostrov Palace (Kamennostrovsky Dvorets)** was built in 1784 for Tsarevich Paul, son of Catherine the Great, and features a church at its entrance covered with the Masonic symbolism in which he was so interested before he became Tsar. It was used by Alexander I during the crisis year of 1812 and later became a military hospital.

A further bridge north-westwards leads to Yelagin Island and **Yelagin Palace (Yelagin Dvorets)** built originally by Rossi in 1818 for Alexander's neglected wife Empress Elizabeth. The whole island was landscaped for her and it was sometimes used by later tsars as a summer retreat.

Turning back south we come to the largest of the islands in the Neva delta Vasilevsky Ostrov, which separated the Malaya and Bolshaya Nevas. The sharper landward corner of this triangular island is known as the **Strelka** or **Arrow** and is embellished with two Rostral Columns (Rostralni Kolonni) decorated with the bows of ships to commemorate Russia's naval victories. The imposing classical **Bourse (Stock Exchange)**, now a naval museum, dates from 1855. Behind are the **Twelve Colleges** – the original administration blocks built for Peter in 1718 by Trezzini. There is the **Kunsthammer** – Peter's original scientific museum and the **Menshikov Palace (Dvorets)** built by Peter's long-term ally and supervisor for building the city, Alexander Menshikov who was given the unpromising Vasilevsky Island in 1707 and built this huge, luxurious Dutch-style residence, much grander than that of his master. He virtually ran Russia from here during the reign of Peter's widow Catherine, his one time mistress.

Overall the style of building favoured by Peter was for a Dutch style of roof, French lay-out and German decor, whereas the dominant colour of façades was to be orange-yellow with the detail picked out in white. As it turned out the high water-table meant that paint soon peeled off the outside walls and had to be renewed very frequently.

Amongst the other key early building projects were the **Admiralty Wharf, Foundry (Liteiny Dvor)** and **Tar Yard (Smolny Dvor)** (now replaced by the Smolny Institute) as essentials for defence.

Initially Peter, with his usual obsession, put a low priority on the building of bridges so that the new inhabitants would be forced to learn to sail and would have pontoons beside their homes. The first bridge over the Neva was the **Lieutenant Schmidt (Most Leytenanta Shmidta)** only completed in 1850. It leads to the small triangular island of New Holland (Novaya Gollandiya) where warehouses and a shipyard were built in the 1760s, with a massive archway decorated with Tuscan columns and designed by the architect de la Mothe who also built one of the elegant new bridges over the Moika. Beyond it over the Moyka River is the **Theatre Square**

(**Teatralnaya Ploshchad**) with its statue of Glinka, composer of the patriotic opera *A Life for the Tsar*, and the **Conservatoire**, which since 1880 has occupied the site of the old Bolshoe Theatre and where Tchaikovsky was a student. The circular **Mariinsky Theatre**, home of the Kirov Ballet and scene of the triumphs of dancers such as Anna Pavlova and singers such as Feodor Shalyapin, was built in 1860 for Maria, the wife of Alexander II. The Empress Anna had set up the first ballet school in the 1730s and her sister Elizabeth even had a dance theatre made of ice on the Neva during the cold winter of 1740 but also built a more lasting stone one.

There is a group of disused minor Romanov palaces in this area including **Xenia's Palace** built for the sister of Nicholas II, **Bobinsky's Palace** built for a bastard son of Catherine the Great and the **Palace of Alexis** built by the playboy Admiral Alexis, brother of Alexander III. Nearby is a statue of Catherine the Great.

South of this theatre quarter is the five-golden-domed, classically columned, blue and white **Naval Cathedral of St Nicholas (Nikolo-Bogoyavlensky Morskoe Sobor)** built in the 1753 as a special church for seafarers. Hence the decorative theme of anchors above the gate and perhaps its appropriately watery setting as it sits in a loop of the Griboyedov Canal. Nearby across the Fontanka is the blue-domed **Trinity Cathedral (Troitsky Sobor)** built in 1828 as a shrine for the Ismailovsky Guards, a twin to the **Transfiguration (Preobrazhensky Sobor)** built soon afterwards east of the Summer Palace for the other great guards regiment founded by Peter the Great.

Returning to the embankment of the Bolshaya Neva from the Lieutenant Schmidt Bridge, and heading eastwards, we come to the **Decembrists' Square (Ploshchad Dekabristov)**, which was the scene of the attempted rising of army officers and intellectuals in December 1825, just after the death of Alexander I. It had the aim of preventing his reactionary brother Nicholas from succeeding him. Many of the participants were hung or exiled to Siberia. In the centre of the square is the Statue of Peter the Great or **The Bronze Horseman (Medny Vsadnik)**, designed by Falconet and paid for by Catherine the Great in 1780. Its base stone weighing 275 tons was dragged from a bog. Across the square on one side is the **Senate**, which was the object of the Decembrists' attack. On the other side, facing the river, is the massive **St Isaacs's Cathedral (Isaakievsky Sobor)** begun in 1818 under Alexander I and completed thirty years later under Nicholas I, suppressor of the Decembrists and whose aggressive equestrian statue rears up on two legs from its plinth in the square beyond, the Isaakievskaya Ploshchad. The cathedral could hold 14,000 people, required huge quantities of different marbles, and its golden dome was covered with 100kg of pure gold. Many serfs forced to work on the project died of poisoning. On the other side of its square, which includes the wide bridge over the Moyka River, is the **Mariinsky Palace (Mariinsky Dvorets)**, built by Nicholas I for his daughter Maria, and after her death used for the Tsarist Council.

The Moyka River embankment was lined with palaces and apartments for the early settlers in the city. Kondraty Ryleev, the radical mastermind behind the plot against Nicholas I in December 1825, lived at number 72 and held his final ill-starred meeting here before his arrest and subsequent execution. Number 94 is the **Yusupov Palace (Yusupovsky Dvorets)**, a vast and grandiose building of classical design by de la Mothe in the 1760s to whose basement the plutocratic Prince Felix Yusupov lured Rasputin in 1916 to eat poisoned cakes, before shooting and then pushing him under the ice of the Neva. The change in policy by the Tsar that was expected to result from the murder sadly did not materialise. With a private theatre, huge hall and banqueting suite it shows the enormous wealth of the Yusupov family. Yusupov himself was never punished for the murder and escaped after the revolution to enjoy the rest of his long life in Paris.

Returning to the Neva and heading eastwards again along the elegant embankment built by the Empress Elizabeth, we come to the **Admiralty** (*Admiralteystvo*), originally a fortified shipyard that was replaced by the present massive yellow and white office block in 1823 as headquarters of the navy. Worked on both by Cameron and Zacharov under the Emperor Paul its façade stretches 500m and Talbot Rice refers to it as 'one of the world's finest buildings'. Its spire is appropriately crowned by a frigate and it is decorated with numerous sculptures symbolising Russian control of the seas.

From the landward side of the Admiralty radiate the three main streets of the city as planned with such care by Peter, thus making this and adjacent public buildings its focal point. The most spectacular is the **Nevsky Prospekt** which thus cuts right across the peninsula formed by the Neva. One side is dominated by the 245ft high **Our lady of Kazan Cathedral (Kazansky Sobor)**, begun on the orders of the Emperor Paul in imitation of St Peter's in Rome but not finished until 1811, six years after his untimely death. Marshall Kutuzov, the hero of 1812 is buried here and there are numerous war trophies. Nearby on the Moyka is Rastrelli's elegant green **Stroganov Palace** (*Dvorets*), once owned by the great merchant family famous for conquering Siberia, for their huge wealth and for their beef cuisine. It now houses a display of waxwork Romanovs.

Back to the Neva and beyond the Admiralty heading eastwards is the **Palace Square (Dvoretsovaya Ploshchad)** the focal point of the entire city. On one side is the massive **Winter Palace (Zeemny Dvorets)** begun by Peter the Great but regularly altered and extended by his successors, mainly completed by Rastrelli for Catherine the Great in 1762 and used as the main palace by all subsequent emperors except her son Paul. Its lavish baroque façade some 200m long is painted green with the detail picked out in white and decorated with numerous statues. Catherine also in 1764 built the gallery annexe, the **Hermitage (Ermitazh)** to house her huge collection of paintings and this function has now taken over the rest of the Winter Palace. The Hermitage Theatre, built for Catherine by Giacomo Quarenghi, replaced the earlier building where Peter the Great died. Because the Winter Palace was used after the March 1917 revolution by the Provisional Government, the storming of the palace by the Bolsheviks was a key moment during the October Revolution eight months later.

In the middle of the Palace Square is the monument celebrating the victory over the French in 1812, the **Alexander Column (Aleksanderskaya Kolonna)**, aptly a huge monolith cut from the rockface and dragged here by over 2,000 men. The angel on top has the face of Alexander I. The south side of the square is occupied by the **General Staff Building**, built in classical style in 1819 and incorporating a massive **Triumphal Arch** also celebrating the painful triumphs of 1812.

Carrying on up the Neva embankment opposite the Fortress of St Peter and Paul we come to the **Field of Mars (Marsovo Pole)**, originally a parade ground where many of the tsars liked to indulge their passion for military drill. The statue of Mars is General Suvorov and the area later became a monument to those who died in the February/March 1917 revolution. Beyond it, over a bridge spanning the Swans Canal (Lebyazhi Kanal) is the **Summer Garden (Letny Sad)**, which Peter the Great began in 1704 to provide himself with an impressive out-of-town residence in imitation of Versailles, though it is now surrounded by town. The Dutch-style **Summer Palace (Letny Dvorets Petra I)** was designed by Trezzini in 1710, with murals of naval victories. It was extended by Elizabeth.

The **Marble Palace** facing the Marsovo Pole was built in 1768 on the orders of Catherine by Rinaldi for her lover Gregori Orlov and incorporated thirty-six different varieties of marble. Outside is an equestrian statue of a somewhat overweight Alexander III put up in 1909 and described unkindly by the sculptor as 'one animal on top of another'.

At the southern end of the gardens across the River Fontanka there is the **St Panteleimon Church** built to celebrate Peter's first sea victories over the Swedes and this area known as the **Partikularny Wharf (Verf)** was where he encouraged the early inhabitants to build their own boats and which was later used for wine and salt warehousing, hence the name **Salt Quarter (Solyanoy Gorodok)**. Nearby was the infamous and well-hidden **Third Department**, which in tsarist times was used for the interrogation of political prisoners such as Herzen, Dostoyevsky and Lenin. Nearby also is the classical **Cathedral of the Transfiguration (Preobrazhensky Sobor)** surrounded by upturned cannon barrels celebrating the defeat of the Turks under Catherine the Great and dedicated to the Preobrazhensky Guards.

Nearby where the Moyka joins the Fontanka is the forbidding **Mikhailovsky Castle (Zamok)**, a fortress built in 1810 by the paranoid Emperor Paul, who hated the Winter Palace because of its associations with his mother Catherine the Great whom he blamed for the murder of his father Peter III and for almost every other aspect of his life. Outside he put up a statue of his grandfather Peter the Great in opposition to the Bronze Horseman version which she had put up by the Neva. Paul barely managed six weeks' residence in his new castle and its fortifications helped him little, for it was here that he was murdered by his own close associates with the tacit agreement of his son, the future Alexander I. The castle was later turned into an engineering college where Dostoyevsky was a student.

Across the gardens is the **Mikhailovsky Palace (Dvorets)** built by the Emperor Alexander for his younger brother Grand Duke Mikhail, now a museum set in fine gardens. It is one of a number of palaces that lined the banks of the picturesque Fontanka River with its numerous ornate stone bridges. The overall consistency of style and elegance of the buildings, pavements and railings is due to the detailed supervision of Alexander I who was more autocratic in this respect than any modern planning department. He also commissioned his architect Rossi to design the Theatre Street with the **Imperial Ballet School**.

The **Anichkov Palace** (*Dvorets*) built in 1741 by Rastrelli and others facing the Fontanka River was first given by Empress Elizabeth to her lover Razumovsky, then by Catherine to her favourite Potemkin. It was regularly used by later Romanovs including Alexander III who was living here at the time of his accession. Since 1936 it has mainly been a centre for youth activity.

West of the Mikhailovsky Palace is the **Church of the Resurrection or Our Saviour on the Spilled Blood** (*Tserkov Spasitelya-na-Krovi*), which was built in 1883 on the spot where the reforming Emperor Alexander II was killed by a terrorist bomb two years earlier. Unlike other St Petersburg cathedrals, which all follow Western styles of architecture, classical or baroque, this one is decidedly Muscovite with assorted multi-coloured onion domes.

Returning yet again to the banks of the Neva a mile further up the main river from the Summer Palace is the **Tauride Palace** (*Tavrichesky Dvorets*) another fine classical building given by Catherine the Great to her lover Gregori Potemkin for his victory over the Turks – he had been made Prince of Tauris for his conquest of the Crimea in 1788. It had a ground-breaking internal colonnade and huge Catherine Hall. In his Winter Gardens, Potemkin staged a huge garden party to impress Catherine when she began to tire of him as a lover. The Tauride was hardly ever used again as a palace as Catherine's son Paul hated Potemkin and used it for his stables. In 1906 it became the headquarters of the *Duma* and in 1917 was simultaneously used both by the Provisional Government and its deadly rival, the Soviet of Petrograd Workers and Peasants.

Across the Neva is the **Finland Station** (*Finlandsky Vokzal*) – famous for the dramatic arrival of Lenin back in Russia from Germany in April 1917 and again from Finland in October. His original train carriage is still preserved here.

Another ¾ mile round the bend of the Neva is the **Smolny Convent (Smolny Monastir)**, which was built by Rastrelli for the Empress Elizabeth in 1748 on the site of Peter the Great's original Tar Yard **(Smolny Dvor)**. The building is brilliant blue and white, highly ornate baroque and was almost immediately converted to a school for upper class girls, in its time a revolutionary step in Russia. One of the young pupils later became the mistress of Alexander II. The classical **Smolny Institute** was added to the complex in 1808 and was to achieve great fame after the fall of the Romanovs when the Petrograd Soviet moved here from the Tauride Palace in 1917. It was here that Trotsky and Lenin planned the October revolution and from here that Lenin ran Russia for the four months up to March 1918 when the seat of government was moved to the Kremlin in Moscow. On the opposite bank of the Neva at the mouth of the river Ochta was the original Swedish **Fort Nienschantz** captured for Peter in 1703.

Halfway between the Tauride palace and the Smolny are **Kikin's Chambers** – the house of the Boyar Kikin who was put in charge of the original Tar Yard or ship repair depot by Peter the Great but subsequently objected to his westernising tendencies and joined in a rather half-baked plot instigated by the Tsar's son Alexis. Like the wretched Tsarevich, poor Kikin was executed or tortured to death.

Another 1½ miles along the Neva and dominating the far end of the Nevsky Prospekt is the **Alexander Nevsky Monastery (Aleksandro-Nevskaya Lavra)**, the first major ecclesiastical foundation by Peter in his new city built in 1710. It celebrated the canonisation of one of his role models, Prince Alexander Nevsky of Novgorod, who had defeated the Teutonic knights on Lake Ladoga and thus conquered a gateway to the Baltic for Russia just as, many years later, Peter had achieved the same by beating the Swedes. The huge complex contains two cathedrals, the classical Annunciation by Trezzini and the baroque Trinity by Rastorguyev. Beside it is the **Lazarevskoe Cemetery (Kladoyshche)** and two other cemeteries where amongst other notables Glinka, Tchaikovsky, Rimsky-Korsakov and Dostoyevsky are buried.

The Out of Town Palaces round St Petersburg

Petrodvorets
Twenty miles west of St Petersburg on a pleasant piece of coastline by the Gulf of Finland, Peter organised a **Wooden Palace (Derevyany Dvorets Petra I)** for himself as a summer retreat and also a vantage point to watch construction work on the fortifications of **Kronstadt**, on Kotlin Island, dominating the approaches to his new city and itself a useful naval base. It is at Strelna where the river Strelka flows down through the later Orlov Park to the sea. Also here is **Konstantinovsky Palace**, built by Rastrelli for Elizabeth and more recently chosen by Vladimir Putin to be a new summer residence for Russian presidents.

In 1714 Peter began building a more substantial palace further to the west, looking down on terraced gardens running down to the shore with fountains and cascades like Versailles. His Upper Chambers were to become the **Great Palace (Bolshoe Dvorets)** and down on the shoreline he had his seaside hideaway **Montplaisir (Monplesir)**, parts of which he built himself. Nearby was a bath house as Peter enjoyed a sauna followed by a dip in cold water or snow. The Great Palace was substantially rebuilt and massively extended a mere thirty years later in 1745 by the Empress Elizabeth and her favourite architect Rastrelli, who added the exotic baroque flourishes. The **Chesme Hall** has extravagant murals advertising Catherine the Great's naval victory over the Turks in the Aegean. The Great Palace was badly damaged by the Germans during the siege of Leningrad and had to be reconstructed.

The **Great Cascade (Bolshoe Kaskad)** celebrated the victory of the new Russian fleet against the Swedes with a Russian Samson opening the jaws of a Swedish lion to make the main fountain spurt high into the air. In the Lower Park (Nizhny Park) in 1723 Peter added the **Marly Palace (Marly Dvorets)** as accommodation for his extended family and then the pink and white **Hermitage (Ermitazh)** as a playground for his courtiers. It was fitted with round lifts to hoist plates of food from below without the need for butlers. Guests who misbehaved in any way were forced to drink huge amounts of wine as a punishment. The park also has its own private cathedral – **Petropavlovsky Sobor** – overlooking the ornamental lake.

Beside Montplaisir is a small palace used by Catherine the Great as she waited on tenterhooks for the violent dethronement of her husband Peter III. Up the hill from here are some trick fountains which were designed to soak innocent passers-by and a dragon-guarded grotto known as the **Chessboard Water (Shachmatnaya Voda)** as the water runs down a giant chessboard. Beyond this to the east, and above a fine sandy beach, is the **Aleksandrovsky Park** an area of less-stylised landscaping originally given by Peter to Menshikov and later by Nicholas I to his wife Alexandra. The garden is scattered with romantic follies. In it also is the Tsarina Alexandra's own exquisite nineteenth-century palace the **Cottage (Kottedzh)** and the tall gothic monument to Alexander Nevsky, the Chapelle (Kapella). The **English Palace (Anglisky Dvorets)** and park were built by Quaranghi for Alexander I and his wife.

A few miles to the west of Petrodvorets at Lomonosov is another vast complex of palaces centred on the **Oranienbaum** originally given by

Peter to Menshikov who, as in St Petersburg, initially outdid his master in the size and luxury of his new palace, the **Great Menshikov Palace (Veliky Menshikovsky Dvorets)**. Later it was given by the Empress Elizabeth to Grand Prince Peter and his new wife, the future Catherine the Great. **Peter's Palace (Dvorets Petra III)** was in his day part of his fortress Peterstadt where he could practice drilling his squads of tame soldiers. It was here that he was staying without her when the coup took place that ended his reign as Tsar and it was from here that he made a fruitless attempt to sail over to Kronstadt to avoid the murderous attentions of the Orlovs. Catherine who had been waiting on the far side of Petrodvorets retained her liking for Oranienbaum and added several more palaces designed by her architect Rinaldi such as the elaborately rococco Catherine or **Chinese Palace (Kitaisky Dvorets)** begun under Elizabeth, which symbolised the Empress's extension of Russia in the far east and the **Knight's Block (Kavalersky Dvorets)**. In addition there is the obligatory cathedral – **Arkhengelsky Sobor**, the **Coasting/Toboganning Hill Pavillion (Salazhkaya Gorka)**, site in 1764 of a pioneering and later much imitated bare-knuckle ride for the royal family that converted for sledging in the winter, and **Skating Hill (Katalnaya Gorka)**.

Ropsha, the small country estate where the Emperor Peter III was murdered by the Orlovs, is about 8 miles south of Peterhof and Krasnoe Selo, the favourite area for Romanov military exercises, about the same distance south east. **Vorobevo** was a tsarist hunting lodge.

Kronstadt, the island naval base built in the Gulf of Finland by Peter the Great and which produced so many revolutionary sailors in 1917, has a magnificent **Naval Cathedral (Morskoe Sobor)** begun in 1903.

Tsarskoye Selo-Pushkin

This is an even larger complex of palaces than the two parks on the Gulf of Finland and eventually acquired its own town to service the needs of the tsars, the first in Russia to have its own railway in 1837 and the first to have electricity.

Some 15 miles south west of St Petersburg it, like Oranienbaum, owed its origin to Menshikov who in 1707 took over a farm on an island (saari is Finnish for island and to this is attributed the name later corrupted to Tsar). In 1710 Peter the Great took it back and gave it instead to his second wife Catherine and the new palace was named after her – **Catherine's Palace (Yekaterinsky Dvorets)**. It was completed under the Empress Elizabeth by her architect Rastrelli, a massive palace in the extravagant baroque style which immediately began to collapse. It was almost completely reconstructed under the orders of Catherine the Great with less of the baroque and more of the classical, with a long façade similar to the Winter Palace but with turquoise instead of green as the main background colour. Inside are huge golden halls and the gilded Great Hall, lined with windows and mirrors was used for banquets and balls.

As a special annex to the palace, Catherine had the **Cameron Gallery (Kameronskaya Galleria)**. Cameron, a Scottish architect who came to Russia in 1779, was also responsible for the ultra exotic Amber Room, Silver Study and Chinese Room in the palace itself.

The **Catherine Park (Yekaterinsky Park)** is landscaped with ponds including her favourite **Great Pond (Bolshoe Prud)** and formal gardens. It contains also the **Hermitage (Ermitazh)**, an additional venue for less formal banquets and dancing, which was fitted with ingenious pulley systems so that the guests could organise self-service meals and keep the servants out of the way. Nearby are a rostral monument for the Russian sea victory over the Turks, an imitation mosque with Turkish baths inside (Catherine famously encouraged Potemkin to join her in her bath houses), a pyramid memorial to Catherine's pet dogs, a Palladian Bridge from 1776 in marble by the architect Neelov and a Chinese Village built by Cameron.

Next door is the Alexander Park – with the somewhat ruined **Alexander Palace** that Catherine had built for her grandson, the future Emperor Alexander I. Nearby are the massive ruins of the **Arsenal**, and the **Elephant Pavillion** where the Tsars kept their elephants. Near the entrance is the late nineteenth-century fake **Kremlin**, a small fortress put up for use by royal guards by Nicholas II who was born in Tsarskoe Selo. Not far away is another pastiche of the same period – **St Feodor's Catheral (Feodorsky Sobor)** with its onion-shaped cupolas.

To the south there is also the huge Babolovsky Park a popular place for the royal family to ride. In it is **Potemkin's Palace** built in gothic style in 1784 for Catherine's favourite.

The **Chesme Palace** was built half-way from St Petersburg to Tsarskoe Selo as a resting place for Catherine the Great and to remind people of her naval victory over the Turks in 1770. Beside it was the exquisite pink and white striped **Chesme Cathedral** built in 1780.

Pavlovsk

Just south of Tsarskoe Selo was the site chosen in 1781 by Catherine for a new palace to house her rebellious son Paul. He took a dislike to the design, was impatient with the slow pace of the architect Cameron who was waiting for a huge variety of different marbles to come from Italy, and with his lack of budgeting, so he replaced him with his own architect Vincenzo Brenna who started again almost from scratch. It is square with a classical façade and dome and approached by a Treble Lime Alley. The interior is redolent of Paul's passion for freemasonry and military drill, the emblems of war. The rooms occupied by Tsarina Maria on the other hand have a more feminine and peaceful aspect. In the once superbly landscaped gardens carved from the valley of the river Slavyanka there is a pavilion on an island in the lake, a Centaur's Bridge and numerous follies such as a Temple of Friendship and a Temple of the Three Graces. Like so many palaces round St Petersburg, Pavlovsk had to be virtually rebuilt after the German siege of Leningrad in 1941-2.

Gatchina

Gatchina Palace (Dvorets), 25 miles south of St Petersburg, was originally built for Count Gregori Orlov, the man who helped Catherine the Great to seize power from her husband, organised his murder and became her lover. It was remodelled by Emperor Paul who hated the Orlovs for the murder of his father. Considering his later militarist period as Tsar, Paul was a remarkably forward-thinking landlord, treating his 6,000 mainly Finnish Lutheran serfs with reasonable generosity. Later because Gatchina was more easily defended than the other country palaces it became a main residence for Emperor Alexander III after the murder of his father. The high park walls were constantly patrolled by guards. Like the others it had huge landscaped parks including a lake with a Pavilion of Venus. It also has a Pavlovsky Sobor and Birch House. The palace had to be rebuilt after the Second World War.

Gruzino

This palace on the way to Novgorod is most associated with the reactionary martinet Arakcheev who experimented here with new ideas for the housing of serf soldiers. It was destroyed by the Germans in 1941.

Other Romanov Memories near St Petersburg and Further North

Ivangorod was built as a massive fortress and port at the mouth of the Narva River in 1492 when Tsar Ivan III first conquered a slice of the Baltic coast for Muscovy. It was recovered for Russia by Peter as was **Vyborg**, the old Swedish-Finnish town on the other side of the Gulf of Finland which has an island fortress, **Vyborg Castle**, built originally by the Swedes in 1293 but modernised by Peter the Great. **Anna Krepost** is an additional fortress built to keep out the Swedes under Empress Anna. The cathedral dates from Catherine the Great. The native Finnish population were all cleared out by Stalin.

Another major fortress, **Fort Noteborg**, renamed **Schlusselburg** won back from the Swedes for Peter by Sheremeteev was on the nut-shaped island of Oreshek (Noteborg means nut fortress in Swedish) on Lake Ladoga near the entrance to the River Neva. Built originally by the Novogrod Russians to defend their trade routes in 1323 the fortress ceased to be part of the frontier once St Petersburg was built, so Peter and his successors used it as a prison. Famously, the former emperor Ivan VI was imprisoned here for eighteen years, reduced to an almost vegetable state and murdered in 1764 after a rumour that he might be helped to escape. The Secret House block was added in 1798. It even had a cathedral. Lenin's brother Alexander Ulyanov was executed here as were many other revolutionaries.

By contrast Peter helped establish a monastery on **Valaam Island** and its neighbouring small islands in Lake Ladoga whose remoteness appealed to an extreme order of ascetic monks who wanted to live in cells, avoid washing, changing their clothes, meat and conversation.

Also dating from Peter's reign is the extraordinary wooden monastery **Spassky Pogost** with its twenty-three-domed cathedral on Kizhi Island, Lake Onega. Nearby **Petrozavodsk** was founded by Peter the Great the same year as St Petersburg as a cannon-manufacturing town. At Kem, also in Karelia, is another cathedral inspired by Peter the Great's victories, the huge **Assumption Cathedral**. Peter also popularised the Spa village of **Martsialniye Vodi (Martial Waters)** whose iron-rich waters were discovered in 1714. He had a small wooden church built here.

Vologda to the east on the edge of the *taiga* was used by Peter as a stopping point on his journeys northwards. It had an ancient **Kremlin** visited by Ivan IV and Anastasia. Peter stayed here in the home of a Dutch merchant called Ivan Gutman. Peter later invested in the town's expansion but despite offering him the money for stone the residents mainly produced stone-look-alike buildings made in wood.

Arkhangelsk to the far north, founded by Ivan the Terrible in 1594, was the place where Peter the Great launched Russia's first ocean-going fleet in 1694 and he considered building the new capital here before he found the site of St Petersburg. The cottage he lived in was later moved to Moscow but a monument marks the spot.

The original name for **Murmansk** was Romanovo-on-the-Murman as it was founded in 1914 under Nicholas II because Germany had closed the Baltic and Russia needed a new port.

Towards Moscow

As a resting point en route between St Petersburg and Moscow Catherine the Great built a new palace at **Tver**, one of the old medieval cities on the Volga. The **Royal Palace (Putevoe Dvorets)** is now a museum. Much of the rest of the town had to be rebuilt after a fire in 1763 but many fine buildings survived. Another popular stopping place was **Torzhok**, an old Russian trading town with its own **Kremlin** on the river Tvertsa, two cathedrals and eleven monasteries including the magnificent **Monastery of SS Boris and Gleb** built by Lvov in the 1790s. As her overnight stopping place Catherine had her new Royal Palace by Kazakov.

Yaroslavl was another old Volga trading city visited on pilgrimage by Ivan IV and Anastasia. It was given a facelift by Catherine the Great. In pre-Muscovite times it was an independent princedom with its own **Kremlin** founded by Yaroslav the Wise and embellished with a large number of fine churches and monasteries.

Rostov played a key role in the early rise of the Romanovs for here Filaret, the father of the first Romanov tsar, was bishop and with Polish help plotted the downfall of Tsar Vasily. The impressive **Kremlin** was built by his predecessor Iona.

Uglich also had a fine **Kremlin** on the Volga though little of it is left except for the beautiful **Church of Demetrius on Spilled Blood** with its blue and red cupolas and recalling the strange death of Ivan the Terrible's younger son during the Time of Troubles.

Nizhny Novgorod is another old medieval city on the Volga. Its Kremlin was the birthplace of the butcher Kosma Minin who helped raise an army to drive out the Poles from Russia in 1612 and thus create a situation where the Romanovs could assume power a year later. Peter the Great stayed the night here in the house of the merchant Chapygin (**Dom Chapigina**) in 1695 on his way to the Azov campaign and the **Olisov Chambers** where he returned for his fiftieth birthday. Allegedly Peter visited the new **Church of the Nativity (Stroganovskaya Tserkov)**, just finished at vast expense by local mining plutocrat Gregori Stroganov. He was so shocked to see an icon of the Archangel Michael that was an exact portrait of Stroganov that he frightened the rich man into closing the church until after Peter was dead.

Pereslavl on Lake Plescheevo was the town chosen to be his first ship-building centre as he planned a river-borne expedition to attack the Turks in Azov. One of his boats, the *Fortuna*, was allegedly partly built by the Tsar himself and still survives in the **Botik Museum** by the lake. Pereslavl has its own Red Square, its white stone **Transfiguration Cathedral** and the magnificent **Goritsky Monastery** built by Empress Elizabeth for her confessor.

South of Moscow

Voronezh was founded in 1585 as a fort to guard against the Tartars, was part of the Stenka Razin Cossack rebellion and used as a naval ship-building base by Peter the Great in 1696.

Alexandrov and its huge fortress **Aleksandrovskaya Sloboda** was used as a major base and later terror squad headquarters by Ivan the Terrible. Its convent was used by Peter the Great as a place to imprison his sister Marfa for joining in the *Streltsi* rebellion of 1692.

Because of its closeness to coal and iron deposits south of Moscow, the then border fortress of **Tula** and its gunsmiths were given special status in 1595 and produced large numbers of *arquebuses* for the tsars. Peter the Great expanded the industry greatly in 1712 and a century later it was one of the important military targets in Russia that Napoleon never quite reached. The cathedral is now a weapons museum. Nearby was the country estate of Leo Tolstoy.

Bogoroditsdk has the palace built in 1771 by Catherine the Great for her bastard son born during her relationship with Gregori Orlov, Count Bobrinski.

Kaluga became known as the 'little St Petersburg' largely because of the investment in planning a new town by Catherine the Great who turned it into a provincial capital in 1776. The **Monastery of Optina Pustyn** became a centre for religious revival soon afterwards and produced a number of wandering holy men or **startsy**.

The ancient forest and fur-trading city of **Bryansk** near the Ukrainian border was another place chosen by Peter the Great to help build up his navy and he stayed at the **Sven Monastery** during his Poltava campaign.

To the West

Smolensk the old frontier city on the Dnieper had Russia's largest stone **Kremlin** built by Boris Godunov in 1609 though it was captured and held by the Poles till 1649. Its role as the first bastion of Russian defence was repeated against Napoleon in 1812 and Hitler in 1941. Its massive green-coloured **Assumption Cathedral (Uspensky Sobor)** was commissioned by the second Romanov tsar, Alexei, to commemorate the defeat of the Poles.

Pskov at the junction of the Velikaya and Pskova Rivers was similarly an early bastion against Poland and Lithuania and also has a most imposing **Kremlin**. It had to be evacuated at the very beginning of the Romanov era in 1615 when the struggle was against the Swedish army of Gustavus Adolphus. Peter the Great used it as his base for the attack on Narva but once the frontier was moved to the Baltic it became less important. It was here in a railway siding that Nicholas II signed his abdication in March 1917.

Sovietsk (Tilsit) near Kaliningrad at the mouth of the Niemen was where Alexander I met Napoleon on a raft in the middle of the river.

Towards the Black Sea and Eastwards

Taganrog port at the mouth of the Don was built by Peter as a base for constructing his Black Sea fleet. **Azov** itself was a major Turkish-Tartar fort which had been captured and destroyed by the Cossacks during his father's reign and was captured by Peter's own army in 1698, only for him to have to give it back after his disaster on the Pruth.

Starocherkask near Rostov on Don has the fortified home of the Cossack opponent of Peter the Great, Kondraty Bulavin, and several other Cossack fort houses. Stenka Razin was based here in 1670 and captured here. Peter helped build the **Resurrection Cathedral**.

Orenburg, 360 miles from Moscow, was a major fort built in 1730 to control the eastern Cossacks and captured by Pugachev during his 1773 rebellion. **Tsaritsyn**/Stalingrad/Volgograd was founded by Ivan IV to control the Volga Tartars. It was captured by both Stenka Razin and Pugachev.

The Caucasus

Astrakhan on the Volga was captured and rebuilt by Ivan IV in 1558 but its **kremlin** and **Assumption Cathedral** date from 1698 and Peter the Great.

Grozny is the capital of the small but rebellious enclave of Chechnya which was absorbed by Russia under Catherine the Great and first declared jihad in 1795. Unlike most of its neighbours it was kept inside the Russian federation after 1991. Dagestan famously has eighty-one ethnic groups in this mountainous area and at least thirty different languages, but the main rivalry has been between the pro-Russian Ingush and the Chechen.

Siberia

The colonisation of Siberia was begun by Cossack fur trappers and traders working for the Stroganovs during the late sixteenth century. They were soon joined by escaped serfs, some of them carrying the smallpox infection which soon decimated the native Altaic tribes of the area. **Tomsk**, founded in 1604, has had its wooden fort reconstructed. **Novokuznetz** founded in 1618 on the Tom River had a major early fortress rebuilt in 1810. **Kolorovo** founded as Spasskoe in 1620 is an example of a caravan way-station.

Yekaterinburg founded in 1723 by Peter the Great as a factory-fort was named after his empress and Catherine, the patron saint of miners. It had **Ipatiev House**, the final prison chosen for Nicholas II and his family and where they were all almost certainly shot in 1918. It has been demolished but a new cathedral, **Church on the Blood (Tserkov na Krovy)**, has been built on the spot. The bones of five of the family were exhumed in 1976 near Porosinko Log (and identified with over 98 per cent certainty by the UK Forensic Sciences Centre in 1992) where they had been buried in an unmarked grave in the **Koptyaki Forest**. In 2007, Russian archaeologists found the remains of two bodies, a boy and a girl fitting the description of the two remaining members of the Tsar's family. Nearby is the **Ganina Yama** mineshaft where some or all of them were perhaps originally buried and which now has a **Monastery of the Holy Martyrs** and wooden chapel commemorating the event. **Alapaevsk**, the small town where the Empress's sister Ella and others were also murdered is just to the north.

Tobolsk, where the last tsar and his family spent ten months, lies 9 miles from the ruins of the old Tartar capital of Siberia, Isker or Sibir. It was founded in the reign of the half-Romanov Tsar Feodor I as an *ostrog* or stockaded fur collection point by Cossacks in the employ of the Stroganov trading family. It grew into the main trading centre for western Siberia and was one of a long line of forts stretching eastwards that consolidated Muscovite control of the area. An expedition led by Cossack captain Peter Beketov in 1632 founded **Yakutsk** in the far north east on the Lena River with the usual stockade or *ostrog*, and it grew to be the main trading station in eastern Siberia as well as an open prison for rebels such as the Decembrists. He also founded the **Lensky Fortress**. The original native tribes of the area were gradually absorbed or eliminated. Yakutsk has an eighteenth-century **kremlin**, two cathedrals and parts of the old wooden town. **Omsk** was founded by Peter the Great in 1716.

Novosibirsk, originally **Novonikolayevsk**, was named after its founder Nicholas II in the 1890s and has a golden-domed cathedral of 1898. **Abakan** to its east was a town captured under Peter the Great in 1701 and used as a fortress base for the invasion of Kazakhstan. **Irkutsk**, a Cossack town founded in 1651 some 1,500 miles east of the Urals, became the base from which the Russians controlled Alaska. Known as the 'Paris of Siberia' it has its old fortress tower, a cathedral and many traditional wooden houses with delicate fretwork embellishment.

THE FAR EAST

Tyva to the south is a Mongolian Chinese area with a largely Buddhist population snatched by Nicholas II in 1911 when China was weak. To the east is **Chita**, a silver mining town founded in 1653 and also used as a dumping ground for tsarist prisoners.

Okhotsk was the first town founded on the Pacific Coast by the Stroganov-employed Cossacks in 1648. They put up an *ostrog* or fort. The same year Simeon Dezhnev rounded the eastern-most point of Asia by sea. From 1733-43 Titus Bering, on orders from Peter the Great, organised his huge expedition of nearly 600 men looking for the North East Passage. **Petropavlovsk** on remote Kamchatka was founded by Bering in 1741 It still has its green-domed orthodox church and was the scene of a remarkable defeat of the British navy by the Russians in 1855 during the Crimean crisis. **Sakhalin Island** was taken over from Japan in 1853 and in 1882 Alexander III turned it into a penal colony which Chekhov described as 'hell'.

Khabarovsk was founded as a forward base by Muraviev in 1858 as he masterminded the conquest of a slice of Manchuria from the Chinese. This resulted in the acquisition of the site of **Vladivostok** 5,000 miles from Moscow, founded as a naval base in 1861 on a newly acquired coastal strip by the Amur River on the Sea of Japan. The vast **Fortress (Bezymyanaya) Battery** took seventy years to build, guarding the Golden Horn Harbour and the terminus of the Trans-Siberian Railway, itself an enormous construction project. Fort Seven, one of the seventeen component forts, is particularly impressive with its mile of tunnels. Immigrant Russians largely displaced the original Chinese and Japanese indigenous peoples.

THE BALTIC STATES

Ironically the three Baltic States that suffered such suppression both in tsarist and communist times probably included the original home of the Romanovs, known then as Prus, in what is now Lithuania or the small portion of Baltic coast round Kaliningrad which is still part of Russia. The ancestors of the Romanovs seem to have moved from this area east to Moscow around about 1346 when the German knights took over Estonia and suppressed an uprising in what is now Latvia and Lithuania.

The whole area was badly devastated during the wars of Peter the Great when a commentator wrote, 'there is neither bark of dog nor crow of cock from Narva to Riga.' Peter annexed both Estonia and most of Latvia in 1710 and they remained under Russian control till 1918 when they were freed by Lenin. During much of this period the Russians gave enhanced privileges to the ethnically German upper class that provided many able officers and civil servants for the Russian Empire. Both nations were conquered by the Germans in 1941, recovered by Stalin in 1944 and became independent again in 1991.

Lithuania's period under Russian rule was shorter, as it resulted from the Polish partition of 1795, but it was more traumatic because the Lithuanains were regarded as troublemakers like the Poles and involved in the violent suppression of rebellions in 1830 and 1863.

All three nations suffered in the nineteenth century from enforced russification, with their native languages, institutions and cultures suppressed. This accounts for the large number of Russian Orthodox cathedrals and churches planted in their cities in the 1890s.

ESTONIA

Narva on the west side of the River Narva was the small fortified town built by the Teutonic Knights in the thirteenth century. During the Russian siege here Peter the Great suffered his worst defeat during a surprise attack in a snow storm by Charles XII of Sweden. It has a **Voskresensky Cathedral** built in 1898 during the russification period.

Tallinn, (Reval) was captured by the Russians from the Swedes in 1710 and remained in Russian hands until 1918, then again from 1944 till 1991. Most of its fine buildings date from its period under the Teutonic Knights but Catherine rebuilt **Toompea Castle** and the **Alexander Nevsky Cathedral** dates from 1894. Tallinn became one of the largest ports in the Russian Empire. Nearby it also had **Kadriorg Palace** built for Peter the Great by Michetti 1718-25 but never finished and never used after 1750, as well as Peter's cottage. Tallinn saw the execution of seventy-two peasants after an uprising in 1806.

The beautiful **Puhitsa Convent** at Kuremae comes from the 1885 drive to russify Estonia.

Tartu/Dorpat was all but destroyed by Peter the Great in 1708 and its people deported to Russia. The old university town was badly burned in 1775 and rebuilt by the Romanovs in classical style.

Haapsalu has curative mud baths which were patronised by the Romanovs and Tchaikovsky.

Parnu has its Russian **Catherine Church** built in 1760 and named after the Empress.

LATVIA

Riga, originally a Viking trading post, then headquarters of the Livonian Knights who built Riga castle in 1320, then a Swedish colony, became Russian in 1710 and grew into one of Russia's largest industrial cities and ports. It had a large German population living in the old town until 1920 after Lenin had granted independence in 1918. Russia reacquired it in 1944 but once more let it become independent in 1991. It has numerous medieval buildings but the Russian imperial period left it with an **Alexander Nevsky** church and a Russian cathedral. One tower survives from the old city walls and has nine Russian canon balls embedded in its walls, from the era of Peter the Great when it was besieged. Peter the Great had a house at **Palata Iela** where he kept a carriage and could do his own garden. It was rebuilt by Rastrelli in 1745.

Marienburg/Aluksne was where Catherine, the future second wife of Peter the Great, first appeared as the widow of a Swedish soldier and later mistress of Marshall Sheremeteev who captured it from the Swedes.

Mitau/Jelgava, capital of Courland, was captured by Peter the Great and was where Empress Anna lived for many years as the widowed duchess of Courland before being summoned to take power. Her tame architect Rastrelli built two new palaces here, one for her former lover and riding master Ernst von Buhren or Biren, whom she made Duke of Courland, and one for herself – **Jelgava Palace** with 300 rooms. Biren also had **Rundale Palace** built by Rastrelli near Bauska with 120 rooms and it was later given by Catherine the Great to her last lover Platon Zubov. This area became part of tsarist Russia forty years later along with Lithuania and northern Poland in 1795.

LITHUANIA

Vilnius became Russian in 1795 after the partition of Poland and grew to be Russia's third largest industrial city with its mixture of German, Jewish and Lithuanian inhabitants. It was where Emperor Alexander was attending a ball with his generals the night that Napoleon crossed the river Niemen and invaded Russia. The cathedral was rebuilt under Emperor Paul. In 1655 Russian soldiers allegedly hid a cache of jewels in the walls of the **Chapel of St Casimir.** The **Bishops/President's Palace** was used by both Kutuzov and Napoleon during 1812. Vilnius and the rest of Lithuania regained independence in 1918, lost it again from 1941-1990 and then it once more became the capital. It was the scene of ruthless repression by the Romanovs after it joined in the Polish rebellion of 1863 and Muraviev known as 'the Hangman of Vilnius' executed some 200 people. A chapel commemorates the victims.

Kaunas has its Ninth Fort built in the late nineteenth century by the Romanovs to help defend their western frontier. It was later used by the Germans as an extermination camp for Jews, including 1,600 children, and by the Russians to imprison Lithuanian political offenders.

Siauliai has a former Russian church, **St George's** built in 1909, and a monument by the market for the Lithuanians who were hung for their part in the 1863 uprising against the tsarist oppressors.

Finland

Alexander I took over Finland from Sweden after bloody fighting during the Napoleonic Wars in 1809 and initially allowed it a substantial degree of self-government which proved successful. So the Finns did not take part in the insurrections of 1830 and 1863. However, Nicholas II changed the policy in 1895 and tried to replace Finnish with Russian as the official language, ended self-government and conscripted Finns into the Russian army. Four years later Sibelius wrote *Finlandia*.

Helsinki was founded as a small town by Gustavus Vasa of Sweden but turned into the capital by Alexander I as it was closer to Russia. He employed German architects to completely rebuild it as a classical city with a fine Orthodox cathedral.

Belarus

White Russia had been Russian in the pre-Tartar days but language and customs diverged in the intervening centuries before it became part of Russia with the partitions of Poland (1772-96). Its indigenous population were mainly illiterate peasants with a Polish land-owning class and a high proportion of Jews working in the towns. Thus it became part of the Pale. After 1839 it underwent repression under Nicholas I, its Church was abolished and its language discouraged. The Bolsheviks were similarly repressive so it sought independence in 1991.

Minsk the capital founded in 1067 had to be virtually rebuilt after the Second World War so there are virtually no historic remains.

Mogilev/Mahilyow, is the location of the Stavka or army headquarters in railway carriages hidden in the forest where Nicholas II spent his final months in power acting as Commander in Chief of the army. It was badly contaminated by the disaster at the nearby Chernobyl nuclear plant.

UKRAINE

While Kiev and most of the Ukraine were very much part of the original state of Russia they became separated from Moscovy during the Tartar conquest and were subsequently ruled by the Poles and Lithuanians until recovered under Alexei and Peter the Great. Meanwhile they had grown apart linguistically and culturally. Because they were used for several centuries as a source of slaves by the Tartar and Turkish slave traders they remained a dangerous area and were settled by Russian runaway serfs and hunter-gatherers who became known as Cossacks. They played off the Muscovites against the Poles or Swedes to try to keep their independence. It was in 1648 that the Cossacks made their first move in shifting alliance from the Catholic Poles to the Orthodox Tsar Alexei. Thereafter, by a slow process of attrition, the Ukrainians were ground down by the Romanovs, their language and customs discouraged. They won independence briefly after the 1917 revolution and then again in 1991 though there remains an unstable mixture of Russian and Ukrainian speakers.

Kiev, at one point 'the mother of Russia' and centre of the Russian Orthodox Church, has the superb blue and cream **Mariinsky Palace (Dvorets)** built by Rastrelli for Empress Elizabeth in 1755. The **St Sofia Cathedral** was remodelled in 1690 at the same time as the **St Nicholas**. **St Vladimir's Cathedral** is also here. Mussorgsky composed his *Great Gates of Kiev* in 1874 to celebrate the fact that Alexander II had survived an assassination attempt here in 1866.

Poltava has an obelisk marking the place where Peter the Great stayed before his most important victory and a **Church of the Transfiguration** built in celebration two years later in 1711. Poltava was also a disastrous defeat for the Cossack hetman Mazeppa who had joined up with the Swedes and this was a severe blow to Ukrainian hopes of devolution.

Ekaterinoslav, later renamed **Dniepropetrovsk**, was a model town founded south of Poltava by Potemkin as he opened up new territory towards the Crimea. He used Kazakov who had done similar work in Tver and Moscow as a town planner to impress Empress Catherine to whom the new town was dedicated.

Livadiya Palace on the slopes of Mount Mogabi is 2 miles south of Yalta and was purchased by Alexander II for his wife in 1861 to enjoy the warm climate and beautiful gardens in an unspoilt area. It was rebuilt by Nicholas II in 1911. The famous Yalta conference between Stalin, Roosevelt and Churchill took place here. Nearby was another palace belonging to Nicholas II's sister Xenia.

Sebastopol is the fortified port built by Potemkin in 1788. It has the remains of a circular fort and a monument to the Russian ships that were scuttled to stop the invaders in 1855. **Balaclava** is to the east.

Odesa was founded by Catherine the Great in 1795 after the capture of the Turkish fort at Hadji Bey and built up rapidly as a port on the Black Sea. The famous **Potemkin Steps** used to such effect in the Eisenstein film of the mutiny of the battleship *Potemkin* date from 1837. **Primorsky Boulevard** and **St Panteleimon Monastery** are highlights as are its legendary catacombs. It was famous for Jewish *pogroms*, industrial unrest and fierce underground resistance during the Second World War.

POLAND

Between them Catherine the Great and Frederick of Prussia master-minded the three partitions of Poland which resulted in Russia by 1796 getting the largest area It meant a significant increase in population, predominantly Polish nationals and Catholics but also a large Jewish minority. From the start the Poles were distrusted and repressed, so they responded with regular rebellions particularly in 1830 and 1863.

Krakow has Wawel Castle where Filaret, father of the first Romanov tsar, was kept prisoner by the Poles for eight years until 1619. It was in the Austrian part of Poland after the partitions.

Warsaw was captured by Alexander I in 1814 and kept by him after the Congress of Vienna. It has its reconstructed **Royal Castle (Zamek Krolevski)** and the **Radziwill Palace** used by Russian governors gen-erally sent here by the Romanovs including Konstantin the brother of Alexander I who was proclaimed Tsar briefly in 1825. Konstantin was ejected during the 1830 uprising and died of cholera during the siege that followed. The next tsar's brother, also called Konstantin, was sent here as Governor in 1863 but failed to suppress the rebels. One hundred and seventy-seven Poles were executed including their leader Romuald Traugutt who was hung in 1864 in front of a crowd of 30,000 people. There is also **Palace on the Isle (Palac na Wyspie)** the summer palace of Empress Catherine's former lover King Stanislaw August Poniatowski, last king of Poland.

Tannenberg/Stebark, site of the huge battle in which the Germans under Hindenburg and Ludendorf heavily defeated the Russians in 1914. This was followed up with another victory at the **Masurian Lakes**. **Stettin/Szczecin**, a Hanseatic port city sold by Sweden to Prussia in 1720, birthplace of Catherine the Great whose father was in charge of the Prussian army garrison here at the **Palace of Duke of Pomerania**. It was also the birthplace of Empress Maria, wife of Tsar Paul.

Bialowieza and **Spala** – little remains of the Romanovs' two hunting lodges associated with the severe illness of Alexander III and of Tsarevich Alexis just before the First World War. They are near the current Belarus border and incorporated in a large forest National Park, the sole breeding ground for European bison or aurocks.

MOLDAVIA

The northern half of Moldova with it mainly Rumanian population was conquered by Russia in 1812, lost again in 1860 after the Crimean War but regained in 1878. **Chisinau** had to be rebuilt after the Second World War including its 1836 Orthodox Cathedral. **Iasi** was Peter the Great's base during his disastrous Prut campaign and his worst defeat was at **Stanilesti**. This area also saw heavy campaigning by Alexander II and his son in 1878. **Tirasopol** was founded in 1792 to encourage Russians to settle in the area which was mixed-race Moldovan/Rumanian and Ukrainian with a few Russians.

GEORGIA

The Georgians unwisely sought protection from the Russians against the Persians in 1783, a trust that was abused when Russia took over control in 1801 and kept it until 1918. There were, however, benefits in terms of stability and economic growth. After a brief post-revolution period of independence it was taken over by the Soviet Union and remained part of Russia until 1991.

Tiflis/Tbilisi, known as 'the Paris of Russia', still has the tsarist governor's palace built in 1807 and **Meteckhi Church** on the site of the prison and fortress used to deter rebellion. Its hot springs were enjoyed by Pushkin who spent his exile here. Nearby is **Gori**, the birthplace of Stalin, who attended theology seminary at Tbilisi. The **Georgia Military Highway** was a remarkable piece of Russian engineering necessary to bring down the troops to control to awkward Caucasian colonies. At 180 miles long and guarded by forts it reaches a height of 7,000 meters at the Krestovy Pass.

ABKHAZIA

This is most famous for the number of centenarians produced by its clean mountain air.

ARMENIA

Yerevan the capital of Armenia along with its two northern provinces was captured by Nicholas I in 1828 after a war with the Persians and Turks. The Russians rebuilt most of the city and many Armenians previously living in the Turkish part of Armenia fled here to avoid persecution which eventually developed into genocide in 1896. **Gyumri** the second biggest city was in tsarist times the garrison town of Alexandropol.

AZERBAIJAN

Baku and the surrounding area became Russian in 1806 though Peter the Great had conquered it temporarily in 1723. After 1872 when oil was discovered it grew rapidly into a major city. **Naxcivan** a mountainous enclave between Armenia and Iran became Russian in 1828.

KAZAKHSTAN

This vast area of over 1 million square miles with a population of 9 million, like Georgia unwisely sought Russian protection during a civil war in 1730 and was gradually absorbed thereafter. In 1748 the Yaik army of seven regiments was installed to defend the Orenburg line. The tsarist fort of **Verny** built in 1854 as part of the expansion plan at **Alma Ata**, now Almaty, which became the country's capital. Its original inhabitants were mainly Turkic-speaking Sunni Muslims descended form the Tartars of the Golden Horde. Nearby was another Russian fort, **Zailysky**.

UZBEKISTAN

Tashkent, its capital, became a Russian city in 1865 and Kaufman made it his capital when he became the aggressive first governor of the Russian province of Turkestan. The other historic Tartar cities **Bokhara** and **Samarkand** followed the usual pattern of seeking Russian protection. The area was taken over by Alexander II in the 1860s partly for economic reasons as Russia needed its own cotton-growing area during the American Civil War. **Kokad** was built as a Russian dormitory town with cathedral and gambling house. There was no effort to Russianise or Christianise this area, the Khans of Khiva and Emirs of Bukhara kept nominal power, but there was substantial Russian immigration which caused unrest amongst the indigenous population. In 1898 under Nicholas II eighteen Andijani rebels were publicly hung and 300 sent to Siberia.

TURKMENISTAN

Mary (Merv), an old oasis town with mud brick houses on the ancient Silk Road was the base chosen by the Russians for their dangerous infiltration of Afghanistan in the 1880s and they had a garrison fort nearby.

Tajikistan

Dushanbe was another Russian base for the attack on Afghanistan.

The Rest of the World

France

Nice has the onion-domed Russian church, Cathedrale Orthodoxe Russe St Nicholas, erected to mark the premature death of the Tsarevich after a riding accident here in 1865.

Paris has its **Alexander Nevsky Cathedral** built in 1860 in the Monceau quarter to cater for the Russian aristocrats living in Paris.

Holland

Zaandam has the preserved cottage where Peter the Great lived while working in the nearby shipyards.

Germany

Kiel is where Peter III, possibly the last genuine Romanov emperor, was born son of Anna Romanova, daughter of Peter the Great and the Duke of Holstein Gottorp. The small surviving **Schloss** overlooks the promenade.

Anhalt Zerbst, near Dessau south west of Berlin was the home of Catherine the Great. **Zerbst Castle** is partially ruined.

Baden-Baden was the home of Princess Louise who became Empress Elizabeth, wife of Alexander I. The **Neues Schloss** still survives.

Wurttemberg and Monbeliard in the French Alps were the homes of Empress Maria, wife of Paul, though she was born like his mother at Stettin.

Darmstadt was the birthplace of Empress Maria, wife of Alexander II. She was daughter of the Princess of Hesse Darmstadt but probably not of the Grand Duke who, at the time of her birth, had been separated from his wife for some years. The **Schloss** dates from around 1300 and has been restored. Nicholas II's Empress Alexandra was also from Hesse Darmstadt and he used to come here with her in the summer, hence the gold-domed **Russiche Kapelle** that he had built here in 1898.

Wiesbaden has an onion-domed Russian church which was built by Elizabeth of Nassau, daughter of Grand Duke Mikhail. She had died at the age of nineteen in childbirth after marrying a Dutch prince. Olga, daughter of Alexander II, died here in 1925. There is a Russian cemetery nearby.

Great Britain

Deptford, Sayes Court, is where Peter the Great lived in the home of John Evelyn while he worked at the nearby shipyards. Sadly the original house was demolished though the name is preserved in the current building.

Denmark

Fredensborg Castle, on Lake Esrum north of Copenhagen, home of Dagmar, Empress Maria wife of Alexander III and mother of Nicholas II, a baroque palace built in 1719 where Nicholas II and his family came for holidays almost every year.

Israel

Jerusalem. The **Russian Church on the Mount of Olives** was built by Emperor Alexander III and his brothers in honour of their mother Tsarina Maria who died in 1880. Grand Duchess Elizabeth, sister of the last empress and like her murdered in 1918, is buried here.

China

Russia's long border with China was settled by treaty in 1689 so that trade could be conducted in peace but in the nineteenth century, when the Manchu dynasty was weakened, the Russians began to encroach on Chinese territory first in the Amur valley in 1857 then in Manchuria in 1900, then Mongolian Tyva in 1911. In the portions they retained they tended to drive out the native populations – perhaps overall running into millions of people – and replace them with Russians.

Huiyuan in Huocheng on the Mongolian frontier was occupied by the tsarist troops of Kolpakovsky from 1871-81.

Dalnya still has its Russian name meaning faraway and is in the most easterly part of China close to the North Korean frontier. Nearby **Port Arthur (Lushun)** was a warm water port much coveted by the Russians but lost in a Japanese attack in 1905. The half-finished Russian fortifications still survive. Meanwhile in 1904 the Russians lost the battle of Liao-Yang in August 1904. **Mukden (Shenyang)** to the north was a major Russian military base and railway depot as they tried to edge south of Manchuria towards the Pacific Coast west of Korea and scene of a major battle between the Russians and Japanese in 1905. **Harbin**, another former Russian railway junction and garrison town, still has numerous former Russian buildings.

UNITED STATES

Alaska was first invaded by Russians in 1741 during the reign of Ivan VI. Further expeditions followed under Catherine the Great and the Russian-American Company took over administration of the territory north of the 55th parallel in 1799. The company's licence expired in 1862 shortly before the discovery of gold and by this time the colony was severely neglected by the Russians who sold it to the United States five years later.

Sitka was originally founded on Baranof Island by Alexander Baranov in 1799 with the name of **(New) Novo Arkhangelsk** after a battle with the local Tlingit tribe. Baranov was the Russian governor of the Alaska colony 1804-8. The Tlingit fort of Kiksadi was 'bombed' by Russians under Lisianki in 1804. Sitka has a Russian **St Michael's Cathedral** rebuilt after a fire in 1966 and a church at Nihilchik Kenai. There was a Tlingit totem pole erected on the site of **Fort Shiiski**.

Fort Ross (Fort Rossiya) in California was founded in 1812 on the orders of Alexander I who was later involved in trying to create a

Russian whaling monopoly in the North Pacific. It was a fur collection centre exploiting the local sea otters and intended to grow crops to feed the bases in Alaska. The fort with its reconstructed Orthodox chapel was sold to Captain John Sutter in 1841 and is now part of the Fort Ross Historic Park near Jenner, 70 miles north of San Francisco.

New York has the **Cathedral of Our lady of the Sign** where the dead Romanovs as the 'New Martyrs of Russia' were glorified as saints by the church in 1981.

HAWAII

In 1817 an officer of the Russian-American Company called Schaeffer captured Kauai and built **Fort Elizabeth** on the Waimea River as one of a series of Russian forts designed to turn Hawaii into a Russian colonial base.

AUSTRALIA

As a result of the strong belief that the Russians were about to invade Australia in 1877, a number of special forts were built including Fort **Denison** and **Bare Island** near Sydney. The invasion did not materialise.

JAPAN

Tsushima Island in the Korean Strait gave its name to the decisive naval battle lost by Russia in 1905.

GLOSSARY

Aleksandr, diminutive Sasha – Alexander
Apparatchik – Civil Servant
Archiepiskop – Archbishop
Arquebus - Handgun originally used by *Streltsi*
Ataman – Cossack Leader
Baltiskoe More – Baltic Sea
Banya – Bath
Bashnya – Tower
Batyushka – Priest
Beli – White
Bistro – Quick
Blini – Pancake
Bogaty – Rich
Bolshoe – Big
Bolshevik – Majority party member
Borshch – Beetroot soup
Boyar – Aristocratic landowner
Cheka – Acronym for secret police
Cherka – The pale, regions to which Jews were restricted
Cherniy – Black
Chernoye more – Black Sea
Chleb – Bread
Dacha – Country cottage
Dom – Home
Dukhobors – Pacifist religious sect
Duma – Parliament
Dvorets – Palace
Gertsog – Duke
Gorod – Town
Gosudar – sovereign
Grozniy – Formidable or terrible as applied to Ivan IV and the capital of Chechnya

Glossary

Imperator – Emperor
Iskra – Spark, name of communist newspaper
Kadet – Member of social democrat party
Kasha – Porridge
Kazak – Cossack
Khlysti – Extreme religious sect, flagellants
Kitai – Chinese
Kitaigorod – Foreign quarter of Moscow
Knyaz – Prince
Knyt – Whip, knout, a multi-tailed whip of twisted leather, sometimes metal wire
Kokoshnik – Gable
Kolokol – Bell
Krasniy – Red or beautiful as in Red Square etc
Kreml – Fortified town
Krepost – Fort
Kulak – Prosperous peasant
Lavra – Monastery
Maliy – Small
Mestnichestro – System of ranks
Mir – World or peace
Mikhail – Michael
Monastir – Convent
More – Sea
Moskva – Moscow
Most – Bridge
Nakaz – Decree
Narod – Nation
Narodnik – Member of national reform movement
Nemetski – Dumb people, Germans
Nikolai, diminutive Nikolasha – Nicholas
Okhrana – Security, Secret Police
Ostrog – Fort
Ostrov – Island
Pereulok – Side street
Polsha – Polish
Ploshchad – Square
Pobeda – Victory
Pogrom – Devastation, specifically attacks on the Jews
Pomeshchiki – Service aristocrats
Pravda – Truth, faith
Raskolnik – Sectarian
Reka – River
Sad – Garden
Samovar – Tea boiler
Selo – Village
Shakhmata – Chess
Shchee – Cabbage soup
Skoptsi – Religious sect believing in self-castration

Sloboda – District, village
Sobor – Cathedral
Soviet – Council
Soyuz – Union
Starets – Old man, wandering priest
Strelka – Arrow
Strelets, plural *Streltsi* – Marksmen, later musketeers
Taiga – Sub-arctic forest
Terem – Women's quarters
Troika – Sledge
Troitsa – Trinity
Tsar – Caesar i.e. emperor
Tsarevitch – Eldest son of tsar
Tsarevna – Daughter of tsar
Tsarina – Wife of tsar
Tserkov – Church
Ukaz – Order
Vasili – Basil (Greek king)
Velikiy – Great
Vino – Wine
Voda – Water
Vodka – Vodka
Voena – War
Voevod – Governor
Vokzal – Railway station
Yekaterina – Catherine
Yelizaveta – Elizabeth
Zamok – Castle
Zemski – Peoples
Zemstvo – Assembly

BIBLIOGRAPHY

Alexander, John T., *Catherine the Great*, Oxford, 1989.

Anderson, M.S., *Peter the Great*, London, 1990.

Bain, R.N., *The First Romanovs*, London, 1905.

Bergamini, John D., *The Tragic Dynasty, A History of the Romanovs*, London, 1970.

Bushkovich, Paul, *Peter the Great*, Cambridge, 2001.

Catherine, Empress, *Memoirs*, trans. M. Budbeg, New York, 1967.

Dmytryshin, B., *Imperial Russia, a Source Book*, New York, 1967.

Dukes, Paul, *The Making of Russian Absolutism*, London, 1990.

Dunning, Chester S.L., *Russia's First Civil War*, Pennsylvania, 2001.

Ferro, Marc, *Nicholas II, last of the Tsars*, Oxford, 1993.

Figes, Orlando, *A People's Tragedy*, New Haven, 1999.

Fuller, W.C., *Strategy and Power in Russia 1600-1914*, New York, 1992.

Greenall, Robert, *An Explorer's Guide to Russia*, Edinburgh, 1994.

Grey, Ian, *The Romanovs, The Rise and Fall of a Russian Dynasty*, Newton Abbot, 1970.

Grey, Michael, *Blood Relative*, London, 1998.

Hartley, Janet M., *Alexander I*, London, 1994.

Hosking, Geoffrey, *Russia, People and Empire 1552-1917*, London, 1997.

Hughes, Lindsey, *Peter the Great*, Yale, 2002.

Hughes, Lindsey, *Russia in the Age of Peter the Great*, Yale.

Hughes, Lindsey, *Sophia, Regent of Russia*, New Haven, 1990.

Kappelen, Andrew, *The Russian Empire*, trans. A. Clayton, Harlow 2001.

King, Greg and Wilson, P., *The Fate of the Romanovs*, New Jersey, 2003

Klyuchevsky, Vasili, *The Rise of the Romanovs*, trans. L. Archibald, London, 1970.

Kokker, Steve, *St Petersburg*, Melbourne, 2002.

Kochan, Lionel, *The Making of Modern Russia*, London, 1977.

Lieven, Dominic, Empire, *The Russian Empire and its Rivals*, London, 2000.

Lincoln, W. Bruce, *The Romanovs*, New York, 1981.

Liria, Duc de, *Pisma o Rossii v Ispania*, Moscow, 1869.

Longley, David, *Imperial Russia 1689-1917*, Harlow, 2000.

Longworth, P., *Alexis Tsar of all the Russias*, London, 1984.

Longworth, P., *Russian Empire*, London, 2006.

Madariaga, Isabel de, *Russia in the Age of Catherine the Great*, London, 1981.

McGraw, Roderick E., *Paul I of Russia*, Oxford, 1992.

Massie, Robert K., *Nicholas and Alexandra*, London, 1968.

Modern Encyclopaedia of Russian and Soviet History, Gulf Breeze, 1976-94.

Montefiore, Simon, *Prince of Princes: Potemkin*, London, 2001.

Moss, W.E., *Alexander III*, Taurus, 1992.

Pereira, N.G.O., *Tsar Liberator – Alexander II of Russia*, Gulf Breeze, 1983.

Pipes, R., *Russia under the Old Regime*, London, 1982.

Rice, Christopher and Melanie, eds, *Moscow*, London, 2004.

Rogger, Hans, *Russia in the Age of Modernisation and Revolution*, London, 1983.

Royle, Trevor, *Crimea*, London, 1997.

Sumner, B.H., *Peter the Great and the Emergence of Russia*, London, 1951.

Talbot Rice, Tamara, *Russian Art*, London, 1949.

Tolstoy, Leo, *War and Peace*, trans. Maude, London, 1943.

Van der Kiste, John, *The Romanovs 1818-1959*, Stroud, 1998.

Whelan, H.W., *Alexander III and the State Council*, New Brunswick, 1982.

Williams, Nicola, et al., *Estonia, Latvia and Lithuania*, Melbourne, 2003.

INDEX